Ambiguous Justice

Native American Series

Clifford Trafzer, Series Editor

Ambiguous Justice

Native Americans and the Law
in Southern California, 1848–1890

Vanessa Ann Gunther

MICHIGAN STATE UNIVERSITY PRESS
EAST LANSING

∞ The paper used in this publication meets the minimum requirements of ANSI/NISO
Z39.48-1992 (R 1997) (Permanence of Paper).

Michigan State University Press
East Lansing, Michigan 48823-5245

Printed and bound in the United States of America.

12 11 10 09 08 07 06   1 2 3 4 5 6 7 8 9 10

Library of Congress Cataloging-in-Publication Data

Gunther, Vanessa Ann.
    Ambiguous justice : Native Americans and the law in Southern California, 1848–1890
/Vanessa Ann Gunther.
        p.   cm. — (Native American series)
    Includes biblographical references and index.
    ISBN-13: 978-0-87013-779-2 (pbk. 13dig : alk. paper)
    ISBN-10: 0-87013-779-4 (pbk. 10dig. : alk. paper)
    1. Indians of North America—Legal status, laws,etc.—California—History—19th
century. I. Title.
    KFC940.G86 2006
    342.79408'72—dc22   2006021702

Cover design by Heather Truelove Aiston
Book design by Bookcomp, Inc
Front cover art is a photograph of General Jose Pachito and his captains at Pala, July 1885.
Back cover art is a broadside seeking the arrest of an unidentified Indian for murder.
These items are reproduced by permission of the Huntington Library, San Marino,
California.

Michigan State University Press is a member of the Green Press Initiative and is
committed to developing and encouraging ecologically responsible publishing practices.
For more information about the Green Press Initiative and the use of recycled paper in
book publishing, please visit www.greenpressinitiative.org.

Visit Michigan State University Press on the World Wide Web at:
www.msupress.msu.edu

For Vera, Hester, and Linda
Strong Women All

Contents

Preface

IN 1987, PATRICIA LIMERICK EXPANDED THE CONCEPT OF WEST-
ern history with her work *The Legacy of Conquest*. Limerick's contention was that the expansion of the United States had not occurred, as
had been popularly idealized, merely from the hard work and sacrifice of
farmers and pioneers. Instead, America's amber fields were first conquered
by land speculators. This wily group of businessmen initially purchased
the lands that would be farmed and developed by the coming masses, and
then sold them for a tidy profit. From their business acumen, our nation
developed, and has continued in many regards to develop along the same
vein. The importance of the land speculators, however, had been ignored in
history books, and their significance almost lost to history. History seems
to be like that. With each generation of historians comes a new idea that
changes our perspective of what we previously thought we knew. From that
germ of a new idea come more ideas, some of which turn our view of the
past on its head. The gender and social histories of the 1960s and 1970s had
this impact. However, despite the seemingly all-encompassing breadth of
these and other methods of studying history, still more avenues have yet to
be strolled in search of a clearer image of the past. One such avenue is the
study of law, and how it has been used to shape the culture and society that
we share.

This study uses the law to explain the social and economic conditions
that existed in southern California from 1849 to 1890. As in Limerick's study,
land lies at the heart of the issue. For Americans, land and money often
went hand in hand. In California, when the value of the land increased,
the legal system was often used to remove undesirable people from the

region. A nineteenth-century version of "Not in My Back Yard" developed, with Indians forced into the role of the undesirables. In the first forty years of American dominance, Native Americans and Anglo-Americans often found themselves at cross-purposes. At the time the state passed from Mexican to American hands, California's aboriginal people had already been exposed to the concepts of European law for almost three-quarters of a century. Many tribes had obtained land grants, and had adapted their traditional practices of social control and punishment to resemble those of the Mexican government. However, little could have prepared them for the new way Americans would use the legal system to ensure that their grasping, petulant desires were met.

In our modern society, the law is often seen as a nebulous concept that passively warns people against traveling too fast, or punishes others who flout the standards of society. In the middle to late nineteenth century, the law also showed a remarkable capacity to reflect the mores and desires of local communities. Often it was used to ensure the fortunes of one social group over another. While this study does not reflect the rigid structural functionalism of sociology, the law in nineteenth-century California certainly filled the social needs of the dominant society. Those needs, as for any organic body, evolved over time. Sadly for California's native people, they became the pawns of the larger society—their actions largely controlled through the expansive reach of the law as the needs of the Anglo society changed.

To fully explore the reach of the law as it impacted the lives of California's aboriginal people, the judicial records from the lower courts that operated in Southern California have been widely examined. California is blessed with a large contingent of pack rats and stubborn archivists who for years preserved the judicial records of the justice, circuit, district, and superior courts, despite protestations from bureaucrats who could not see the value in preserving hundred-year-old cases that involved petty theft or rape. To them I am indebted. However, despite their efforts, many of the records that recount California's early judicial history have forever been lost. Even those that have been preserved on microfilm have been corrupted over time, rendering them virtually unreadable. In an attempt to recreate this history as accurately as possible, newspaper articles, Indian-agent reports, prison registers, and personal papers from California's Anglo pioneers have also been used. Cultural histories and anthropological studies, especially those that focus on the traditional law practices of California's southern tribes, have also been consulted. While these sources certainly add more flesh to the story, they can only give a sketchy sense of those whose lives have been reduced to a few written words on paper. For the Indians of southern California, the years in prison or the fines incurred were part of a steady onslaught against their culture and their birthright to the land of their ancestors. It is these people I hope to bring to life in the following pages.

No book is ever written by one person, and without the assistance of several colleagues and friends, this volume would have remained only an idea. For their help, encouragement, and friendship I am truly grateful. These few lines of acknowledgment cannot fully express their contribution or my gratitude. To my family and friends, who accepted my excuses for missed gatherings without qualm only to later be forced to listen patiently as I monopolized their attention with impromptu lectures on the importance of one document or idea over another, thank you. Your support has been invaluable, and could not pass without acknowledgment.

My thanks to Fred Bohm, director of Michigan State University Press, who had the vision to begin the American Indian Series in an attempt to further our understanding of First Nations people, and in doing so to also understand more of the world we currently occupy. To Professor Rebecca Kugel, who, while her own research was divergent from my own, provided counsel and feedback that I will long remember. To the librarians and support staff at the National Archives—especially Paul Wormser, who took the time to ensure that no stone was left unturned and who provided an environment in which to fully explore the documents in his care, even when the results of our labors proved fruitless.

The Huntington Library in San Marino, California, provided invaluable assistance and support over many long months through their willingness to aid in my research, and their professionalism. Their dedication to scholars and their scholarship have resulted in not only this tome, but in the flowering of numerous other projects that have furthered our understanding of the past. To share equally in the kudos are the archivists at the County of San Bernardino, the County of San Diego, and the State of California. Each provided me with assistance and direction in the face of a daunting task. The staff and volunteers of the historical societies in the respective counties, San Diego, Los Angeles, and San Bernardino, were instrumental in pointing me in new directions and providing me with new ideas. The staff at the Sherman Institute in Riverside graciously took time from their schedules to allow me access to their facilities. The librarians at the Bancroft Library, the Riverside County Library, and the University of California, Riverside also deserve special mention for the aid they have provided in helping me to locate obscure letters and reference works that otherwise might have been overlooked.

Finally, I would like to extend my most heartfelt thanks to two men who have been unstinting in their support and guidance over the years: Dr. Gordon Morris Bakken, whose stalwart belief in my abilities as a scholar induced him to provide countless hours of guidance and encouragement—all of which was offset by his disarming sense of humor—and who reminded me of the human element in the papers I was perusing. His passion for history is as infectious and powerful as the support he has provided. And Dr. Clifford E. Trafzer, who has been my mentor, professor, and friend throughout this process. His humanity and kindness mark him as a uniquely special man. He was able to see the value in the research I was engaged in, even when there were times I was blinded by the magnitude of the task. His quiet but persistent perseverance is largely responsible for making these pages come to life. I consider myself truly lucky to count them both as friends.

Introduction

BY THE MIDDLE OF THE EIGHTEENTH CENTURY, SPAIN GREATLY feared the loss of her northern territories in the New World to other grasping and aggressive European powers. She could not have been more right in her concerns. Following the conclusion of the Seven Years' War in 1763, Spain was forced to abandon her claims to Florida. Not satisfied by the acquisition of this prime piece of territory, England quickly turned her gaze to the northwest coast of the continent, to an area that was already being exploited by Russian fur traders. The lucrative fur trade could greatly bolster the sagging coffers of Britain's treasury, and a western port could provide England with access to additional markets in Asia.

Faced with a challenge to her sovereignty, in 1769 Spain took action to solidify control over her northern territories by establishing a series of missions and presidios in what is now modern California. Through a series of military and religious excursions, Spain established twenty-one missions and four presidios along California's coast. To populate these remote establishments, the Spanish crown relied on the talents of Franciscan priests to convince the native Californian population to abandon their traditional religious practices and adopt Catholicism. The priests' success in achieving this mandate was mixed; while the missions recorded approximately 79,000 baptisms during the sixty-five years the missions operated it is also estimated that the native population declined by as much as 75 percent in areas where missions were established. Those Indians who survived their tutelage would be indoctrinated into Spanish society, where they would learn obedience to the church and crown. Eventually it was hoped they would abandon their traditional cultural practices and Spain would find herself with a loyal indigenous population, albeit one that was destined to forever occupy the lower rungs of Spanish society. These newest of Spain's citizens would provide the bulk of the labor for the Spanish colonies in the region.

Spain's attempt to occupy California and to use the indigenous population to her advantage would be similar to the behavior of the Americans seventy-nine years later. Like the Spanish, Anglo-Americans saw the Indian as a potential labor source, one that could be cheaply exploited and then abandoned. Indians could be used to develop the land and thus increase its value. Europeans held fast to the contention that since Indian people did not own the land, but merely took from it its rich resources, they could be enjoined from holding title to the land. Instead, the title to the land would be held by a European, an individual who would develop the land and harvest its rich bounty in accordance with God's wish that mankind would be the master of the earth. To merely live upon the land without significantly altering the terrain was thought to be proof that the Indian was closer to an animal in his relationship to the land. The abundance of land in the New World also resulted in a perverse trend among Europeans, to take from the land what they needed, and to move on to another unexploited parcel of land once the resources had been exhausted. Unfortunately, the Europeans treated the Indians with similar contempt. When their usefulness had been exhausted, the Indians could be released from their labor commitments, but the decision was one-sided.

Any attempts by the Indians to abandon the missions and return to their relatives in the interior were met with harsh reprisals. Spanish soldiers, often accompanied by a mission priest, would hunt down the neophytes, or Indian converts, and forcibly return them to the missions. Initially, the presidio soldiers had little choice but to comply with the demands of the priests to hunt down the neophytes, as the food the presidios consumed largely came from the missions. Once Indians had been lured into the mission system, they became part of an economy upon which the Spanish heavily relied, an economy largely controlled by the mission fathers. Any attempt by an Indian to flee what was seen as their duty to the crown and church was viewed with little sympathy by the mission fathers or the Spanish settlers. In a few short years, California's native population had been rapidly coerced into a system of slavery that permeated all of Spain's southwestern possessions. To further exacerbate the woes of California's native population, diseases introduced by Europeans found ready hosts among the Indians, who had no natural immunity. In many areas, smallpox and other diseases decimated up to half of the Indian tribes within the state. The mistreatment of California's native population became so pronounced that in 1787, Governor Pedro Fages enacted an ordinance that outlawed the forced labor of Indians and insisted that their complaints be heard in the Spanish courts. For the most part, Fages' decree fell on deaf ears. The Spanish courts that would have heard the complaints were deep within Mexico, and since the Indians were largely unaware of the rights granted to them by the Spanish crown, no action was taken.

Between 1810 and 1813, further attempts to protect the Indians who occupied Spain's southwestern possessions continued with several decrees from the Cortes of Cadiz, a legislative body that sat when the king was unable to fulfill his duties as sovereign. The Cortes abolished Indian tribute, promised Indians equality within society, ordered the distribution of vacant lands to the Indians, and abolished flogging as a punishment. As with Fages' earlier edict, the rights granted to the Indians would be quietly buried by the Spanish bureaucracy and recalcitrant priesthood, which had other designs on the aboriginal population.

By 1816 the abuses inherent in the mission system had generated enough attention that Spain decreed that any mission that had been in existence for over ten years was to begin the process of secularization. This decree was largely ignored by the Franciscan fathers, but enjoyed increasing support among the non-Indian secular population in the state, who stood ready to claim the livestock and the developed lands that had been accumulated by the missions over the years. Their patience would soon be rewarded.

A mere fifty-two years after embarking on its grand scheme for regional domination, Spain's designs for its northwestern territories were lost amid the crown's struggle for survival. By the time Mexico proclaimed her independence from Spain in 1821, the authority of the feudal theocracy that had developed in the state was waning. In 1824 the new constitution of the Federal Republic of Mexico established the rights of the people of Mexico. Heavily influenced by the Enlightenment ideas that had resulted in the United States' revolution forty-five years earlier, Mexico adopted, at least on paper, the same guiding principles that governed the United

States—namely, equality and the inherent rights of men. However, the precepts that laid the foundation for Mexican democracy were as selectively applied as those within the American legal system.

Using the Constitution of the United States as a blueprint, the nascent government asserted that the authority to govern rested in the hands of the governed. In recognition of its large indigenous population, the Mexican government decreed that Indians would be granted citizenship in the new country, and as such would be considered the equals of all members of the society. Predictably the new laws, like the old ones, drew fire from the mission fathers, who contended that the Indians continued to require their oversight, or more aptly their exploitation. The mission fathers held considerable power within the small communities that developed in California during the years of Mexican domination. The non-Indian population heavily relied on the food and other goods produced by the Indians within the missions. This reliance gave the priests authority out of context to their positions as religious leaders, and resulted in animosity between the secular and the religious populations in the region. The secular population, seeing an opportunity to seize the wealth of the missions and control the labor of the Indians, supported the proposal to secularize the missions. The de facto reality of life in California would be less about freedom for the Indians and more about a change in masters. Despite the protestations of the Franciscans, the final secularization of the missions would be completed by 1834.

The overthrow of the Spanish crown and the installation of a new Mexican government promised a better life for the Indians of the state, at least on paper. However, the new government proved to be equally as disinclined to oversee the workings of the state. Conditions within the Mexican government in Mexico City were fraught with political intrigue and rebellion; as a result, a sparsely populated region to the north that had limited economic development and relied upon an Indian population to sustain itself barely earned the attention of the government. Without the active oversight of the government in Mexico City the Indians in southern California were powerless to press for the privileges they had been granted. Despite their elevation to full citizenship, Native Americans in California were still hunted by the secular population and forced to labor for new masters. Mexican entrepreneurs quickly began to exploit California's verdant grasslands, and within a few years, a vibrant cattle industry evolved from the abandoned shell of the mission system. With the promise of profit as a guiding force, the Mexican government began issuing land grants to settlers. From 1820 to 1846, the number of grants increased from twenty to over seven hundred. Exports in hides and tallow fueled the developing economy. Drawn by the prospect of wealth, a growing number of expatriate Americans began to drift into the state. Despite California's continued importance as a buffer to aggressive European nations who might seek additional territorial concessions, and its growing economic importance, Mexico devoted little to the defense or political oversight of the state.

All this only dimly impacted the few thousand individuals of European descent living in the state. As the economy of California grew, large *ranchos* dominated the landscape. Their proprietors, the *rancheros*, ruled the developing state both economically and judicially. While they assumed the roles of both judge and jury in disputes that occurred on their lands, judicial impartiality was largely a myth. Within the towns and pueblos, disputes were settled by *alcaldes*, individuals appointed to serve dually as the chief judicial and civil authority in the area. To appease local Indian chiefs, many traditional tribal leaders were nominally granted this title over their own people. However, the final authority within the state continued to rest primarily with the large landholders.

As it became clear that Mexico had little interest or money to invest in the further development or protection of the state, many Mexicans and Americans began to call for the annexation of the region to the United States. California's sweeping coastline offered opportunities to expand trade to Asia, and her ranchos stood ready to supply the raw materials needed for export. When congress agreed to the annexation of Texas in 1845, hopes within the state rose to match the expectations of what the American government could do for the region. Mexico refused to accept the loss of Texas to the United States, and both nations moved deliberately toward war.

The annexation of Texas served as a catalyst for Americans who bowed to the dictates of Manifest Destiny. Led by Stephen Watts Kearney, Americans began to claim title to California even before war had been declared. The clumsily enacted Bear Flag Revolt of 1846 claimed the state prematurely. For two weeks, California stood apart from Mexico and the United States as an independent nation before war was declared and the Mexican-American War commenced. In California, this disjointed and spiritless war resulted in few battles between loyalist Mexican citizens and the invading

American and pro-American Mexican forces. By 10 January 1847, Andres Pico, the brother of the last governor of California, was forced to sign the Cahuenga Capitulation which surrendered California to the United States. The following year, on 2 February 1848, the Treaty of Guadalupe Hidalgo ended Mexico's brief sovereignty over California and much of the Southwest.

A new legal system, based on common-law tenets, replaced the civil law of the Spanish. However, the exchange of legal traditions initially meant little to the Indian people living within the state. Those acculturated to the Mexican system of *alcaldes* continued to practice with the assumption that this system was still intact. Well into the 1850s, there were reports of Indian chiefs, attesting to be *alcaldes*, who attempted to intercede on behalf of tribal members who had been accused of crimes after California's annexation to the United States. Those tribes that had not yet been indoctrinated into the Mexican legal system continued to practice their traditional legal culture. To many of the tribes who had yet to be dominated by Anglo-Europeans, the changes wrought by the war were secondary to their own struggle for survival. Unfortunately for the Indians of California, the legal traditions of America would soon be used to challenge that survival further.

Despite the differences between the English and Spanish legal traditions, several similarities appear in how these European traditions dealt with Indians within the colonies.[1] The change in governments did not result in a change in the economy, and the region still heavily depended on the labor of Indians to survive. Subsequently, changing the status of the Indians within the new society would prove to be financially and socially disastrous. Despite the provisions of the Treaty of Guadalupe Hidalgo, which insisted that all Indians were citizens of the Mexican state and therefore would be citizens of the American state, Indians were not granted the privilege of citizenship, and as such they had no authority within the new American government.

The use of Indians as a source of exploitable labor was a concept that found considerable favor among the early white Californians. Although the option existed of forcing Indians to perform tribute labor, as the Spanish had, the Americans would prove adept in finding legal ways to compel Indians to labor for free. In this regard, California Indians who witnessed the transition of government from Spain to Mexico to the United States might have had a difficult time in determining when each regime ended and the next began.[2]

American Law, 1850–1865

T HE TRANSITION OF POLITICAL POWER FROM MEXICO TO THE United States resulted in a myriad of changes for the inhabitants of California, not all of which were directed at Indians. Many of the resulting changes occurred because of the arrogant beliefs of the Americans who flooded into the state. These new masters of California saw the immeasurable possibilities that awaited them in the region, if only they had control of the land. However, the Treaty of Guadalupe Hidalgo had guaranteed that the vast tracts of land held by the Mexican land grantees would not be sacrificed to the avarice of the incoming Anglo-Americans. With much of the state's most profitable lands held by not only another national group, but also another racial group, this racialized the issue of land control. In order to ensure that Americans had access to the land, first the military and then the law were resorted to.

The Americans regarded the retention of so much land in the hands of so few as a social evil, and an impediment to the development of the region.[1] Opposed to a single individual, especially one of Spanish descent, holding so much land, the advancing Anglo-Americans fell back on arguments about the barbarity of letting the land lie undeveloped. Ironically, these were the same arguments that the Spanish had used to dispossess the Indians when they first came to the region. As their predecessors had done, the Americans ignored the current land-use patterns of the Mexicans, who primarily used the land for raising stock, and established a hierarchy of land use that gave preference to agriculture. To accommodate these opinions, the fledgling American military government, which governed the state from 1847 to 1849, made it clear it would represent the rights of the

Anglo-Americans, not the incumbents. Many of the policies established by the military would be codified in the new California Constitution of 1850.

For the Indians, legislation to deprive them of their rights followed a direct route from the military to the state government. Under the rubric of the Act for the Government and Protection of Indians, Anglo-Americans systematically prevented Native Americans from engaging in almost any activity that did not require them to be subservient to the dominant culture. Through legislation that strongly resembled the Black Codes of the Deep South, Americans relegated Indians to a degraded position in the new society, their worth measured by their ability to labor, not their humanity.[2] Within this new society, Americans often ignored the Indian's basic human rights. While the Americans recognized that Indians had a "natural right" to their lands, they also felt this right could be extinguished through conquest or treaty.

During the first twenty years of American occupation, the California Indian population found itself increasingly under attack. Denied the basic right of citizenship—as was called for under the Treaty of Guadalupe Hidalgo—the Indians had no voice in the courts, no right to defend themselves, and no right to educate their children. The growing Anglo population viewed the Indian in one of two ways: as a marauding criminal, or as a debased but useful labor source. Either way, as the decades passed, and the Anglo population increased, the Indians became more expendable.

The development of the new state government was not purely the imposition of Anglo ideas on the former Mexican and Indian residents. When Americans assumed control of the state, many of the characteristics of the Mexican regime, such as the compulsory labor of the Indians in service to the community, were codified into law. Within this environment, Anglos did not readily discern between Mexican and Indian, and as a result, former Mexican citizens found themselves at the mercy of a government many had helped to create. For California, the pivotal years from 1847 to 1865 set the tone for how Indians would be treated in the state. As the only state in the union that refused to relinquish control of its native inhabitants wholly to the federal government, California's legislators viewed the Indian in the same context as Southerners viewed the African American in the South; like their Southern brethren, Anglo-Americans also codified these opinions into law.

From the Cahuenga Capitulation in 1847, when Mexico surrendered to the American forces, until late 1849, California's government was a hybrid of the United States military and Mexican civil authorities. The Mexican *alcaldes* continued to oversee most of the civil needs of the developing state, while Anglo-American military courts primarily attended to serious criminal infractions.[3] The rapid influx of Americans after the discovery of gold in 1848 doomed this reciprocal relationship. As Americans flooded the state and came into contact with the remnants of the Mexican judicial system, they insisted that the old system be replaced with an American judicial system. American prejudices, which viewed all non-whites as inferior, forced many Mexican civil servants out of their positions in local government. In practice, the removal of Mexican civil authorities occurred primarily in the north. In the south, where limited migration occurred, the *alcaldes* continued to serve their communities as before.

During the 1847–1849 military occupation and administration of the state, the policies adopted to control the Indians presaged the government's preferential treatment of Anglo-Americans over Indians. Historian Albert Hurtado argued that Stephen W. Kearney, California's first territorial governor, expressed an "attitude toward the Indian [that was] almost wholly punitive."[4] As dual civil administrator and military commander, Kearney employed his military forces to control Indians who protested the annexation of their lands by the Americans, as well as to secure control of the land from Mexico. Under the military government, the United States prohibited Indians from going about in crowds without written permission from the military. Additionally, military Indian agents served as liaisons between the government and the tribes, with the agent's goal being to "reclaim the old Mission Indians to habits of Industry."[5] Except under extraordinary circumstances, only the Indian agents would hear Indian grievances. This further impacted the authority of the *net* and the coherence of tribal society. Conversely, Anglos would be subject to punishment by their local *alcaldes*, who practiced in accordance with the law, not the whim of an individual. In addition to the dictates of the Indian agents, American authorities also subjected Indians to municipal regulations. These regulations were also open to the whims of those who enforced them, and punishment was often more stringent than that allotted to non-Indians. According to Lieutenant Henry Hallack, then acting as secretary of state, those Indians who were caught stealing should be shot on sight.[6] For the Indians, it was clear what their position in society would be.

The massive migratory change that resulted from the gold rush in 1849 highlighted the obvious inadequacy of the military to provide for the legal needs of the area. The remnants of the Mexican civil law system was poorly understood, and as such failed to provide a cogent plan to ensure the orderly functioning of society. To ensure that the newly acquired territory did not devolve into anarchy, residents of California began to consider whether to petition the United States government to establish the region as either a state or a formal territory. For the Indians within California, this would prove to be an important distinction. As a territory, the area would be regulated under federal jurisdiction, and Indian relations would be governed by treaty and prior practice. As a state, California's legislators could establish laws that would accommodate the needs of the state. For the Indian, the needs of the state invariably overshadowed any concern for native rights to land or justice.

The Monterey Convention of 1849 hammered out the laws and regulations that would govern the new state. The development of the new government was not a purely Anglo affair, as several of the delegates to the convention were former Mexican citizens who now swore allegiance to the United States.[7] Many of the Anglo delegates at the convention had also been in California during the Mexican period and had adopted Mexican culture, and to some extent its worldview.[8] It is not surprising, then, that several elements of the Monterey Constitution reflected elements of Mexican law; the most pronounced were the idea of common law and the idea of using Indians as a servile labor force.

Despite the influence of the Californios (the former Mexican citizens who remained in the state) and the Hispanicized Americans, the bulk of the civil and criminal codes had a decidedly American flair. Stephen J. Field, who would be appointed to the United States Supreme Court in 1863, crafted most of the laws of the new state. These new laws, not coincidentally, reflected the statutes of his native New York.[9] Despite Field's influence, and New York's abolitionist traditions, many of the laws that initially governed California reflected the biases held by Anglos of the era, that non-white people were inferior. The presence of California's new laws, however, meant little unless there was a mechanism by which to enforce them, such as capital and an infrastructure that had been allowed to develop over a period of years, as in the other territories and states. California was sorely lacking in both.

When the state's new laws went into effect in 1850, it became clear that California would be a land whose bounty would serve the Anglo-American population. The first step in this realization came as American jurists debated the status of the Indian following the adoption of the state constitution. Despite being considered citizens by the Mexican government and granted the privileges and protections afforded Mexican citizens under the conditions of the Treaty of Guadalupe Hidalgo, Indians were denied these same privileges under the new American regime.

Additionally, the possibility of placing the California Indians in the same category as all other U.S. Indians—that of noncitizens who were members of a domestic, dependent nation—was also rejected. Instead, the government ignored their initial status as a group deserving protection. As a result, Indians were the first to feel the effects of the new laws.[10] Without a voice in judicial proceedings, Indians found themselves in a nebulous position in California society: they were not citizens and therefore had no rights, but at the same time were bound by the laws of the state. The new California government further separated Indians from the rest of the state's population with the all-encompassing Act for the Government and Protection of Indians. Passed on 22 April 1850, this collection of statutes sought to regulate all aspects of Indian/Anglo interaction.

The law stated that all Indian matters fell under the jurisdiction of the justice of the peace for "all complaints by, for, or against Indians." Complaints could be made by "white persons or Indians; but in no case shall a white man be convicted of any offense upon the testimony of an Indian."[11] Justices of the peace would instruct local Indians on aspects of the law that pertained to them, and if "any village or tribe refused or neglected" to obey the laws, the justice could punish the tribal chiefs. In its purist form the law established by the Americans did as much, if not more damage to the traditional authority held by the tribal leaders, and thereby undermined the customs of the Indians in the state. Setting fire to the land, an age-old method among the Native Americans to clear brush, flush out game, and encourage new plant growth, also found censure in the act. The new statute made many of the Indians' traditional techniques of land husbandry illegal under the state's constitution. By preventing native people from practicing traditional subsistence techniques, Anglos forced Indians to either learn all new subsistence patterns of survival, which in many cases would still be inadequate to sustain the tribe due to the influx of Americans onto their traditional lands, or to depend on Anglo techniques of land husbandry, which in many cases was also proved to be inadequate as Indians were frequently dispossessed of their lands, and what lands they did retain were too poor for agriculture.

In addition to the attack on the political and economic traditions of the tribes, the punishment for Indians was draconian and swift. Indians convicted of "stealing horses, mules, cattle or any valuable thing" were subject to whipping, which was not to exceed twenty-five lashes, or a fine of up to two hundred dollars. Juries could be used if needed, but they would be composed of Anglo men. Additionally, Indian chiefs were now compelled to bring any Indian accused of a crime before the justice of the peace, or face a fine. Those Indians who were found guilty of a crime and were unable to pay their assigned fine could be hired out by the justice of the peace to anyone who could pay the fine; the Indians would then labor for their "benefactor" until the fine was paid. Indian children could be bound out to a responsible Anglo adult until they reached their majority.[12] The act prohibited vagrancy, and any Indian who was found "loitering" about could be hired out for as much as four months.[13] Through legislative fiat, the new State of California had reduced Indians to the status of perpetual minors—minors whose very presence in their homelands could be considered a criminal act. Previous patterns of land use would not be respected, nor would the autonomy of the tribe to judge and control its own members. Instead, Indians found within Anglo settlements were little more than a convenient labor source. Native people, whether convicted of a crime or not, found themselves subject to the labor demands of the larger Anglo society.

The prohibitions against Anglo mistreatment of Indians seemed minor in comparison to the rules imposed on the natives. Anglo-Americans could be convicted of kidnapping Indians or giving them alcohol or forcing them to work.[14] Fines for kidnapping started at fifty dollars. Individuals caught selling liquor to Indians netted fines starting at twenty dollars for each offense, or five days in jail. Despite the presence of these laws they were only infrequently enforced, especially in the early years of statehood. It was only after the Anglo population increased sufficiently to no longer rely on Indians for labor that enforcement of the prohibition on the sale of alcohol was routinely enforced. Clearly the state legislature codified a double standard in its regulation of Anglo and Indian criminal behavior. However, in deference to the state of penury that most Indians existed in, in most cases when an Indian was convicted of a crime and given the option of paying a fine, the rate of reimbursement stood at one dollar a day, not the four dollars charged to Anglos. Despite this minor concession, the law of 1850 had one clear intent: to create a subservient labor force in the state at the expense of the aboriginal population. The codification of these discriminatory practices was an affront to California's status as a free state. Unfortunately, the precedent established by the state in its treatment of Indians as slave laborers was readily embraced at the local level as well. Quite possibly these statutes also served as a blueprint for the Black Codes that were enacted in the South following the Civil War.

California's confused position in regard to her status as a free state, as exhibited by the development of the quasi-slave statutes that regulated Indian behavior, also resulted in some conflict with the federal government over the regulation of Indian affairs within the state. In all other states and territories, the regulation of Indian affairs fell to the federal government, as Indian tribes, following the 1831 *Cherokee Nation v. Georgia* case, were considered to be sovereign nations residing within the United States.[15] When the federal government attempted to assume this position within the state, conflict arose.

The acceptance of California statehood in 1850 resulted in a period of time in which the federal government, because of a dearth of information about Indians living in the state, reacted blindly to the situation that existed between Indians and Anglos. The state's newest residents, the gold seekers in the northern territories, inflamed hostilities between the two groups by wantonly attacking Indians who they felt challenged their access to the placers. The callous and often cruel behavior of these individuals strained Anglo/Indian relations to the breaking point. With the remote location of the gold fields, the limited governmental authority that existed within the state failed to regulate the behavior of its new Anglo citizens, resulting in open warfare between Indians and gold seekers in many areas. In the gold camps, attempts to regulate the behavior of the miners in the absence of a judiciary resulted in the enactment of several "miner's laws." However, as with the newly written state laws, the Indians who fell under the "jurisdiction" of these courts were subject to a double standard when it came time to mete out justice.

When an Indian stood accused of a crime, the Anglo mining communities punished Indians swiftly and completely. If an Indian committed a murder, "miner's law" called for the "destruction of the rancho to which the criminal belonged and its inhabitants if known. If not known, by that of those nearest the spot." If Anglos suspected an Indian of robbery, the simple destruction of the Indian camp would be sufficient punishment.[16] In contrast, a jury of their peers would determine the punishment of Anglos who were accused of crimes against Indians. Since most miners viewed Indians as competitors for the scare gold and resources in the region, the punishment extended to Anglo miners was often light or nonexistent. Because of these draconian and unfair practices, Anglos, armed with the flimsiest of evidence that supposed an Indian had committed a crime, committed untold atrocities against California's aboriginal population. As Governor Peter Burnett remarked in 1851, "The white man, to whom time is money . . . after being robbed a few times he becomes desperate, and resolves upon a war of extermination."[17] With Anglo miners literally getting away with murder, commandeering resources, and forcing Indians off their lands, the situation began to spiral out of control. As the year progressed, rumors began to circulate about a general Indian uprising. In central California, conflict between miners in the southern Sierra mining camps and the local Miwok and Yokut peoples had already resulted in violence that would escalate into the Mariposa Indian War. Concerned that a widespread conflict would devastate the growing economic importance of the region, the federal government finally acted. Three agents were dispatched to California to negotiate land concessions and peace treaties with the hostile Indians.

In the spring of 1851, Redick McKee, George Barbour, and Oliver Wozencraft began the task of negotiating peace with the Indians throughout the state. Altogether, the commissioners negotiated eighteen treaties, which reserved a total of 7,488,000 acres for the Indians of California. Only one of these treaties addressed a tribe in southern California. The treaties guaranteed that the United States would provide Indians with livestock, provisions, and training in husbandry so that the tribes could become "civilized." In exchange, Native Americans promised to recognize the United States as the sovereign government over the tribes, cede all other lands, and maintain peace with the Americans. Concern arose immediately from Anglo Californians that if the United States ratified the treaties, Indians would no longer need to work on the ranches for Anglo landholders, thus depriving the economy of a cheap source of labor. Additionally, the lands secured by the Indians encroached on some of the mining districts claimed by Anglo miners. This would have deprived the state and the miners of revenue. With the issue of money being brought to the fore, the treaties were doomed to fail.

While the commissioners were zealous in their work, their level of accuracy in tackling the quagmire of Indian/white issues in the state left something to be desired. Of the 139 groups of California Indians they reported to be represented in the treaties, 67 were tribelets, 45 were village names, 14 were duplicates, and 13 were personal names or unidentifiable. In 1926, an enumeration acknowledged that 175 tribes were not even represented in the treaties.[18] Many of those missing from the rolls were found in San Bernardino, Los Angeles, and San Diego counties. Only the Treaty of Temecula in 1852 included any of the major Indian tribes in southern California, and then only the Luisenos and Cahuillas were represented. To further complicate the issue, while these tribal groups were represented, the treaty did not take into account that several bands of Luisenos and Cahuillas occupied the territory, nor did it acknowledge the other tribes in the region. Despite the limited accuracy of their work, amid the chaos and violence that characterized the first years of California's statehood, the treaties produced by the commissioners were probably the best the United States could have hoped for at the time.

During the year the treaty commission operated, the commissioners were almost constantly at a disadvantage. The gold rush in the north made it almost impossible to hire anyone who had first-hand knowledge of the California Indians. In addition, because of the dramatically inflated prices in the gold fields, the gifts the commissioners were supposed to provide as indicators of the good intentions of the United States had to be purchased at rates that far exceeded the limits of their budget.[19] In an effort to reduce growing conflict between Anglos and the California Indians, the commissioners found themselves constantly rushing to hot spots to negotiate for peace between the encroaching Anglos and the Indians. Originally the activities of the commissioners focused on the northern and central districts of the state, where conflict between Anglos and Indians were most acute; the Indians of southern California did not present an immediate threat to the Anglo-American populace, and as such they did not merit consideration by the commissioners. However, the same corrupt influences of violence and land seizures that had come to characterize Anglo/Indian relations in the north also came to a head in the south; the result was a threatened Indian war. To dissuade the Indian population in southern California from attacking the small settlements, Oliver Wozencraft was dispatched to negotiate what would become the Treaty of Temecula.

In 1851, to support a flagging local tax base, Sheriff Agoston Haraszthy of San Diego had decreed that the Indians of San Diego County should pay taxes, regardless of whether they were considered citizens of the state or not.[20] Haraszthy asserted, "There is no doubt that the possessions, real and personal, of Christianized Indians, are taxable." If Indians proved unable to pay the taxes, their lands would be forfeited to the county in payment of the debt. Many Indians in southern California, however, disagreed with this arrangement, and under the leadership of Antonio Garra of the Cupeno Indians, some Indians fomented a revolt.[21] For the heavily outnumbered whites, a large-scale revolt would have been disastrous. Four whites had already been killed in skirmishes near Warner's Ranch in the heart of Cupeno and Cahuilla country. When Oliver Wozencraft arrived, the conflict showed all the promise of exploding into a regional war. Had this occurred, the limited military presence in the state would have been forced to further divide its troops. With numbers inadequate to address the conflict, a cascade of failure to control the violence between the Anglo and Indian communities in the state would have resulted. Protection of Anglo communities would have reverted to the local population, which in all likelihood would have responded with more viciousness in defending their families and possessions than would have been perpetrated by a trained military force. Because of these concerns, Wozencraft traveled to the area to negotiate a "Treaty of Peace and Friendship."[22] As with the other seventeen treaties, Wozencraft promised the Indians land, livestock, and provisions. His agreement allowed most southern California tribes to remain in their same village sites, as well as providing a preserve for them in the mountains. Satisfied by the concessions made by the United States, some Luisenos, Cahuillas, Kumeyaays, and Cupenos put down their weapons and eventually turned in the leaders of the revolt to Anglo authorities in a show of good faith. They then settled back to enjoy the benefits of their new agreement with the United States. It would be a long wait.

The Treaty of Temecula, like the other seventeen treaties negotiated by the commissioners, was steeped in controversy. Alarmed by the growing list of vouchers for supplies, salaries, and livestock, the secretary of the interior called a halt to all further proceedings and called the commissioners back to Washington. The two years that separated the call for the commission in 1850 and its final reporting to the Senate in 1852 had been a time of incredible change in the American concept of Indian land rights. Within that brief period of time, the rapidly rising Anglo population had changed the balance of power within the state from one in which Indians held the majority to one in which the Anglo-American population dominated. Additionally, in 1849 the secretary of the interior had dispatched Thomas Butler King and William Carey Jones to California on a fact-finding mission. King and Jones operated in the state at the same time as the commissioners; however, the purpose of their visit was not to quell Anglo/Indian hostilities, but to report on the condition of the Indians and address the issue of aboriginal land title.[23] When their reports were presented to the Senate in the spring of 1851, proponents of land acquisition had something to smile about.

King's report bluntly stated that the Indians "never pretended to hold any interests in the soil," while Jones's report conceded that the Mission Indians probably did have some legal right to the land, as they had been engaged in agriculture. Their reports, coupled with an argument presented by California senator Thomas Hart Benton, set the Senate to thinking about Indian land rights. Benton argued that the United States government was under no obligation to quiet Indian land claims before allowing settlement in disputed areas. Benton, like the Puritan John Winthrop before him, insisted that Indians did not have the right to own land, but merely a right to enjoy the bounty of the land, because they did not husband the soil. Because Indians did not manipulate the land by planting crops, even their right to enjoy the bounty of the land was abandoned when the Indians removed themselves from an area where they had been collecting foodstuffs. Since the Indians of southern California migrated to collect food, and the agricultural activity they engaged in was not recognized by Anglos, it would have been difficult for any tribe, save one that was wholly agriculturally based, to claim land for any period of time.[24] The arguments put forth by Senator Benton echoed those of the Spanish and Mexican governments, which had begun the process of dispossessing the Indians in the late eighteenth century.

In a state that was promising to be wealthy and immensely successful, the ideas presented by Benton and the Indian Office agents were seductive. While the Indian commissioners were busy scurrying around the state, public opinion was making its way more quickly across the continent. Public opinion in California as expressed by the state's representatives strongly opposed the ratification of the California treaties. As the Anglo population in California grew, its tolerance of Indian land claims fell. It is therefore not surprising that Commissioner Redick McKee's report, which stated, "We gave them all the land they asked for," was not met with great enthusiasm in the changing political climate. When the treaties came before the Senate in June 1852, the Senate unanimously defeated them in a closed session. In its 1852 majority report, the Senate stated, "In examining this subject, they may have been surprised to find, that the policy of the Indian Commissioners is not sustained, either by practice of the Mexican Republic, or that for the last forty-five years of our own. It is well known to all those who are reacquainted with the history of the Indian policy of Spain and Mexico, that the right of the Indian in the soil was never admitted or recognized."[25]

While many Americans who plied the gold placers in California wanted Indian removal, not treaties or accommodation, theirs was not the only opinion that garnered attention during the debates. Removing Indians from their traditional territories produced new issues that needed to be addressed—such as where to send the Indians, and how to absorb the cost of the enterprise. While Indian removal would have certainly solved the issue of Indian land rights, Californians, at least those in southern California, were more divided on the issue. Rancher J. J. Warner, also a Mexican land grantee, wrote a minority opinion following the rejection of the Treaty of Temecula. Warner suggested an alternative to Indian removal that would be less costly to implement, and at the same time would be beneficial to the Anglo communities that were expanding in the state. Moving the Indians, he reasoned, would deprive the local economy of a needed source of labor. In light of the labor demands generated by the gold rush in the north, if the Indians were removed from the state, the labor they provided would be impossible to replace. He suggested instead allowing local Indians to remain on their traditional village sites, but not giving them title.[26] In this way Indians could continue to meet the state's labor needs, which would allow the Anglo communities to flourish, and eventually the Indian question would be resolved when the Indians were absorbed into the rapidly expanding Anglo society. While the treaties generated a considerable amount of discussion at the time, their rejection withdrew them from further debates over the status of Indians in the state, but also resulted in accusations of a conspiracy of silence that has continued to the present day.

When the treaties were summarily rejected, the Senate returned the treaties to the Department of the Interior. Since the treaties dealt with Indian tribes, the Department of the Interior eventually forwarded the documents to the Bureau of Indian Affairs, where government bureaucrats unceremoniously filed them with other unratified treaties. Because it was clear that the issue of what to do with the California Indians would be resolved in another way, the treaties faded from memory. However, while the treaties passed into the dead-letter file of the U.S. government, they were still very much active in the minds of the tribes who had made the agreements. Many Indians believed that the negotiations had secured them perpetual possession of their lands, and the protection of the United States government against encroaching Anglos. None of the tribes had been made aware that the treaties required ratification by the U.S. Senate to make them valid. The summary dismissal of the treaties has resulted in some discussion that a conspiracy of silence occurred within the government, with the intent to deprive Native Americans of their lands. As historian Harry Kelsey has convincingly related in his rebuttal to this contention, the idea is little more than a fairy tale.[27] However, the fairy tale had been given credence, since Anglo officials did not inform the Indians of California that the Senate had rejected the treaties. Until the mid-1860s, many tribes continued to believe they had secured their lands as a result of the agreements they had made.

What the treaties did manage to do was to provide an interlude in the hostilities that had existed between Anglo-Americans and the Indians, especially the hostilities that had broken out in southern California. What remained to be addressed, however, was what to do with the Indians while still serving the needs of the growing Anglo population. Granting Indians title to the lands they had inhabited for centuries was not seriously considered. This left the creation of reservations as the only viable option for dealing with the state's Indian population. However, the placement of the reservations needed to be sensitive to the resource needs of the Anglo communities, while still allowing access to the labor provided by the Indians. To resolve this dilemma, in 1852 President Millard Fillmore appointed a former naval lieutenant, Edward Beale, as the California superintendent of Indian Affairs. His appointment boded ill for the Indians of the state. Beale had close personal and financial ties with California senators John C. Fremont and Thomas Hart Benton. His choice obviously presented a conflict of interest for the government and the Indians of the state.[28]

Beale arrived in California just as the treaty commission concluded its business. Disgusted with the "mismanagement" of the treaty commissioners in their cession of almost eight million acres of land, Beale suggested the establishment of five reservations of 25,000 acres each to accommodate the needs of the Indian population within the state. On 31 March 1853, Congress authorized the creation of the reservations, and appropriated $250,000 for the removal of the Indians and for their support on the reservations. Despite the original call for the establishment of five reservations, the United States created only one reservation near Fort Tejon in northern Los Angeles County, and a small farm near Fresno.[29]

Beale's reservation system failed for a number of reasons, not the least of which involved the suspicion natives harbored about the intentions of Anglo-Americans. Many had already suffered the loss of family members and their homelands. Additionally, the remote location of the reservation would have forced the majority of Indians to relocate to an unfamiliar area and forfeit the support they enjoyed from other tribal groups. On the new reservation, Indians were also compelled to labor at tasks that many were unfamiliar with, or that made little sense because of the terrain. Because of these reasons, few Indians left their traditional lands for the designated areas. This only inflamed anti-Indian sentiment among some Californians who saw the reservation as the first necessary step in a process of opening up the region for further Anglo settlement. Because Indians refused to migrate to the reservation, conflicts over land use resumed. At times Indians were prevented from gathering traditional food crops that they needed to sustain them through the winter, and wide-spread hunger resulted. As an incentive to increase migration, Beale refused to provide services to those Indians who would not move onto the reservation; his efforts only met with limited success. At the height of its existence, Beale was only able to convince eight hundred Indians to move onto the Tejon Reservation.[30]

Despite Beale's own criticism of the commissioners and their mismanagement of the treaty crisis, the reservation at Fort Tejon was also mired in corruption and mismanagement. In one instance, Beale used $25,000 to purchase beads from a sum of $100,000 that had been earmarked for use by the Indians.[31] The misappropriation of funds, coupled with the limited quality of the soil and the compulsory labor required by the Indian agents, doomed Beale's plan.[32] By 1858 the federal government had significantly decreased its funding to the reservations, and by 1860 the scheme had been abandoned. The only option available to Indians who chose to remain on their traditional lands was to establish their right of occupancy through the state system.

In order to sort through the various land claims that evolved when the United States assumed control of the ceded Mexican territory, California established a land commission.[33] Under the Act to Ascertain Private Land Claims in California, the state commission examined the various Mexican land grants, determined which ones were valid, and issued the appropriate title to the petitioner. The act was also intended to confirm Indian land claims by determining which lands Native Americans had occupied prior to the signing of the Treaty of Guadalupe Hidalgo. The act did not require the Indians to present their claims before the commission.[34] The question over Indian land rights would soon grow to be one of the largest single most deliberate uses of the law to divest the Indians in the state of their lands and subsequent rights. While the duties of the commission were clearly laid out, the results were less than favorable. Of the 155 southern California cases that were presented before the land commission, approximately 80 percent of the cases were confirmed either by the commission or after appeal to the district court. Many of these land grants included Indian villages—which, according to Mexican law, meant that the Indians were protected in their right to the land they occupied unless they chose to abandon the site. The land commission made no such distinction in its rulings, and of the hundreds of Indian villages that dotted the landscape, few received assurances of their title to the land.[35] In many cases, Indians who claimed to have received a land grant were denied title to the land, as in the case of Pablo Apis of the Luisenos.[36] In other cases title was confirmed, but the heirs of the grantee would later sell the land out from under the other members of the tribe, as was the case with Maria Juana, also of the Luisenos.[37]

The provision that excused Indians from presenting their claims before the commission did not excuse them from petitioning for the retention of their lands. This legal doublespeak left many Indians with the false impression that they did not need to prove title to their ancestral lands, or even seek to confirm title to the lands that had been given to them under the Mexican government. Additionally, while as many as fifty land grants had been made to Indians in the southern California area by the Mexican government, many tribes did not pursue their claims before the commission, because they remained under the impression that the issue of land tenure had been resolved by the signing of the treaties with the United States.[38] For the Indians, it seemed the retention of their ancestral lands was destined to be a confusing and protracted battle. To compound the complexity of the issue, most Indians primarily spoke their native language, Spanish, or a combination of the two languages. Few were literate. Since English would have been an unfamiliar language to the Indians, the distinction between appearing in court to plead their case versus filing a claim would have been beyond the ability of the Indians (or anyone not fluent in the language) to understand. California land commissioners spoke primarily English and dealt with laws written in English. As a result, the Indians in California were summarily denied their rights to their land because they did not understand the nuances of the English language or American law.

For those claimants who did come before the commission, each had to provide proof that they had been the recipient of a land grant. Most of the grantees provided titles that were either based on a system of metes and bounds—wherein boundaries were identified by physical characteristics in the land, not compass points—or on oral testimony. Most of the Indians of southern California had not received paper title to their lands; their only proof of possessory right came from oral testimony or past habitation. This proof could be easily refuted by Mexican land grantees who coveted the improvements that had been made on native lands, or by incoming Anglo-Americans who claimed they had purchased the land.[39]

Because of their lack of paper title and clear understanding of the new rules and regulations that governed the land commission, the Indians of southern California labored under a heavy burden to prove their right to the land. As for the few Indians who managed to meet the requirements of the land commission, they faced yet another obstacle to overcome in retaining their claim to the land. This obstacle came from the very treaty that presumed to protect their rights. While article 10 of the Treaty of Guadalupe Hidalgo stated that "all grants of land made by the Mexican government . . . shall be respected as valid," the United States Senate struck out this provision during the ratification of the treaty. According to historian Lisbeth Haas, the government then interpreted article 11 of the treaty as granting Indians "no land rights whatsoever." Under this article, the United States assumed the responsibility of preventing Indian raids on both American and Mexican citizens, and placing the Indians into "new homes." Haas contends that the phrase "new homes" implicitly denied Indians their "rightful possession of land or claim on ancestral territory."[40] To compound the difficulties faced by the Indians of southern California, in the 1860s the California land commission adopted a provision that maintained that those claims brought before the land commission that relied on oral testimony were "presumed to be invalid, if not fraudulent."[41]

An incomplete understanding of the law and the language, lack of paper title, and a prohibition on oral testimony resulted in discriminatory actions against the land claims of the Indians of southern California, and of all tribes throughout the state. No other racial group was so targeted by the new California legislature. Despite the effectiveness of these laws in quieting Indian land titles, two other laws affecting Indian land rights were passed by the California legislature in the early years of the state. In 1853, the legislature approved a preemptive act "which opened all land where title was unverified by the land court to settlement as public domain."[42] This act officially sanctioned "squatting" on Indian lands. As the number of Indians living in traditional village settings dwindled, and their very existence became more precarious because of a lack of access to traditional food crops, squatters knew that time was on their side. To prevent further decimation of their society, many Indians moved off traditional lands and onto less-productive acreage; many others abandoned their traditional societies and sought work in the growing Anglo towns.

The state's disregard for the land rights of its native inhabitants was further impacted by a second piece of legislation, the so-called "squatter's law" of 26 March 1855. This law allowed newly arrived Anglos to challenge the land rights of the Mexican land grantees, and individuals who had purchased portions of their grant lands. The law maintained that all lands were regarded as public until the claimants could prove legal title. Under this law, even if the original landholder prevailed in his claim on the land, he was obligated to reimburse the squatter for any improvements that might have been made on the land. For many of the Mexican land grantees, this provision alone could push them into bankruptcy. Coupled with the litigation costs, many Mexican land grantees either chose not to pursue their claims in court, or abandoned their attempts before the commission had made a decision. This law, while directly impacting Mexican land grantees, also indirectly impacted Indians living on the lands in question. Since many Mexican land grantees had encouraged Indians to reside on their lands in order to secure a ready supply of labor, when the grantee lost his land, the Indians also lost their homes. Finally, for the Indians who had refused to be integrated into the mission system, the California legislature summarily denied their rights to possess their traditional lands.[43] In the end, Indians found themselves either viewed as interlopers on their own lands, or pushed onto less-desirable properties where subsistence became increasingly more difficult. Under the Americans, both the federal and state governments during the first years of California statehood had been unsuccessful in humanely addressing the needs of the native population within the state, due to the duplicity of the Americans who had been charged with overseeing this activity. The behavior exhibited by the officers of the state and federal government were mirrored at the local level as well.

In the County of Los Angeles, the lawless behavior that characterized the northern mining districts struck a familiar note. In northern mining communities, the absence of a trained judiciary forced the development of "miner's codes" to govern the behavior of unruly miners. On the surface, these codes appeared to support the traditional legal structures that existed in the East; however, beneath the surface, the "laws" and rulings that came from the miner's courts were based as much on personal prejudice as on distantly remembered statutes. In southern California during the first decade of the state's existence, the limited tax revenue generated by the sparsely populated region and a lack of trained judicial representatives forced the local courts to operate in conditions that often mimicked the miner's courts. Many of the courts in southern California were forced to perform their duties without access to copies of legal works that discussed judicial precedents or the finer points of English law.[44] This resulted in a hodgepodge of rulings and court antics that in 1852 led the district court to annul all business being addressed by the local courts.[45] Additionally, the language barrier that existed because a primarily Spanish-speaking population was now being governed by an English-speaking legislature only added to the confusion.

To accommodate for these shortcomings in the judicial system, the counties of southern California, like the mining camps of northern California, fell back on the use of popular justice in their early years.[46] The use of vigilance committees, while illegal according to the new state statutes, also proved to be quite popular. In 1854–1855, Los Angeles recorded twenty lynchings due to vigilante activity, with the practice continuing well into the 1860s. The call for vigilante justice was not limited to the growing urban areas, or solely used as a means of controlling the non-Anglo community. In most instances, the use of extralegal justice was born out of the frustration Anglo-Americans felt when their attempts to control the rampant crime in their communities failed. The anonymous nature of most of the crimes committed in the area led many to find an easy scapegoat for the disintegration of their communities. In many instances, Indians were seen as the primary perpetrators of crime.[47] Many times Indians were accused of perpetrating a crime despite evidence to the contrary. Unfortunately for the Indians, the difference between belief and reality all too often resulted in vigilante justice.[48]

The fickleness of vigilante justice did not limit the actions of the participants to Indian victims. On occasion, vigilantes used extralegal punishment to protest the rough treatment of Indians, but in these examples, the victim of the vigilantes was usually non-white. A characteristic incident occurred on 31 July 1852. The *Los Angeles Star* reported that a "Mexican who stabbed an Indian at the Mission San Gabriel was taken by the citizens and upon examination sentenced to sixty lashes."[49] For the most part, however, the only reaction against a crime visited on an Indian was occasional condemnation in the press.[50] Such an example occurred in San Gabriel in 1852. In a news article, the *Los Angeles Star* reported that three Anglo men had "visited the rancheria at San Gabriel, and cruelly abused some Indian women." Several Indian men who heard their cries for help rescued the women. However, aside from the condemnation of the press, no assistance was forthcoming from the authorities.[51] Despite occasional assistance from the vigilance committee, Indians were primarily seen by the fledgling society as a ready source of labor.

Four months after the passage of the Act for the Government and Protection of Indians, the Los Angeles City Council approved an ordinance that mirrored the state's decision to legislate compulsory labor. The result was the establishment of a virtual "slave market" within the city, with the Indians serving as the slaves.[52] In the early years of the city, a limited supply of currency encouraged the payment of Indian workers in alcohol, a practice that had been established by the Spanish missionaries and continued through the Mexican period. Continuing this "tradition," Anglo-Americans paid Indian laborers their wages in cash and *aguardiente*, a potent alcoholic beverage. Wages were most often paid on a Saturday evening, so that by Sunday the now drunken Indians could be rounded up by the police and held in jail until Monday. As a group, those Indians incarcerated in the sweeps for public intoxication were marched to the courthouse, where those who were unable to pay their fines had to submit to being auctioned off to the highest bidder in a labor auction.[53] This demeaning process continued in Los Angeles for almost twenty years. Its demise was more the result of the dwindling supply of Indians than a change of heart on the part of the citizenry. The "participants" in these labor auctions remained solely Indian; law enforcement did not auction off Anglo prisoners.

As the first decade of California's statehood progressed, the conflict between Indians and whites prompted Anglos to demand action from all levels of the government. The laws that had been established by the state legislature favored Anglo-American rights over Indian rights, and federal intervention within the state remained weak. It is not surprising, then, that even the pitiful laws regulating Anglo behavior toward Indians were frequently ignored. During the 1850s, two schools of thought dominated the region. The first, supported by California's first two governors, advocated exterminating the Indians within the territory.[54] By exterminating Indians, Anglos could conveniently quiet all land claims they might make, thus preserving Anglo hegemony in the state. The other position held by the Americans determined that Indians should be removed from contact with the encroaching Anglos. Since the early reservation system left a great deal to be desired during the early years of California's existence, it seemed as though extermination would win out over removal. However, a distinction was made between those Indians who were beneficial to the Anglo society, since they provided needed labor, and those Indians who refused to relinquish their land and cultural traditions to encroaching Anglo-Americans.

Through the 1850s and 1860s, the depredations by the Indians who had not been assimilated nominally into the growing American society reached a fevered pitch. Pushed off their traditional lands and frequently lacking the ability to feed themselves, many resorted to violence to retain access to their lands, and to protect their families from the wanton violence that characterized Indian/Anglo contact. In southern California, the theft of livestock and raids on settlements by "non-civilized" Indians from the Mojave Desert threatened the development of the region. As a result, punitive forays into Indian land by Americans occurred with some frequency. In Los Angeles, the city deputized its own rangers to assist law enforcement with Indian control.[55] Unfortunately, the rangers and private citizens who took to the field to confront the marauding Indians were often indiscriminate as to whom they attacked.

During the 1850s, the California state legislature, not the United States Army, called for several military campaigns against the Indians. Normally, the burden of conducting a military raid against a hostile foe would have been left to the discretion of the United States military. However, in California, private raids were often the rule. In San Bernardino, the famed Mormon Battalion served as rangers for the County of Los Angeles against Indians who raided the area.[56] Their brutality proved to be very effective at controlling the depredations of nonresident Indians. However, their harassment of innocent Indians was also commonplace.

These quasi-military groups were not alone in their attempt to eliminate "non-beneficial" Indians from the region. Several townships created their own temporary extermination squads to hunt down Indian groups suspected in the depredations. These squads maintained that it was the responsibility of the state to protect their property rights over those of the Indians. After determining that something needed to be done, these squads operated independently of any state oversight to secure their goals. Once they had achieved their objective, most military units billed and received compensation from the state for their efforts. Coinciding with these orchestrated campaigns against Indians were the private wars that literally littered the landscape with the bodies of murdered Indians. To many Indians living in the state during the 1850s, it would have seemed that Anglo-Americans had launched a "crusade" to exterminate them. While most of the atrocities occurred in the north, where contact between Anglos and Indians was greatest, southern California shared in this grisly war. In Los Angeles, the discovery of dead Indians in the streets became so commonplace that the newspapers frequently only reported that the dead individual had been handled in the "usual way," which was to ignore him.[57] In San Diego, the frequency with which Indians were found shot dead by Anglo men led one news reporter to quip that San Diego "should not be surprised at the arrival of parties from San Francisco to practice before goin' out a shootin' duels."[58] By the middle of the 1850s, the widespread and unpunished murders of so many human beings prompted local papers to decry the deaths.[59] This moral outrage had little effect on quelling the violence, except perhaps to assuage the consciences of those involved, or those who sanctioned the behavior by their silence. Instead, the violent contact between Anglos and Indians fostered support for additional legislation that would hinder the Indian's ability to defend himself, instead of addressing the issue of Anglo-Indian violence.

In 1854, the state legislature passed a law prohibiting the sale of firearms or ammunition to Indians, or anyone associated with Indians—such as an Anglo spouse. The impact of this law was to effectively leave the Indians within the state virtually defenseless against a better-armed foe. It also served to limit the rights of citizens who willingly associated with Indians. The effectiveness of the law was staggering; court documents reported that the vast majority of Indians brought into court on assault charges most often used a knife as a weapon, whereas during this time period Indians found dead on the streets were often the victims of gunshot wounds or beating. This pattern of weapon use suggests an Anglo perpetrator and not an Indian.

By 1860, California celebrated its first decade as a state. During that time, the gold fields in the north had consistently yielded less and less to the miners who remained in the diggings. Forsaking the search for gold, many of these former miners left the placers and settled onto farms and ranches. Families were reunited, and the State of California enjoyed a consistent period of economic prosperity. In the southern portion of the state, the large-scale ranching economy that had dominated the region since the Spanish conquest had started to give way to smaller individual landholdings. In part, this restructuring of landownership was the result of laws that hampered Mexican land grantees from retaining their lands. Protracted legal battles over the lands they claimed had to be fought in courts, and legal fees bankrupted many of the previous land barons. With the smaller landholdings, the region started to concentrate more on agriculture instead of ranching. However, the division of the lands in the region did not result in any improvement of the status of the state's Indian population.

On 22 April 1860, the state legislature amended the infamous 1850 Law for the Protection of the Indian. The new amendments expanded the control the state could exercise over Indians, to allow for the indenture of Indians who were held as "prisoners of war." This same law extended the rules against Indian vagrants to all of those who had not "placed themselves under the protection of any white person." The length of time an

Indian minor could be held in bondage was also extended. Upon application to the county recorder, an Anglo individual could control the labor
of an Indian male until age twenty-five and females until age twenty-one,
if they were indentured before the age of fourteen. Also under this new
revision, the age for indentured service increased to thirty years for men
and twenty-five years for women, if the Indian was over fourteen at the
time of their indenture. Previously, it had been eighteen and fifteen years
old respectively. Additionally, the forcible conveyance of any Indian within
or outside the state for the purposes of labor was still prohibited, but fines
were increased to not less than $100 or more than $500.[60] The fines were
to be equally divided between the prosecutor and the county in which the
conviction was made. No provisions for the Indians were made.[61] In 1863,
the legislature eventually repealed the law compelling the bondage of Indians, in keeping with the federal Emancipation Proclamation Act.

The 1850s and 1860s saw a change in the way the Anglo population
of California dealt with the Indians within the state. Previous proposals
had called for the extermination of Indians, or their removal to federal
reservations. No doubt each proposal served as a cost- and time-saving
measure, encouraged by the limited resources of the new administration
and the persistent insistence by some Anglos that Indians had no place in
the land of their birth. Under California law, only those Indians who were
in direct contact with Anglos were subject to local control. The presence
of unregulated Indians, coupled with lingering questions over land rights,
had inhibited development in some areas and led to increased vigilante
activity. Much of this activity had been sanctioned by the state through the
payment of charges claimed by the vigilantes. The willingness of the state
to act to address its "Indian problem" received further support from the
federal government, which in 1860 attempted to shunt the sole responsibility for the California Indians onto the state. The federal legislature offered
the state an annual sum of $50,000 if the state would "agree to take charge
of and maintain within the State the Indians now within her jurisdiction,
to the satisfaction of the President, and to relieve the United States from all
liability or responsibility connected with the same for the period of twenty
years."[62] The proposal was vilified in the California press as too cost-prohibitive and went down to defeat in the Congress.

Through the 1850s and into the 1860s, the residents of southern California lived a largely isolated existence from the rest of the state. For the

Indians in southern California, the 1850s opened with a devastating small-pox epidemic that decimated the tribes of the region. Many tribes were unable to sustain themselves on their traditional lands because of the loss of so many of their members. As a result, many native people in south-ern California either moved away from the sites where the outbreaks had occurred, or relocated near Anglo settlements where they continued to serve as laborers. For those who moved, their abandonment of their tradi-tional lands added fuel to the land issues that still linger in the state. Still other Indians refused to leave and fought to eke out an existence on their traditional lands.

The increased dependence on Anglos for survival was offset by chang-ing conditions in the north. By the mid-1850s, Anglo miners had depleted gold supplies, and they used increasingly harsh extractive methods to remove the ore. In 1848 the average daily wage for a miner had been twenty dollars; by 1856 this had dropped to three dollars.[63] As former miners aban-doned their claims, many assumed respectable positions within their new communities as farmers and businessmen. The overall result was a reduc-tion in the demand for the beef of the ranchos, and subsequently of the need for Indian labor. Those Indian laborers now faced increasing compe-tition from Anglos for the positions they once held. During the 1860s, the southern California region was rocked by a series of punishing droughts and floods. In 1860–1861, the area suffered a series of devastating floods that washed away much of the pastureland for cattle and made transporta-tion in some areas impossible. The devastation wrought by the rain was countered in 1862–1864, when a prolonged drought further reduced the ranching capacity of the area by destroying the fodder for grazing ani-mals. These environmental changes further reduced the need for Indian labor and concomitantly made it more difficult for those Indians who still attempted to live a traditional existence. Increased irrigation in Los Ange-les and San Bernardino encouraged the development of agriculture, but the distribution of this produce was limited to the region because of the lack of rail service. It would not be until 1869, when the city of Los Angeles was connected to its nearest port in San Pedro Harbor, that this issue was elimi-nated. However, the recognition of the economic importance of a rail line in the region was not lost on the local Anglo residents. By the mid-1860s, the push to get more extensive rail service to the southern California area intensified. To ensure that nothing would hinder the advancement of the rails, those individuals deemed "undesirable" would again fall under the punishing gaze of the law. Despite their best efforts, another seven years would lapse before the railroad connected Los Angeles to the north. For San Diego and San Bernardino, the railroads would not arrive until the late 1880s. Another drawback to the influx of Americans and the withdrawal of land from native control was the loss of native foods that the indigenous population relied on to survive, a situation that further enhanced the misery endured by the Indians.

Throughout the first fifteen years of its existence, the California Land Commission was still debating title questions stemming from the Mexican land grants in the southern California region. By the mid-1860s, most Indians had abandoned any hope of seeing their claims approved through the system and had stopped petitioning the commission for the return of their lands. This opened the land to purchase and further encouraged Anglos to enter the region. The entrance of still more people into the area served to further destroy the fabric of Indian life that had existed prior to contact. Unfortunately, the devastating legislative and environmental events of the 1850s and 1860s, coupled with the persistent violence against local Indians, only served as the precursor to the continued attacks on native peoples by the state and federal governments, and by private individuals within the state.

American Law, 1865–1890

B Y THE TIME CALIFORNIA WAS BEGINNING ITS SECOND DECADE as a state, the condition of the Indians within its borders had deteriorated dramatically. The Indian population in the southern region prior to contact with the Spanish in 1769 is estimated to have been between 15,200 and 35,000.[1] By 1860 these numbers had dropped to approximately 8,474.[2] Conversely, in the same year the Anglo population in southern California was approximately 20,000.[3] The number of Anglo individuals seems of limited consequence when compared to today's modern census figures, but in the nineteenth century California's economy was based on agriculture, and as such, one farmer could claim hundreds of acres of land. To ensure their success, farmers undertook several irrigation schemes that diverted water away from Indian villages. Additionally, farmers limited access of Native Americans to lands that had once been open during the rancho period. The introduction of non-native plants and livestock to the fragile ecosystem destroyed native plant forms. Those most impacted by these changes were the Indians who had once depended on these plants for sustenance.

Many of the conditions that characterized the decade between 1850 and 1860 continued into the final decades of the century. Vigilantism, while declining in incidence as the Anglo population increased and the judicial and police presence solidified, continued to be a persistent condition through the 1870s. State law that prohibited Indians from testifying in court against Anglos had been withdrawn by 1875, but the daily practice of this newfound privilege was limited.[4]

A dramatic shift occurred in national policy during the Civil War era, from one that allowed compulsory labor to one that condemned it. This development had a significant impact in southern California. The de facto slavery of the Indian that had been codified by the first California legislature clashed with a national policy that forbade forced labor. By 1865, California abandoned the earlier legislation that supported the forced labor of Indians. In 1879, when state delegates set about writing the second California Constitution, provisions for the forced labor of Indians had been stricken from the final document. In addition to the national changes, the rapidly changing demographics of the region resulted in a flood of Anglos into the southern California region, and increased the cultivation of the land by non-natives. As more Americans entered the area, the sight of starving, landless Indians greeted many. These newcomers began agitating for federal assistance in dealing with the "Indian problem." By 1870, the federal government capitulated and agreed to reestablish a reservation system in the area.[5]

As the last years of the nineteenth century waned, the presence of the Indian in the judicial system decreased significantly. In part, this was because of the declining Indian population and the shunting of the native population onto reservations. Faced with declining rights if they retained their identity as members of tribes, untold numbers of Indians also assimilated into the burgeoning Latino population. Reports from Indian agents chronicle the devastating effect malnutrition had on the already weakened Indian population.[6] Finally, the effects of the murderous behavior of Anglo-Americans against Indians continued to take its toll on the native population. The final result was the decimation of the Indian people of southern California. By 1910, the number of Indian people in the southern California region had declined to approximately 3,000.[7]

As more Indians sought refuge on the new reservations, native people found themselves confronted with another foe: the Indian agent. Within the federal enclaves of the reservation, the Indian agent increasingly assumed the function of the tribal captain or the local justice of the peace in the punishment of minor offenses.[8] This progression in how Indians were treated in the courts was not a forward progression for the Indians. Instead, the prejudices of the agent often resulted in the punishment of an Indian for behavior that would not be considered a crime in the larger

Anglo society. Additionally, since the justice court had served as the referring court for higher court action against Native Americans, the presence of Indians in the county and district courts decreased. This meant that any of their complaints would be addressed in an informal manner and without judicial oversight. As the nineteenth century neared its conclusion, the federal courts became increasingly involved in the judicial proceedings against Indians living on federal reservations, but largely left the decision on whether to refer to a higher court to the agent. The combination of these factors served to greatly remove the California Indians from the control of the local judiciary, and in doing so also removed them from much judicial oversight. For the Anglo population of southern California, however, this resulted in an "out-of-sight, out-of-mind" dichotomy.

By the late 1860s, the whole of southern California was teetering on the cusp of hard times, the result of almost a decade of setbacks. However, what affected the Anglo population seemed to disproportionately impact the Indian population at a greater level. A virulent outbreak of smallpox in 1862–1863 had decimated the Indian population. In the Akagchemem (Juaneno) village near present-day San Juan Capistrano, 129 out of a population of only 227 Indians died in one month alone.[9] This loss was followed in 1867 by a devastating flood, which prevented the growth of fodder for livestock and all but destroyed the cattle industry in the area.[10] For the Indians, these environmental changes would have a profound effect, as many had worked and lived on the ranches.

Environmental changes were compounded by the national economic depression that wracked the nation beginning in 1873. Because of these issues and the increasing Anglo population in the region, Indians faced increased competition for the manual-labor jobs they had traditionally performed. The competition for jobs inflamed Anglo prejudices against non-whites, and Nativist rhetoric often found its voice in a rising worker's-rights movement that violently opposed any non-whites who competed with Anglo-Americans for work. A combination of these forces ensured that Indians who had survived the dispossession of their lands through the land commission and fraud, as well as the decimation of their tribes from violence and disease, would have little choice but to assimilate into the Anglo society or migrate to the reservations that the United States government had created in the mid-1870s. By the end of the nineteenth century, the Indians of southern California were a people under siege from many sides, not the least of which was the judiciary.

By the late 1860s, previous state legislation that had been aimed at the native population, such as the Act for the Government and Protection of Indians, came under increased scrutiny from the population at large. No longer in need of controlling the labor activities of the Indians by legislative fiat, and flush with a Anglo population willing to perform the same services, California's interest in perpetuating the availability of a native labor force began to wane. To ensure the steady removal of Indians from the presence of the burgeoning Anglo population, in 1860 the federal government enacted legislation that divided the state into two Indian districts. Under the provisions of this statute, the government would support those Indians who agreed to abandon their traditional lifestyles, learn to farm, and assimilate into American society. For this group, the government would provide agricultural tools and the advice of a seasoned farmer. While these Indians attempted to establish themselves as agriculturists, the government would feed and clothe them.[11]

By 1865, Congress, in an attempt to get out of the California Indian business, proposed further revisions to this 1860 federal law. Under the revised law, the Indian Department of California would be reorganized under one superintendent, instead of two, and the government would limit the number of reservations within the state to four, a net reduction of one reservation. The 1865 federal bill also called for a single agent to oversee each reservation. Aware that the quality of life on the reservations had been declining significantly over the previous years, and that many Indians refused to live on them, the statute also allowed abandoned reservations to be appraised and sold at auction. The only reservation for the southern portion of the state would be on the Tule River in Tulare County, several hundred miles to the north of the main Indian population centers in southern California.[12] Indians who refused to go to the reservations would forfeit any protection they might have been afforded by the government. However, while this draconian bill had support from the California politicians, the federal government never executed its provisions. Had the bill passed, the Indians of southern California would have lost much of their cultural identity as they meshed with other tribes. Additionally, any hopes of retaining their traditional lands would have suffered a setback, as the land that they had occupied would be subject to sale at auction.

While the reservations attracted much of the public's attention regarding the "Indian question," most Indians lived within the Anglo population as laborers. This growing assimilation resulted in many Indians becoming estranged from their tribes, and subsequently resulted in a further deterioration of the cultural traditions that had once bound the native people of southern California together. In 1865, the Supreme Court of California struck down the provisions of the 1850 Law for the Protection of the Indian that specifically addressed those Indians who lived independent of their tribal affiliations. While the court's decision initially seemed to favor these Indians by pushing them into the mainstream society, it also removed the limited protection these individuals had—namely, the use of county courts. Because of a wider financial base, the county court system could provide greater oversight to judicial proceedings. In contrast, the local courts labored under limited judicial oversight, and consequently the Indians were subject to local prejudice.[13]

As California entered the 1870s, the single most important government policy became the Grant Peace Policy. Ulysses S. Grant, unlike many individuals of his age, believed that Indians had a right to their own lands, a right that should not be abridged by the states, territories, or federal government. However, while these progressive ideas would meet with a nod of approval in today's multicultural world, the caveat had always been that Indians would have to move aside for the greater Anglo society if need be. Despite this acknowledgment, Grant's policies were not purely motivated by altruism and goodwill.

Several religious denominations within the country had long agitated for a greater role in Indian affairs. These groups believed it was their duty to enlighten native people on Christianity, and felt that the corruption endemic among the Indian agents was a deterrent to the religious and cultural assimilation of native people. Additionally, the still-bloody battlefields of the Civil War had resulted in a desire by American politicians to limit further bloodshed within the nation. A protracted war against the Indians would surely result in more soldiers dying on the battlefield. A less militaristic solution to the "Indian problem" would also allow the country to recover economically from the financial burden left over from the Civil War, and to deal with the "Indian problem" in as cost-effective a manner as possible. As conflict between the Plains Indians and the westward settlements increased, Grant's policies called for the extension of an olive branch instead of the gun. Under his administration, the government created a Board of Indian Commissioners to oversee the treatment and status of the Indians. To prevent further conflict between Anglo-Americans and Indians, and to assist in assimilation, Ulysses Grant also created several reservations by executive order. Grant believed the army needed to divest itself of the burden of managing Indians, a burden that was willingly assumed by many religious groups. To assure the success of his peace initiative, religious groups began to assume control of the Indian agencies, often with ministers appointed as agents.[14] While Grant's policies served to hasten the assimilation of Indians and to prevent further bloodshed, it still did not ameliorate the prejudices of many Americans. Instead, in many cases it placed the Indians in direct competition with the growing Anglo population in southern California.

Initially hoping to placate the settlers who viewed Indians as a degraded people and wanted them removed from the public domain, Grant authorized the creation of two reservations in what is now San Diego County. By executive order, on 31 January 1870, the president created the San Pasqual Reservation, which encompassed over 92,000 acres of land, and the Pala Reservation, which included about 46,000 acres.[15] Government officials believed that the creation of the two reservations would end the concerns the Anglo leaders of southern California had about their "Indian problem." However, the trouble was just beginning. Almost immediately, local communities rose up against the removal of so much land from the public domain. The outpouring of criticism proved to be considerable, as the commissioner of Indian affairs noted in a communication to the secretary of the interior:

> It appears . . . that the citizens of San Diego County protest against the order of the President setting aside said lands for Indian reservation; that the Indians are unanimously opposed to going on said reservation; that citizens have made valuable improvement thereon; and that there are but few Indians on the lands set apart as foresaid . . . it would be in the best interests and welfare of the Indians, as well as others, that . . . the order of the President . . . should be rescinded.[16]

Bowing to political pressure, on 17 February 1871, Grant revoked the executive order that had created the San Pasqual and Pala reservations.

However, the issues that resulted in the demand for reservations in southern California still existed, despite the revocation of Grant's executive order. Without a treaty stipulating their right to lands, or an executive order creating a reservation for their use, the Indians of southern California had no "legal" right within the American judicial system to demand any land concessions. As a result, the landless status of the Indian resulted in many of the aboriginal people of southern California being forced to beg for subsistence food or labor in a land of abundance. Other Indians chose instead to seize what they felt was rightfully theirs and ran afoul of the law. The degraded conditions forced on the Indians in the southern California region coincided with the negative attitudes that persisted among Anglo-Americans about the criminal natures of Indians or their laziness because they often occupied the lowest rungs of society. These attitudes formed an odd juxtaposition within the Anglo-American society: the newspaper accounts of the day are replete with the acknowledgment that Anglo land seizure prevented Native Americans in the area from being self-sufficient, but also absolved the local community from the responsibility of correcting the issue. Instead, the call was repeated for the creation of reservations for the Indians, which would remove them from the Anglo communities and divest the state from further responsibility in the maintenance of the tribes—a position that stood in opposition to the laws that had been passed in the state only twenty years earlier wherein the state refused to relinquish control of the Indians to the federal government.

On 27 December 1875, Grant complied with these demands and approved the creation of several new federal reservations for the Indians of southern California. Instead of setting aside large tracts of land for aboriginal use, Grant attempted to ameliorate the impact these reservations would have on the local communities by proposing several smaller reservations on plots of land that would be less attractive to the Anglo population. In the end, this approach proved to be palatable to the Anglo-American communities in the southern California region, and a total of nine reservations, including Santa Ysabel, Pala, Agua Caliente, Sycuan, Inaya, Cosmit, Potrero, Cahuilla, and Capitan Grande, were established. The government divided these reservations among the Cahuillas, Cupenos, Luisenos, and Kumeyaays living in Riverside and San Diego counties.[17]

Despite the obvious need for a land base for local Indians, the stability of the reservations remained uncertain into the next several administrations, due to conflicts with local communities that saw the land—and especially water rights—that had been endowed to the reservations as a challenge to Anglo hegemony.[18] In 1880, President Rutherford B. Hayes revoked the executive order for the entire Agua Caliente Reservation and returned almost 2,000 acres of the Santa Ysabel Reservation to the public domain.[19] Rescission of the reservations came at the behest of several non-native landholders. Since the Indians did not have "title" to the lands they occupied, they had no legal ability to fight against this injustice. As the 1870s progressed into the 1880s, more Anglo settlers came into southern California to take advantage of the region's unique agricultural attributes and the promise that the railroads would soon connect the farms to markets in the rest of the United States and beyond. As property values increased, they solidified Anglo prejudices that saw the Indians as a group of individuals who should be moved off the land in order to allow the Anglo-American society to flourish. Confronted with these challenges, Indians had little chance of securing title to the lands they had inhabited for centuries.

In addition to the pressure being exerted by the local communities, Indian land tenure ceased to be a deciding factor in whether Indians might regain access to the land by governmental edict. Land under the American system was normally granted to specific tribes through the use of the treaty. While some of the Indians of California had signed a treaty with the federal government in 1851, the Senate never ratified it; therefore, they had no claim to the lands. The possession of a treaty was not sufficient to guarantee a tribe perpetual control over their lands. Historically, many Indian tribes have had their original treaty agreements abrogated by the Congress without their consent. American law, like European law, assumed that all land ultimately belonged to the government. The government in turn supported the ownership rights of individuals who had tangible proof of land title. In 1875, the county sheriff of San Diego forcibly removed the Indians of Temecula after three local farmers petitioned the courts for title to the land. The Indians waged a court battle against the farmers, but the courts supported the land claims of the Anglo-Americans, and the land was lost.[20] Despite the preceding events, the dispossession of the California Indian still was not complete.

In 1879, due to the significant changes economically, demographically, and socially that had occurred in the state during its first thirty years, California decided to rewrite its state constitution.[21] Policymakers, well aware of the growing Anglo population in the state, no longer needed laws that compelled native people to labor for the Anglo population, as had occurred in the 1850 constitution. Under the new state constitution, compulsory labor was no longer a central feature of the way the state viewed its Indian inhabitants—however, the land was. The new state constitution contained a provision that allowed squatters to continue to claim lands that were reportedly part of the "public domain." For the Indians of southern California, this meant squatters could still challenge their right to reside on lands that many still clung to. Several Indian tribes in the southern California area held documents that indicated they held title to their lands, including the Luisenos of Temecula and the Cahuilla Indians living in San Timoteo Canyon. Many other tribes assumed that they had title because of the Treaty of Temecula (1852). However, since the United States Senate had never ratified this treaty, its provisions were not binding. Unfortunately, the tribes of California that signed the treaty were never advised that the Senate had failed to ratify it—a fact that significantly impacted their status in the state. Additionally, most tribes lacked the level of documentation that would have secured them permanent title to their lands by the California Land Commission. Despite their limited chances for success, several Indians filed suit to preserve their homelands, including the Luiseno and Cahuilla Indians.[22] Each tribe lost their case in court. For the Indians of southern California, this left them little choice but to either move onto the reservations or assimilate into the larger society.

While the labor needs of the growing American communities no longer demanded the same consistent labor supply that had characterized the early years of American settlement, cheap labor was still ardently sought in the region by those who needed an itinerant labor supply. The creation of reservations did not remove local Indians from the influence of the courts or save them from the abuses of the larger Anglo communities. The "slave market" continued to operate into the 1870s in Los Angeles, and while San Diego and San Bernardino were not as blatant in their use of Indians as a community labor source, each city regularly committed Indians to jail for minor infractions and assessed fines they could not pay. When an Indian could not pay the assessed fine, the county hired that person out for work. In Los Angeles, Indian convicts went to the highest bidder, while in San Diego and San Bernardino, those Indians incarcerated exchanged their labor at a rate of one dollar per day. However, it should be noted that only Los Angeles widely embraced this practice. In San Diego, an ordinance against public intoxication passed in 1874 increased the fines for each offender from five to ten dollars.[23] In San Bernardino, the assessment of fines remained the privilege of the justice of the peace and varied from one to ten dollars. All communities had some type of ordinance prohibiting public drunkenness, dating from the 1850s. However, despite their declining numbers in the population, Indians made up a disproportionate number of the cases for public drunkenness brought before the local courts.[24]

The continued use of the Indian as a source of labor, and as such an important component in the development of the community, did not offset the treatment of natives at the hands of Anglos. Indians were still regularly abused and murdered by members of the larger American society. In many instances, the abuse suffered by Indians occurred at the hands of those sworn to uphold the law. Historian Gordon Bakken has discussed the active participation of lawmen in lawless activity in his study of law in California. For many of these lawmen, "vigilante justice was supportive of the formal legal system."[25] Several instances of vigilante justice occurred through the 1870s, many of which were inspired by the atrocities that occurred in the mining districts near Las Vegas, Nevada, which sits forty-five miles from the border with California, or in the mining districts in San Bernardino County. Anglo residents of the local southern California communities were often identified as victims; this personalized the events and undoubtedly generated support for retaliation. The decade opened with the murder of a Los Angeles man who had gone to the mines near Las Vegas to seek his fortune. Unfortunately instead of securing his fortune, he met his death—reportedly at the hands of Piute Jack, "a notorious scoundrel, who has always been hostile to the whites, and has been the chief instigator if not the actual murderer of many white men." The local miners approached Tecoha, the chief of the local Piute tribe, and based on this speculation demanded that Piute Jack be turned over to them. The chief acquiesced to their demands, and Piute Jack was dutifully turned over to the mob. He was systematically tried in a miner's court, found guilty, and sentenced to be shot to death.[26] In San Diego County during the same year, an Indian named Jose had been held in the Julian jail on charges of grand larceny. Sometime during the night, Jose had been taken from the jail and beaten to death. There had been no evidence of a forced entry into the jail, nor any investigation into his death.[27] Jose's death was not an isolated incident.

Two years later, in the San Diego city jail, an Indian named Sole also died under suspicious circumstances. Sole had been placed alone in a jail cell after being arrested for public drunkenness. The following morning, law-enforcement officials found Sole hanging in his cell. Sole had been bound with a rope following his arrest and reportedly had remained bound during his incarceration, which made suicide impossible.[28] Considering the hostile climate between whites and Indians, it is likely that either his jailers hanged him, or they allowed others to do so.

The prevalent image of the Indian as a subhuman entity within the communities of southern California garnered him the enmity of his Anglo neighbors to the point that Anglos claimed Indians committed almost every crime that went unsolved.[29] In 1871, authorities in San Diego County accused Indians of murdering an Anglo man simply because they found barefoot tracks outside of his window.[30] When the San Bernardino city jail caught fire in 1873, officials again blamed Indians for the crime, despite the lack of proof and the absence of any Indians being in the jail at the time.[31] In another incident, in 1879, two Indians stood accused of assault in San Bernardino. Following their trial, a jury acquitted both men; however, before they managed to leave town, they found themselves in court again, accused of another assault. A second trial ensued, and again the jury acquitted both Indian men. In spite of their acquittals, the local newspaper viewed the decision of the court with suspicion, stating, "Where there is so much smoke there must be some fire."[32] The tenuous position of Indians in society, and their convenience as scapegoats for unsolved crimes, encouraged vigilantism. For the remote, undeveloped counties that made up southern California, the perception that they were a lawless region would have retarded investment in the area, and subsequently would have negatively impacted the fortunes of many. Civic and business leaders such as B. D. Wilson, former Indian agent and businessman; Horace Bell, Los Angeles lawyer and journalist; and Phineas Banning, founder of Wilmington and "father of the Los Angeles [San Pedro] Harbor," all participated in vigilante activity in order to lend the perception that the southern California region was safe for investment and growth. The popularity of vigilantism continued at least as late as 1887, when Anglo-Americans continued to demand vigilante justice against the perpetrators of crimes, a position that was widely supported in the newspapers.[33]

Despite the excesses of vigilantism, this was far from the extent of the abuse heaped upon the local Indians during the first forty years of California's existence. Vigilantes were able to operate because of the support of the local Anglo population. The local judiciary, which could be equally insensitive to native rights, also enjoyed widespread support in its mistreatment of Indians. However, instead of receiving their mandate from below as the vigilantes did, the courts had the support of state lawmakers. Non-white individuals within the state had been prevented from testifying against an Anglo in court as per state statute since California was admitted as a state in 1850; however, while the law that prevented non-whites from testifying against Anglos in court had been repealed in 1875, the effect of this act on the actual practices in the local courts remained to be seen. In most of the cases after 1875, it would seem that if Indians were allowed to testify, their testimony was severely discounted. An example occurred in 1877, when two farmers from San Diego County, Chatham Helms and his brother, were scouring the countryside for lost stock. While searching, they encountered a band of Kumeyaays. The two parties exchanged words, and then gunfire erupted. When the dust settled, an Indian named Francisco lay dead. Despite several Indian and Anglo witnesses who supported the Indian version of events, that they had been the victims of an attack by the Helms brothers, local authorities never indicted Helms for his role in Francisco's murder. [34] Had the murder of Francisco been the sole example of a judicial system gone wrong, his death would have been a footnote in California history. Unfortunately, Francisco was not alone in his fate. Free to continue to prey on individuals who were virtually invisible before the judiciary, Chatham Helms would appear in court twice more, each time accused of attacking Indians.

The limited concern that Indians in southern California drew from the local communities and from the courts perpetuated a second-class status for Indians, and resulted in many Indians trying to avoid or limit their contact with Anglos as much as possible. Because much of the prime land in the region was being snapped up by Americans, this left Indians with land that was by many accounts uninhabitable. Unable to support themselves, the Indians of southern California slipped further into untenable living conditions. While the local communities could not be counted on for sympathy for the aboriginal residents of the region, this did not mean that the plight of the Indians in southern California went unnoticed. In 1883, Helen Hunt Jackson arrived in California at the invitation of the commissioner of Indian affairs to examine the conditions of the Mission Indians. Her report is perhaps one of the saddest documents penned describing the conditions of Indians in southern California during the first half-century of American domination. Her report stood as a stark reminder to the government that vigilante justice against Indians occurred all too frequently. Jackson wrote, "The Indians' own lives are in continual danger, it being safe to shoot an Indian at any time when only Indian witnesses are present."[35]

After completing her investigation, Jackson submitted a report of her findings and recommendations to the government. In her report, Jackson encouraged the government to confirm land titles to the Indians as a way of providing for their subsistence, and as a way of keeping them separate from the growing Anglo community. Jackson was aware that eventually, Anglo encroachment would threaten to overwhelm the lands granted to the Indians, and attempts would be made to wrest the land from them. To counter this, she felt that Indians could only survive within the larger society if they were able to function at the same level as the individuals who refused to recognize their land and legal rights. To achieve this, she advocated that lawyers, teachers, and agricultural specialists be provided to assist the Indians in their transition to American culture. Her recommendations were incorporated into a bill by the Office of Indian Affairs and submitted to Congress. While the bill passed in the Senate, the House did not act on it.[36]

For Indians, the limited if not total lack of control they had over their lives left them vulnerable to a rapacious group of Anglos determined to exploit Indian labor while seizing native lands. Even though reservations had been set up for the Indians of southern California, perpetual use of the land had not been guaranteed, as we have seen. As each new generation of lawmakers came to the capital, each seemed to build on the contention that Indian rights were not to be respected, and that legislation could be passed that would effectively and permanently divest the nation, and the state, of its "Indian problem." In the 1880s, the federal government enacted two bills of significance to the Indians of southern California. The first was the Indian Homestead Act which was passed on 4 July 1884, which insisted that in order to receive title to a homestead, individual Indians were required to separate from their tribal group by taking up land on a site away from the reservation. For many Indians, this provision forced them to choose between survival and the continuation of affiliations that supported their language, culture, and religion. What they would receive would be land that was surrounded by a passively, if not actively hostile group that shared none of their cultural attributes, and that in many instances wanted nothing to do with them. Despite the hardships that they faced with their decision, many Indians who had already lost their traditional tribal structures because of encroaching Anglos filed claims.[37]

Following closely on the heels of the Indian Homestead Act was the Dawes Allotment Act of 1887. Hoping to force the Indian to adopt the individuality that characterized the American people through private land ownership, Congress passed the Dawes Allotment Act. Unlike the Indian Homestead Act, which required voluntary separation from the tribe through the acceptance of individual plots of land off the reservation, the Dawes Act forced Indians to accept allotted lands on reservations. In a thinly veiled reiteration of the Indian Homestead Act, the Dawes Act divided up the lands on the reservation into 160 acre plots. Indians were then assigned to these plots of land, but were not given title to them for twenty-five years. The rationale for this delay was to ostensibly ensure that the Indians had proven themselves to be self-sufficient and no longer in need of tutelage from an Anglo overseer. Once the allotment process had been completed, the remaining lands would be sold to Anglos. To ensure that the Indians did not merely combine their lands and continue to live communally, the allotments assigned to the Indians would be non-continuous. The result was that each Indian family found itself to be quite literally isolated from other members of their tribes on lands that they had shared for centuries. The rationale behind the Dawes Act was a convoluted attempt to save the Indian by destroying his culture. The supporters of the Dawes Act were individuals who had grown concerned over the rapidly declining number of Indians within the nation and feared their eventual extermination. It was felt that the crux of the issue lay in the communal nature of tribal societies, which prevented the Indians from adapting to the modern world and as such guaranteed their eventual destruction, especially in light of the tendency displayed by Americans to seize native lands. This movement was led by the Indian Rights Association (IRA), a nineteenth-century group that primarily consisted of Anglo businessmen and civic leaders from around the country who supported the rights of Indians. By the end of the

1880s, the group supported a radical change in how Indian land claims were administered: since treaties and executive orders had failed to secure a permanent home for the Indians in the nation, the group proposed that Indians be given individually allotted land instead of the previous communal allotments. One of the leaders of the IRA was Albert K. Smiley of Redlands, California, who had seen the destruction brought about by the dispossession of the Indians of southern California. While the Dawes Act was a radical proposal that would destroy the communal nature of tribal society, it would also result in the assimilation of native people into the larger American society, and thus their preservation as a people.

Since American society had not yet come to terms with the problem of whether or not to grant Indians title to their traditional lands, the Dawes Act provided a ready compromise. Americans would have access to the lands not distributed to the Indians, and Indians would be saved from destruction by being provided with a means to support themselves.[38] The only groups not satisfied with the act were the Indians who did not want to give up either their traditional lands or their traditional cultures. In the paternalistic world of Gilded Age politics, however, their opinion hardly mattered. The government began by surveying the reservations and dividing the land into individual allotments. The Indian agent would assign the allotment in accordance with the individual's marital status. While the actual allotment varied by reservation, it usually included 160 acres for heads of household, 80 acres for single individuals, and 40 acres for those under age eighteen. Babies born after the end of allotment were not eligible to receive any lands. In southern California, because most reservations lacked enough land to allot according to the national norm, heads of household received up to twenty acres, and unmarried allottees would be allowed only five to ten acres—parcels that would be insufficient for the purpose of farming or livestock raising.

Under the terms of the Dawes Act, Indian allotments were to be held in trust for twenty-five years to allow Indians the opportunity to adjust to private ownership and learn the rudiments of agriculture. During this transitional period, states and territories could not levy taxes on the land; however, once the twenty-five-year period had elapsed, the United States would grant Indians title to the land in fee simple, and all ties to the government would be severed.[39] The cost savings to the United States, which would no longer be responsible for the administration of Indian lands or required to honor past treaty provisions which guaranteed certain services to the tribes cannot be understated. In exchange, the allottee would receive United States (but not necessarily state) citizenship.[40] As evidence of their newfound status within the nation, all future legal actions would come under the jurisdiction of the state in which the Indians resided.[41] In other words, Indians would lose their protected status under the federal government. The land that was not included in the allotment process would then be auctioned to the highest bidder, and the revenue would return to the government. This program resulted in the loss of millions of acres for the tribes.

Many Indians protested the Dawes Act because it intentionally destroyed the primary stabilizing force in their lives—the tribe—and refused to accept allotments. Others, fearful that Anglos would eventually take even the reservations from them, supported the act's provisions. This led to a schism within several tribes that is still felt to this day. Despite the support for the Dawes Act among the Anglo-American communities, only the Sycuan and Pechanga reservations in San Diego County were immediately mapped for allotment. And despite the designation of parcels, the allotment of land in the southern California region did not start until 1892. The allotment process occurred first on the Pechanga Reservation at the request of the Indians living there. The Sycuan Reservation started allotting lands in 1894. Indians quickly came to realize that the allotments would be inadequate for their needs, and often ignored the allotment process altogether, even when they had been assigned land.

On the Capitan Grande Reservation in San Diego County, the allotment map was never approved for distribution. On other reservations such as Mesa Grande and Santa Ysabel, boundary disputes between Anglos and Indians prevented the allotment program from being put into force.[42] In southern California, few Indians spoke English, and fewer still could read the allotment agreements or fully understand what the legislation required of them. The individuals who were responsible for the transition to private ownership among the Indians of southern California were aware of this, but did little to ensure that Indians were given all the information they needed about the allotment process. In many tribal areas of southern California, the confused nature of the act was exacerbated by the status of the reservations themselves. Reservations in southern California had been created by executive order, and as such they essentially existed at the pleasure of the chief executive; questions existed over whether Indians had any rights to these lands at all.

Despite the rescission and the reestablishment of the reservations in southern California during the 1870s and the allotment acts in the 1880s, Anglos continued to challenge native claims to the land. In a report to the commissioner of Indian affairs in 1888, Indian Agent Preston complained of his need to remove "thirty eight persons as trespassers from the Potrero Reservation, near Banning, California." Two of the squatters requested they be forcibly removed from the tribal lands, as they believed to relinquish the land otherwise would have affected their ability to "test the titles in court." At this same time, Preston was already involved in another case in district court to determine squatter's rights on Indian land.[43]

Unfortunately, Agent Preston's frustration with land grabs by Anglos proved to be a frequent occurrence. In 1888, Agent C. H. Yates reported, "Many Indians occupy lands or are entitled to occupy them [lands] which are not included in any reserve. Intruders have 'squatted' upon lands which Indians have occupied for generations." These activities occurred despite a decision that same year in the Supreme Court decision in *Byrne v. Alas et al.* (1888). In this case, the court determined, "If the Indians were entitled to possession before the date of the patent [application filed by Anglos for claim to the land], they were entitled to it afterwards so long as any of the community remained in actual possession."[44] Despite the promising judgment in the *Byrne* case and the potential for Indians to claim lands under the Indian Homestead Act in 1883, Anglo-Americans continued to challenge Indian rights to the land well into the twentieth century.[45]

Government treaties, legal decisions, and tacit federal agreements suggested that Indians held a right to their ancestral lands, but many Anglo-Americans single-mindedly pursued a goal that would have resulted in the total negation of Indian land title. Recognizing the limited options available to them, in southern California many Indians accepted the only option they felt was available to them: they accepted allotments. This resulted in the steady deterioration of tribal culture and life. For many Indians in southern California, the acceptance of allotments divided the tribes along ideological lines—those who feared a total loss of tribal lands and those who insisted that refusal to accept the allotments would mean that the tribes would retain their reservations as a whole. In southern California these differences resulted in the formation of the Mission Indian Federation in the early twentieth century. The focus of this group was to refuse allotments and to renounce the authority of the federal government over the tribe as a whole. Unfortunately the schism created by the Federation and non-Federation Indians is still felt in many tribes today. Despite their attempts to save their people and their culture from destruction, in the end the Federation's activities bore a bitter fruit. The group was successful in halting the distribution of lands on some of the southern California reservations and served as a model for the Indian protest groups of the Civil Rights Era; however, much of the reservation land was nevertheless later seized and sold to Anglos. In many cases despite the debasement of tribal culture that resulted from allotment, many home sites granted in the nineteenth century are still occupied by Indians today.

As the nineteenth century drew to a close, the conditions endured by the Indians in southern California had deteriorated so dramatically that their plight caught the attention of the nation. Work by Indian advocates such as Helen Hunt Jackson contributed significantly to this awareness among the general population. Despite all the half measures that had been enacted to "assist" the Indians, the core reason for the debased conditions they were forced to endure was the loss of their lands. In southern California, this resulted in such a sharp decline in the native populations that many Anglos feared Indians would one day become extinct as a cultural group. Faced with the loss of one of America's adopted cultural symbols, the federal government acted.

In 1891, the federal government finally acted to ensure the continued survival of the Mission Indians. In January 1891, Congress passed the Act for the Relief of the Mission Indians. This act directed the secretary of the interior to appoint three commissioners who would select reservation sites for the Indians, preferably on their traditional lands. Albert K. Smiley, a businessman from Redlands in Riverside County, led the commission, along with Judge Joseph B. Morse of Lapeer, Michigan, and Professor C. C. Painter of Washington, D.C. All three had been active in the Indian Rights Association of Philadelphia, which sought to preserve the rights of the Indians while integrating them into Anglo society. The commissioners toured the southern California area and tried to purchase the lands that had been traditionally used by the Indians. However, many of the Anglo landowners, seeing an opportunity to gain more than the value of the property, attempted to exploit their position by charging exorbitant rates for the land. Their greed, coupled with the time constraints imposed on the commissioners to complete their duties, prevented them from thoroughly reviewing all the pertinent land-claim documents or visiting all the proposed sites. The shortcomings of the commission resulted in an incomplete assessment of, and provision for, the Indians of southern California.

However, the Act for the Relief of the Mission Indians was still unique in its approach to Anglo-Indian land relations in that it combined provisions of the Dawes Allotment Act with an agreement to create reservations for the Indians of southern California. After surveying the land and creating a reservation that "as far as practicable [would include] the lands and villages which have been in actual occupation and possession of said Indians," the government would remove Anglos from the lands in order to prevent future claims on the land, and compensate them for improvements they had made. The result, it was hoped, would be a reduction in the friction between the Anglo and Indian communities. Additionally, in keeping with the provisions of the Dawes Act, "whenever any of the Indians residing upon any reservation . . . be so advanced in civilization as to be capable of owning and managing land in severalty, the Secretary of the Interior may cause allotments to be made to such Indians." The land would then be held in trust for a period of twenty-five years by the United States government and then given to the allottee. While on the surface, the Act for the Relief of the Mission Indians provided homesteads for the Indians of southern California, it also limited their full control over the land by authorizing "any citizen of the United States, firm, or corporation to construct a flume, ditch, canal, pipe or other appliances for the conveyance of water over, across, or through such reservation." The only provision to the Indians to compensate for the loss or destruction of their lands was that they "be supplied with sufficient quantity of water for irrigating and domestic purposes."[46] Unfortunately, this provision of the act was often used to take water from the reservation created by the act, and subsequently quashed all hopes of agriculture on the new reservations.

As the last quarter of the nineteenth century continued, it became apparent that the State of California had significantly changed its opinion regarding the Indians who resided within its borders. No longer was the state willing to assume control over Indians, as had been done in the 1850s, or to share responsibility regarding the status of the Indians as it had evolved by the 1870s; as a result, the federal presence in the area increased. Under the guise of agents and federal legislation, this increased presence offset some of the control the state and local agencies held over the Indian, especially within the local courts. For Indians living on federal lands, agents now dealt with minor infractions of legal codes, such as being drunk in public. Those Indians who committed more serious crimes were referred to the federal courts for prosecution.[47] This transition of authority from local to federal jurisdiction prompted heated debate in the local press, a controversy that local Indians exploited for their gain. In October 1889, local Indians refused to deliver one of their tribal members to a local court for prosecution, arguing instead that the case should be heard in federal court.[48] The actions of these Indians indicate a level of agency that is normally not attributed to native people, but shows a growing awareness of and ability to adapt to the American system, just as native people adapted to the incursions by the Spanish and later the Mexicans. Native defiance of the local courts indicated that native people were well aware that the authority over them had changed from the state to the federal government, and that they had weighed which agency, federal or state, would provide the most advantageous forum for their needs.

As the nineteenth century waned, the debate over jurisdiction continued to persist, and increased in November 1889 following the murder of Petronillo Alvarez at the Soboba village in San Diego County. In this case, federal authorities accused an Indian named Antonio Ales of Alvarez's murder and held him over for trial. While he waited for his case to be heard, Ales was held in the city jail. While Ales awaited the outcome of who would assume jurisdiction over his case, a storm raged in the local press: at issue, according to one newspaper, was not the jurisdiction of a case in "which the white people of the county have only a limited interest," but the contingent fees each constable received when an individual was arrested and tried for a crime. In the end, the Ales case was forwarded to federal court, and the local press, in a face-saving move, determined that the cost of appealing the decision regarding jurisdiction for cases involving Indians to the United States Supreme Court would amount to more than the retention of the contingent fees would be worth.[49] In the end, it simply turned out to be cost-prohibitive for the Anglo community.

By the end of the century, the federal government's power over Indians in southern California had been firmly established. While this would seem to have been a positive transition since Indians would no longer be subject

to local prejudice, the transition came with several drawbacks, the most significant of which were the agents themselves. Several agents stood accused
of—but were never prosecuted for—crimes against their Indian charges.
Newspapers and government reports accused several agents of crimes
ranging from theft to murder.[50] The protection of the federal courts also
only extended to the borders of federal land. Since most Indians worked off
the reservation, they were subject to local and state control. Despite these
drawbacks, the presence of Indians in the courts after the creation of the
reservations declined dramatically.

By the late 1870s and early 1880s, the arrival of the railroads and the
widespread development of irrigation projects to serve the growing agricultural communities further marginalized the position of the Indian
within the developing society in southern California. Despite having no
legal title to the lands they had occupied for generations, Indians still phys-
ically occupied and used the land much as their parents had. On the Pala
Reservation, Indians irrigated their meager crops with water from the San
Luis Rey River and continued to live at a subsistence level. Indian control
of a water source in the arid region proved to be too much for the local
farmers. While Anglos may have grudgingly allowed Indians to occupy the
land, they protested native control of an important resource, water. In 1877,
another devastating drought convinced Anglo-American farmers that a
series of dams would be needed to offset the effects of the next drought.
The fact that the water-diversion project robbed Indians of a significant
resource, violated provisions of the Act for the Relief of the Mission Indians, and prevented Indians from farming for their own survival met with
little sympathy from the local Anglo communities.

The arrival of the railroads, much like the appropriation of water,
would prove to be a devastating blow to the economy and existence of the
Indians of southern California. The first train in the area was a spur line
from Los Angeles to its harbor in San Pedro in 1869. It took another seven
years before the railroads finally connected Los Angeles to the northern
portion of the state, but the impact on the population was significant. In
1870, Los Angeles had 5,700 residents, and by 1880, just four years after
the arrival of the railroad, this number had increased to 11,200. By 1890,
some 50,395 people called the city of Los Angeles home.[51] In contrast, the
city of San Diego, which would not receive its rail connection until 1885,
languished with a population of 2,300 in 1870; by 1880 it had increased

by only 337 souls.[52] Five years after the arrival of the railroad, the population of San Diego had jumped to 16,159.[53] These numbers indicate the significant development of the southern California region, and the increased demand by Anglo-Americans and local governments for land, water, and labor resources. All of these developments had a profound impact on the status of the Indian within the growing society. Whereas Indians had initially been seen as the primary source of labor for the region, as the value of land increased and development in the region expanded, the Indian was an anachronism who no longer had a place in the developing American society. As a result, Indians found themselves disproportionately attacked by the local communities in the one forum that presumed to rise above prejudice: the courts. However, as the following chapters will reveal, as the Anglo population rose and land values increased, the Indian found himself increasingly victimized in the local courts in a not-so-thinly veiled attempt to push him further out of the region that he had called home for centuries.

Native American Law

Aᴀꜰᴛᴇʀ ᴛʜᴇ ᴛʀᴇᴀᴛʏ ᴏꜰ ɢᴜᴀᴅᴀʟᴜᴘᴇ ʜɪᴅᴀʟɢᴏ ʜᴀᴅ ʙᴇᴇɴ signed, the residents of the new territory of California largely returned to the same economic and social structures that had previously sustained them. According to the provisions of the treaty, individuals who had been citizens under the Mexican government would become citizens of the United States, and their property rights would be respected. Initially, it appeared these provisions would be put into practice. Despite California's strategic economic and military importance, widespread plans to occupy the region were left to the initiative of farmers who, like their earlier brethren in the Oregon Territory, moved slowly across the continent in small numbers, seeking a better life in an unspoiled land. All that would change when James Marshall, a former expatriate American who had been living in the state since before the Mexican-American War and who had supported the Bear Flag Revolt, returned to his ranch in northern California to find his stock gone and his land destroyed. To offset this financial setback, Marshall took a position with John Sutter, a Swiss immigrant who had created a community he called New Helvetia near what is now Sacramento. Sutter anticipated a rush of people into the state—all of whom, he reasoned, would need lumber for building homes and stores. To ensure his stake in this potentially lucrative business, Sutter hired Marshall to build a sawmill on the American River.

With the aid of several Indians from the Maidu-Nisenan tribe, Marshall located a likely spot for the sawmill and secured his position in American historical lore by finding gold in the river.[1] Marshall's discovery would result in one of the greatest migrations in American history, the 1849 California Gold Rush. While this moment in American history has found its way into every conceivable medium from monographs to movies, what is often not recounted is the challenging effect this rapid influx of gold seekers had on the traditional societies of the Indians of California. While most of the early immigration occurred in the northern part of the state, many gold seekers traveled up from Mexico or across the Mojave before turning their sights on the northern placers. When the gold began to play out, many of those same individuals returned to the lush rolling hills and chaparral of the south to establish themselves as farmers and ranchers. What they found were intact Indian societies that had their own legal and social traditions. While the Indians of southern California had managed over the years to accommodate, and in many cases assimilate to, the Europeans in their midst, the pervasiveness of the Anglo-American migration left little room for accommodation. Following their seizure of the state from the Mexicans, the Americans showed little inclination to embrace or tolerate any but their own culture. Many Anglo-Americans believed that the Indians they encountered had no culture or formal social structure, and this made their treatment of the Indians easier to justify; however, they ignored the vibrant cultural traditions that had once held sway in the region.

Indian tribes have lived in the southern California area for several thousand years. Over the centuries, their proximity to each other has resulted in many shared cultural attributes, such as a patriarchal social system and similar religious and language practices. The Indians of southern California include the Cupeno[2], Luiseno[3], Gabrielino,[4] Cahuilla,[5] Serrano,[6] Chemehuevi,[7] and Kumeyaay[8] tribes, all of which are subgroups of the Uto-Aztecan linguistic stock. This language group ranges from southern California northward along the eastern ridge of the Sierra Nevada range, and into Nevada and Utah. Uto-Aztecan dialect groups are also found to the east into Arizona, and further south into western Mexico. This widely diverse linguistic group encompasses the Yuman, Serrano, and Shoshonean linguistic families. The Yuman languages dominate the area west of the Colorado River, the Shoshonean languages trend northward and eastward from the Mojave Desert region, and the Serrano group occupies the area east of modern-day Los Angeles. Despite the variation in their languages, the common language-family group among the tribes would indicate that the tribes of southern California at one time shared a common ancestor. The longevity of their residence in the region allowed ample time for diversification and cross-cultural contact with other tribal groups—the result being that by the time of contact, the Indians of southern California shared some traditions with the Indians of the southwestern desert, as well as other California tribes who occupied the coastal and mountainous regions in the central portions of the state. Despite their longevity within the state, re-creating the cultures of the aboriginal people that inhabited the southern California region is replete with hazards.

Determining the pre-contact legal traditions of the native people in southern California with any certainty is clouded by several issues—the first being that the tribes were nonliterate, and as such have not left a record of the traditions that characterized their cultures.[9] Within the first century of contact with Anglo-Europeans, the tribes were decimated by disease and warfare and forced to assimilate to a foreign culture. The result was the massive loss of many individuals within the tribe who knew the stories and laws of their people. Secondly, the loss of these individuals and the push to assimilate by the Europeans in many cases resulted in an almost universal inability to understand their own languages. Since language often serves as a cultural root, with its absence, the few words that tribal members could remember often lost much of their meaning and became more of an anachronism than a barometer of culture.[10] By the time the Americans assumed control of the state, the process of assimilation started by the Franciscan fathers had wide-reaching effects. In 1852, pioneer Hugo Reid addressed a series of letters to the *Los Angeles Star* describing the local Indians. In one missive he states, "Their language has deteriorated so much since the conquest, that this present generation barely comprehend a part of what one of the 'old standards' say, when they speak the original tongue. There is now at San Gabriel an old woman named Bona, who takes a pride in speaking sometimes the 'Court language' to the 'young ones,' to stultify their intelligence."[11] Bona's playful behavior toward the young people in her village highlights how far this assimilation had advanced, and how much of the Gabrielino culture had already been lost.

The second issue that hinders the re-creation of traditional legal customs largely revolves around the Spanish conquerors who invaded the state in 1769. Since the Spanish largely considered the native population as potential converts to Catholicism and also as a possible permanent labor class, they studiously set out to erase all evidence of traditional culture in order to ensure that their new laborers would not have mixed loyalties.

Native Americans who came into prolonged contact with the Spanish and later the Mexican people were encouraged to abandon their own languages in preference for Spanish, to adopt European dress, and to conform to European standards of behavior. Those Indians who resisted the overtures of the Spanish were "picked up immediately, flogged and put in irons until an opportunity presented of returning them to undergo other flagellations. If they stowed themselves away in any of the *rancherias*, the soldiers were monthly in the habit of visiting them; and such was the punishment inflicted on those who attempted to conceal them, that it was rarely essayed."[12]

Despite the treatment they received at the hands of the Spanish and later the Mexican people, some remnants of the Indians' previous cultures doggedly endured. Despite their common ancestors, each individual tribe also had unique cultural attributes and worldviews. However, Anglo-American contempt for the Indians of southern California—and all Indians, for that matter—was as pervasive in the nineteenth century as it can be today. Prior to contact with the Spanish in the latter part of the eighteenth century, the collective number of Indians in southern California was estimated to be between 27,000 and 35,000. At the time America took possession of California in 1848, the native population in the southern portion of the state had dwindled to perhaps a quarter of what it had been prior to contact, due to disease, violence, and infanticide. According to historian Joel Hyer, many native women who had been raped by Spanish soldiers murdered their babies at birth rather than live with the product of a rape.[13] This practice, while tragic, continued into the American period of occupation. The loss of the very young, those who were considered the future of the Indian nations, was only compounded by the loss of the older generations, who for centuries had been the repositories of tribal stories and histories, but who found themselves particularly vulnerable to the diseases brought in by the invaders. With the loss of both these generations, native culture in some areas of southern California teetered on the brink of extinction. However, this destruction was not absolute.

Prior to Anglo-Americans taking control of the state, most Indians lived apart from the missions and presidios that stretched up the coastline of California. In some of the missions—for example, the mission at San Diego—the established Hispanic community was too small to accommodate a large influx of Indian converts. For these Indians, many were "converted" and then released to return to their tribes. Other tribes, especially those in the interior, were too far removed from Spanish settlements to warrant anything more than rare visitations from the mission fathers. This lack of contact allowed the interior tribes to remain culturally intact. However, this lack of direct contact did not remove them from the more devastating aspects of European culture, disease, and violence, or protect them for long.

While many of the Indians along the coastline had been pressed into service for the missions, as their numbers dwindled, the Europeans began to make more frequent forays into the interior of the state in order to secure additional Indians to serve the missions and to be converted to the Catholic faith. Finding the violence and cruelty meted out by the mission fathers to be unreasonably harsh, many of the newly converted Mission Indians, or neophytes, escaped back to their homes or to related tribes who lived beyond the reach of the Europeans. These escaping neophytes would eventually form a bridge that reached from one culture to the other. To their unconverted brethren, these individuals brought the technology of the invaders: their tools, agriculture, and weapons. However, accompanying this largesse were also the diseases, Eurocentric attitudes, and the promise of future expeditions by the Spanish in an attempt to wrest the remaining Indians from their strongholds in the state's interior. Fearful of losing their labor force, and by extension their authority in the region, the mission fathers, with the aid of the presidio soldiers, routinely raided the interior in search of escaping neophytes. Their efforts only infrequently resulted in the assimilation of large numbers of Indians from the southern California region.

Recognizing the threat imposed by the growing presence of the Spanish, many tribes attacked their tormentors. The Kumeyaay Indians who lived in the San Diego area were perhaps the most violently resistant to the incursions onto their lands; they attacked and set fire to the mission at San Diego several times in an attempt to force the Spanish off their land. Despite the valiant efforts by the Kumeyaays and the other native people of southern California to retain their lands, many fell under the control of the missions and over time adopted many aspects of Spanish culture into their own traditions. Their assimilation further threatened the survival of the aboriginal people in the region by withdrawing from the tribes the vital labor and new members needed to perpetuate the tribe and its customs. Despite their assimilation into the mission system, and later into the larger

Spanish or Mexican population, many still retained vestiges of their traditional lives. This resulted in a syncretic blend of traditional and European traditions.

By the time the Anglo-Americans assumed control of the state in 1848, the number of Indians who had lived in the southern California region prior to contact with the Europeans had suffered significant setbacks. While no attempt was made by the American government to count the number of Indians in the region, a newspaper report in 1858 estimated that the Indians in southern California numbered around 15,000. However, this included tribes who frequently crossed the Mojave Desert from Arizona.[14]

As a central recurring theme in the history of the New World, land was (and in many cases remains) the primary indicator of wealth. As Europeans began to spread across the continent, they brought with them concepts of land use and rights of possession which assumed that land, in order to be possessed, must be developed and fully utilized. To the uninitiated European, the lack of regimentation in the pasturelands and food crops that characterized Indian land use was a clear indication that Indians were little more than wild animals who roamed the land and took from its bounty. Since the Indians were not fully utilizing God's gift, their claim to the land was tenuous. This rather short-sighted and prejudicial opinion characterized most Anglo-European/Indian encounters.

Land served as one of the central tenets of the law of the Native Americans in southern California. Instead of roaming freely across a verdant landscape, living primitively off the bounty of the land—as many Europeans, and later Americans, believed—Indians had well-defined rules regarding the possession of land and its products. Land was held in total by the tribe; but within the borders set by the tribe, land was further divided into parcels that were held in common by the patrilineal clans that collectively made up the tribe itself. While the tribe claimed the land as a whole, importance must be given to the clans who further subdivided the land for their own personal use.

The clans or moieties protected access to their lands, because to do otherwise would have reduced the foodstuffs available and could have threatened the very existence of their group. Conversely, the importance of the moiety in maintaining the viability and health of the tribe as a whole cannot be understated. With marriage taboos in place, the moiety served as a means to ensure against birth defects. These defects would have impacted the survival of the society as a whole. Each moiety was free to manipulate the land through planting, burning fields to encourage pastureland for grazing animals, or protecting important plants, such as acorn trees. Among the tribes in southern California, conflicts often exploded over the misuse of land claimed by another tribe, leading to warfare. It was not, as reported by Hubert Howe Bancroft in his study of native people, a "mere pretext for plunder."[15] Instead it was a challenge to the viability of the tribe as a whole. The misappropriation of land could also impact the equanimity of the tribe itself, if one moiety strayed into land claimed by another. In the intratribal conflicts, the viability of the clan would have been threatened.

However, as Native Americans found themselves overwhelmed by the influx of Spanish immigrants, the logic behind their land practices was ignored by the Europeans. To ensure that their access to the land remained unfettered, tribes were forced to adapt to the practices of the invaders, or risk the loss of their land completely. As tribes became more Hispanicized, many permanently embraced Spain's, and later Mexico's, practice of assuming title to the land in order to retain exclusive claim to it. The adoption of the land-title practices of the Europeans also introduced the Indians of southern California to the legal practices of the invaders. Many of the land grants given to Spanish settlers included lands that traditionally had been occupied by the Indians of southern California. These land grants stipulated that the grant excluded the land occupied by the Indians. Only if the tribes abandoned the land could the grantee lay full claim to the land. For the Spanish grantee, this arrangement was rarely protested as it provided a ready supply of peon labor in a region bereft of laborers. However, in order to solidify their control over the Indians on their land grants, *rancheros* often used the laws of Spain to maintain control over the Indians.

Under the minimalist government that had been established by the Spanish crown, prominent land grantees were often given secular legal authority over the land that they had been assigned. Their authority was to be secondary to those secular authorities who largely resided in the presidios or towns. While this distribution of authority theoretically ensured the proper functioning of society, it also reduced the administrative costs of the government. Land grantees were among the few individuals in Spanish society who were literate, or understood the rudiments of Spanish government. As such, it was considered that they would discharge their duties with compassion and neutrality. However, human nature being what it is, often the grantees looked to their own interests before considering the rights of others. Many of the Spanish grantees presided as both judge and jury over their charges, or unduly influenced the *mayordomos* and *alcaldes*, the secular legal authorities who were appointed to dispense justice in the region. In a move that would presage the treatment Indians would receive under the Americans, Indians who were guilty of an infraction such as traveling without permission, stealing, or killing livestock could be sentenced to pay their debt to society by laboring on the ranchos of local grantees.[16] The assumption of this power by the rancho grantees undermined the authority of the traditional tribal leaders, leading to further dissolution of the Indians' traditional culture. However, those Indians who complied with the new laws of the Europeans would be rewarded.

During the Mexican period (1821–48), attempts to integrate Indians further into Mexican society advanced. Indians who had become Christianized were to be granted citizenship and given a plot of land. According to Florence Shipek, who did an extensive study on land grants in southern California, only "a few hispanicized Indian pueblos were founded and a few hispanicized Indians given land grants."[17] Some of these grants, however, were held well into the American period. Shipek also noted that while "few rancho grants" were given to Indians, additional "lots and small grants" were provided to several.[18] A few of those Indians who received title to land during the Mexican period included Victoria, who received a rancho near the San Gabriel Valley in 1838, and Felipe Castillo, who received a rancho near Julian in 1846. According to Joel Hyer, in his study on the status of Indians in southern California, by 1852 "approximately fifty Native Americans possessed Mexican land titles in southern California."[19] While most of these land holdings would be lost because of the shortcomings of the U.S. government, some remained in Indian hands for several years. In 1858, the *Los Angeles Star* reported on the delinquent water taxes owed to the city. On the list is an acre of land owned by an Indian named Benuto. The amount owed was fifty-five cents.[20] For many of the Indians who were granted title to land, the concept of taxation was a foreign one. Why should they continue to pay to enjoy lands that for centuries had sustained them? This cultural difference was compounded by a linguistic one: in many cases, Indians were unable to speak or read in English. These cultural and linguistic traits impaired the Indians' ability to fully function within the Anglo community. When this was compounded by the prejudice of the larger Anglo community, who had more to gain from the Indians' ignorance than his enlightenment, many Indians lost their lands over seemingly trivial issues, such as a delinquent fifty-five cent tax. To the Anglo population the dispossession of the Indian was made easier through these misunderstandings, and provided a ready excuse if the morality of their actions was questioned. To the Anglo mind anyone who would abandon their land over a trivial matter, clearly was not invested in the land to begin with.

To many early settlers, the supposed passivity of traditional southern California societies in adapting to the land-use and labor demands of the Anglo-European invaders was proof of a disjointed and poorly organized grouping of individuals had benefited from the autocratic demands of the Spanish. This eurocentric thinking could not have been more wrong. In the traditional ethnic societies of the Indians of southern California, similarities abound between the various tribes regarding land use and tribute labor. As mentioned earlier, all tribes in the southern California region were divided into affiliated bands that were then divided further along patrilineal lines, with each lineage claiming rights to land and to the bounty of the land. The *net* or *noot*, a tribal chief who was commonly referred to as "captain" by both the Spanish and the Americans, governed each tribe.[21] Since most documents refer to the tribal leader as "captain," this term will be adopted throughout the text to denote tribal leadership. Tribal captains were assisted in their task of governing by a speaker and a council, which largely consisted of shamans who had specialized information about environmental, religious, legal, and political issues that impacted the tribe. In most instances the position of captain was hereditary, but variations on this requirement differed by tribe. According to anthropologist Alfred Kroeber, the "bravest fighters became chiefs," while "Chieftainship was also hereditary in the male line."[22] Because of the services they provided to the tribe, members of the tribal leadership were compensated with goods and labor from members of the band. When the Spanish entered California in the late eighteenth century, their demand for tribute labor and reliance on a dominant individual to direct the activities of the tribe was not completely foreign to the Indians they encountered.

What the Spanish often failed to recognize was the responsibility each tribal captain had in ensuring harmonious relations between tribal members and the outside world. This responsibility extended to serving as a trial judge in the event any band member stepped outside the bounds of acceptable behavior. Both the Spanish and Mexican governments recognized the importance of the traditional power hierarchy and often appointed tribal captains to serve as *alcaldes*, or secular judges, over their people. However, equally as often, they sought to undermine the authority of a recalcitrant captain by appointing another tribe member to serve as *alcalde*; this attack on the *net*'s authority helped to destroy the unity of the tribe.[23] According to Harry James, an amateur historian of the Cahuilla people, Francisco Nombre of the Desert Cahuilla reportedly claimed to have been appointed *alcalde* "over all native peoples from San Gorginio Pass to Los Angeles."[24] While James expresses his doubts about Nombre's claim, newspapers in the early 1850s reported several claims by Indians who stated that they been appointed as *alcaldes* by the Mexican government. In the Chino area, an Indian named Roane claimed to have been appointed as an *alcalde* by the district judge.[25] It is clear that regardless of the title recognized by the Anglo population, the traditional tribal hierarchy continued to operate well beyond the period of time Anglos assumed it to have been obsolete.

Many of the Indians of southern California who willingly acquiesced and brought in tribe members who had been accused of violating American law were actually adhering to the tenets of the 1850 Act for the Government and Protection of Indians, which advised that "if any tribe or village of Indians refuse or neglect to obey the laws, the Justice of the Peace may punish the guilty chiefs or principal men by reprimand or fine, or otherwise reasonably chastise them."[26] For the Indians of southern California, failure to comply with the law would have resulted in punishment of their leaders, and by extension shame the tribe as a whole, something that most societies would balk at. In referring to themselves as *alcaldes*, the Indians in the region were likely adapting terms that they were familiar with to the new demands of the American government. In 1858, further evidence that Indians in southern California continued to operate within the previous system of *alcaldes* occurred when "An Indian who had been confined in prison for horse stealing, broke jail about two weeks since and escaped, taking with him another horse. He was brought back on Sunday last by a party of Indians, and delivered to the sheriff, who put him in irons in prison."[27]

While the term *alcalde* is only infrequently mentioned after the transition of power to the United States, the public record is replete with examples of the importance of tribal captains, who led their people and meted out punishment to those who violated both Indian and Anglo-American law. This importance was underscored by an incident in 1851 in which several members of the Cahuilla tribe met in the office of the county judge and deposed their "distinguished chief, Juan Antonio," because members of the tribe regarded "Juan Antonio as unsafe—they say he is too headstrong." The tribal committee took the opportunity to "elect as successor an Indian who received the approval and recommendation of the deposed captain."[28] Had the Indians not been integrated into the larger political and judicial system of the Mexican, and later Anglo-American, system, it is unlikely that they would have taken the time to arrange a delegation, travel to the city, and formally announce the change in their leadership. The deposing of Juan Antonio and the return of the horse thief demonstrate an expectation among the Indians that they enjoyed at least some equal standing as a group before the law. This almost collegial relationship is further exemplified in a letter from Benjamin Hayes, a judge who served in southern California during the 1850s, to Senator David Atchison in 1853. Hayes, in describing the appointment of Benjamin Davis Wilson to the post of Indian subagent to the southern California region in 1852, notes that "Before his appointment, their Chiefs visiting the City, habitually came to see and talk with him about their business."[29] Wilson was a wealthy landholder who came to the Los Angeles area in 1841 and would later serve as the mayor for the city. His wealth and prominence in local affairs gave him considerable influence over the affairs of the local community. Together with another early Los Angeles pioneer, Judge Benjamin Hayes, he pushed for many of the laws that impacted the daily lives of the local tribes. Wilson structured many of these policies on the model established by the Franciscan missionaries. Because of his position in the Anglo community, Wilson received deference from the Indian communities, as well, and was sought after by the tribes to discuss matters where the two groups intersected. For the tribes of southern California, Wilson likely held a position akin to a council member or respected elder. It is important to note that while the tribes consulted the authorities in the growing cities of southern California, there is no indication that they presumed any innate superiority on the part of the Americans. This would be in keeping with tribal tradition as recalled by Father Geronimo Boscana, one of the early missionaries to California, who lived among the Juanenos for decades, until his death in 1831. A confirmed racist who infamously considered the Indians he ministered to be like monkeys, Boscana's diary still remains one of the few documents that depict the traditions of the Indians in southern California. In his diary, he noted that the tribes of southern California did not "acknowledge any power higher than that of captain or chief."[30]

In the early years of American domination in the state, captains continued to serve as the primary source for justice within their tribes. In 1852 the *Los Angeles Star* reported on a missing San Gabriel Indian named Castro. A search was conducted, but only turned up the missing man's horse. Several days later, Castro reappeared; his only accounting was that he had been directed to perform "some kind of penance."[31] In 1871, two unidentified Indians became embroiled in a fight at an "Indian gambling ground," on the east side of the city of San Bernardino. Knives were drawn, and one of the men later died from wounds sustained in the fight. He was arrested by the local sheriff and held in jail until the next day, when a "mob of his own race" claimed him from the jail. The Indian was later "hanged from a limb of the same tree under which he did the stabbing."[32] A further example of the perseverance of traditional tribal, social, and cultural structure occurred in 1873, when "A striking example of summary justice occurred on Tuesday at the foot of Third street [in San Bernardino]. Two Indians who had engaged in a cutting scrape received 30 lashes each, well laid on, by order of the [*sic*] Captain John."[33] A further confirmation of the authority of the tribal captains can be found in Benjamin Wilson's report to the Indian commissioner in 1852. Wilson noted, "The present chiefs, in general, understand their affairs very well, and appear to be keenly alive to the good of their people. They often come to the towns—to this city, at any rate—and inflict some punishment in particular cases, the merits of which are left to be 'best known to themselves.'"[34] Wilson, true to his age, insisted "I do not wish to covey the idea that they have any regular government, or system of law, or rational grades of punishment, much less that they indulge in very refined distinctions as to guilt."

Unfortunately, despite the relative commonality of the *net* or the tribal captain in maintaining order within the tribe, Wilson's prejudices were not unique. In his seminal study of California, business leader and amateur historian Hubert Howe Bancroft enlisted the assistance of hundreds of historians, linguists, and interviewers to record the history of the region.[35] According to Bancroft, "Each tribe acknowledged one head, whose province it was to settle disputes, levy war, make peace, appoint feasts, and give good advice. Beyond this he had little power." To further support his contention that the Indians of southern California had no legitimate governmental authority, Bancroft quotes an 1869 report from John Stanley, who served as an Indian agent in the southern California region, to the commissioner of Indian affairs. Stanley maintained, "I have found that the captains have very little authority."[36] While Wilson, Stanley, and Bancroft may have been reticent to confirm the presence of an established legal code replete with the responsibilities of judgeship for Native Americans in the region, the real practice among the Indians of southern California belies that contention.

Despite the reticence of Anglo-Americans to acknowledge the presence of a systematic legal code for the Indians of southern California, there is some support for the idea that Anglo behavioral standards impacted native traditions more and more as contact increased. In most pre-contact tribal societies, the physical beating of a grown man would not have been acceptable. Here the record is confusing. In 1852, Hugo Reid, an American who immigrated to California during the Mexican period and established himself among the Gabrielino Indians, remarked about those same Indians that "physical punishment was not known to them." However, in the memoirs of Tom Lucas, a Kumeyaay Indian born in 1903, he reports that the "punishment for stealing was a public flogging with a hard mescal fiber rope. Everyone had to be there, even if they did not actually watch."[37] In Anglo-European tradition, flogging was a ready punishment meted out to individuals considered to be of a lower social standing. Based on the scant information available on the changing values of the tribes in southern California during the latter half of the nineteenth century, it cannot be known for certain whether this represented a change in attitudes regarding the thief's social standing within the tribes, or an adaptation of Anglo punishment techniques. According to reports written by men who routinely dealt with Indians in the region, there is a growing preponderance of material to suggest that native people increasingly adapted to Anglo standards. In a report to the commissioner of Indian affairs in 1852, Benjamin Wilson, noted that "The Cahuillas have not had a head chief . . . since the death of the one they called 'Razon' [White]. He died within two or three years past, at an advanced age. They gave him his name, as they told me, from his always acting so much like a white man, in staying at home and tending his fields and flocks, for he had both."[38] For many of the Indians in southern California, this assimilation process undoubtedly impacted traditional legal standards.

The emphasis of the Anglo-American legal tradition is on the maintenance of property and the preservation of public stability. Within the traditional legal structures of the Indians of southern California, the preservation of property and the maintenance of public harmony were also key to the maintenance of their societies. According to Delfina Cuero, a Kumeyaay woman who lived at the turn of the twentieth century, native law outlined "what (one should) expect from other people in the way of behavior."[39] Further confirmation of this comes from Father Boscana's diary "The young were instructed to love truth, to do good, and to venerate old age." For those children who chafed at this requirement, the punishment was almost out of the Old Testament: "The perverse child, invariably, was destroyed, and the parents of such remained dishonored."[40] The desire to preserve a society free of conflict may account for the willingness of tribal captains to turn over or severely punish band members who were suspected by Anglo authorities of a crime. A further possibility would be that since many of the crimes committed by Indians were offenses against Anglo law, the punishment should fit the standards of the victim. Several sources note that the Indians of southern California abhorred violence and embraced peaceful relations with outside groups. Benjamin Wilson notes that the "Mission Indians . . . have a common spirit of amity for the whites, and that their general inclination is not for war. They want peace with the whites."[41]

In the worldview of the Indians of southern California, the maintenance of harmonious tribal and international relations dominated society. From an early age, children were taught to respect their elders, practice honesty, and refrain from anger. To reinforce these ideas, story, ritual, and demonstration were used to ensure compliance with societal norms. Within each moiety, most issues regarding discipline became the responsibility of the clan or related family members. However, at times the antisocial actions of a few prompted the need for intervention by the tribal captain.[42] In cases where members from different bands or different tribes were involved, the case would be heard by both captains and a decision rendered. In the event a decision could not be made, a third captain was brought in to hear the same arguments. The determination of the captains was binding, and nothing short of war would reverse their decision.

The primary focus was to return the tribe to a state of equanimity, a feat that could only be accomplished with the cooperation of both the accused and the accuser. For a people weaned on the importance of harmony, any imbalance in the society, including that caused by an individual, needed to be identified and rectified so that the tribe itself could continue to function. For this reason, honesty was held in great esteem by the tribes. For the native people of southern California, this propensity for truth on the part of an Indian accused of a crime often carried into the Anglo courts. The public record is replete with instances of Indians who, when accused of a crime, freely admitted their guilt and suffered the punishment without complaint.[43] In 1852, four Indians were charged in a Los Angeles court with stealing a barrel of *aguardiente* (alcohol) and a cloak from a local proprietor. All confessed to the crime, were sentenced to receive twenty-five lashes, and forced to pay court costs.[44] Another case involved an Indian boy named Felipe Valdez who was accused of stealing $40, a pistol, and a bottle of whiskey. Felipe confessed and received thirteen lashes.[45]

It would be impossible not to suppose that as the tribes continued their relationships with the Europeans, the standards of both crime and punishment changed for the Indians. The Eurocentric invaders, convinced of their own superiority and willing to use force to ensure the continuation of their own worldview, were unlikely to undergo a similar change. By the time the Americans assumed control of the state, the Indians' loss of their traditional languages and the imposition of the standards of the Europeans were creating a synchronous blend of European-Indian traditions. Because of the Indians' peon status within the larger Spanish and Mexican cultures, literacy was not considered necessary for the work that had been relegated to them. The result was the loss of first-person accounts of pre-contact life. While archeologists have the advantage of physical remnants to guide their suppositions, physical evidence does not provide assistance here. For these reasons, reconstructing the world of the native people of southern California prior to contact is challenging. Since the native people of southern California were prevented from speaking directly for themselves, other sources must be consulted.

Following the Mexican-American War, a number of American men, who had been Indian fighters or rancheros prior to the war, would prove to be invaluable in meeting this challenge. Through their diaries, letters to newspapers, and reports to the Indian commissioner in Washington, an image of aboriginal culture emerges. These reports provide important insight but must be approached with caution, as they are written from an ethnocentric perspective that can lead to confusion when interpreting events that are being observed. A case in point can be found in a series of letters Hugo Reid submitted to the *Los Angeles Star* in 1852. Reid notes that Indians did not like living in houses and were always "vexed and annoyed with them as debarred the satisfaction of burning them up according to usage, when their observances demanded it."[46] What Reid surmises as a dislike for enclosed spaces may also have been a funerary rite. Following the death of an individual, family members would burn the individual's personal possessions in order to release them into the spirit world, and to prevent him or her from coming back for something. In addition to the accounts written by Anglo-Americans, each tribe has some oral accounts that have been passed down through the generations. Lastly, the public records, newspapers, and judicial records imply what would have been acceptable and unacceptable behavior among the individual tribes. Together, these records provide an imperfect but captivating view of the traditional cultures that inhabited the state.

Perhaps the most significant American chronicler of the Indians of southern California in the middle of the nineteenth century was Hugo Reid. Reid was a Scotsman who came to California to seek his fortune shortly before the complete secularization of the missions in 1834. He later married Victoria, the daughter of a Gabrielino captain, and lived with her near what is now San Gabriel. Over time, he gained prominence in the community because of his business acumen and connection with the local Indians. Beginning on 21 February 1852, the *Los Angeles Star* published a series of letters written by Reid that discussed several aspects of tribal life, including the Indians' response to the invasion by the Spanish, their language, and some of their laws and customs. Reid maintains that "laws in general were made as required, with some few standing ones," and that the "government of the people was invested in the hands of their Chiefs; each captain commanding his own lodge."[47] Reid's assessment stands in concert with other tribal histories that give considerable authority and respect to a hereditary leader.

In the tribes of southern California, cultural norms and laws were passed from one generation to the next through a series of stories, songs, and myths. Each of these narratives expounded on cultural values such as honesty, fidelity, respect for tribal elders, and harmony. When a tribal member moved beyond accepted social behavior, a system of legal precepts awaited him. The legal precepts of the Cahuillas were held within specialized songs that had been given to them by the Creator. All who violated the norms of society were considered to be going "against the song."[48] According to the worldview of the Indians, the world was a series of reciprocal relationships that existed between man and nature, and between the different moieties that made up the tribe as a whole. The belief was that reciprocity was needed to ensure the continued economic, political, social, and religious harmony of the tribe. To ensure that all members were aware of their importance in the overall functioning of society, each particular moiety was responsible for certain aspects of tribal rituals, such as mourning.[49] Much like European myths and fables, tribal stories were told to entertain and to instruct children in the standards of conduct that were expected of them.[50] While Reid incredulously maintained that "their innumerable stories are all legends and more than half believed," each served as a means of ensuring the continuation of social norms.[51] Reid failed to acknowledge that all societies have fables and stories that impart moral lessons. Reid's cultural intolerance is mirrored by Bancroft in his assessment of the Indians of southern California, where he wrote, "They had a great number of traditions, legends, and fables; a few are pointed with a moral; but the majority are puerile, meaningless, to us at least, and filled with obscenities."[52] What each man failed to grasp was the fluidity with which societies that are preliterate pass information from generation to generation.

The importance of the moiety in determining and maintaining the overall equanimity of society was extremely important. Since each moiety held land in trust for the whole clan, any infraction could imperil the moiety. These recognized private land rights often served as the basis for public offenses. However, such an infraction was not simply an offense against one member, it was against the clan as a whole. Once an offense became known, either the *net* alone, or the *net* and the governing council would render a judgment and assign a punishment for the offender.[53] Tribal captains could also take land from tribal members whose actions necessitated punishment from the tribal leadership. Since a scarcity of food literally could impact the survival of a clan, punishment was often harsh and included banishment, whipping, stoning, or death.[54] Despite this carefully structured system of reciprocity, at times things would go wrong and no one was to blame. To address this issue, many clans had traditional enemy or rival clans that they routinely cursed and threatened during the course of a day for things that had gone wrong. This perpetual rivalry could have been an outlet for stress within the clan without needing to resort to violence. However, once rivalries that existed between clans reached a point where they could no longer be controlled, punishment prescribed by the *net* may well have reflected the long-term animosity between these groups and its impact on the society as a whole, as much as any real insult from trespass or poaching.

As members of a culture that prized social equilibrium, many taboos in the cultures of the Indians of southern California revolved around interpersonal relationships. In a culture that was patriarchal in nature, women were not granted the same status in society as men. Marriages were most often arranged by the families and became part of a larger socioeconomic relationship between the clan groups. Because of the reciprocal nature of these relationships, a marriage was literally not just between a man and a woman, but between families, and in a larger sense between the two clans. To offer a woman in marriage to another clan could solidify a mutually beneficial arrangement, one which would have been ardently sought by clans that had a limited power base. In a diary that related his travels up and down the coast of California in 1602, Father Antonio de la Ascencion, a Carmelite priest, noted during an encounter with Indians between San Diego and Los Angeles that a "petty chief seeing that there were no women on board [our ship] then offered by signs to give everyone ten women apiece if they would go to his land."[55] What the good father may have seen as an immoral enticement would likely have been more closely related to an attempt to form an alliance with a group of men who clearly had technological advantages over the Indians. Had the Spanish been willing to engage in such an alliance, the socioeconomic status of the clan they had become associated with would have been elevated.

When an individual had been factored into the socioeconomic structure of the larger group, replacement was often difficult. Men held higher status in the society than women because of their ability to hunt and to fight. While women were primarily, but not exclusively, responsible for gathering and maintaining agricultural products, these foodstuffs did not provide sufficient protein for the long-term survival of the tribe. Because of this, a man's hunting prowess could dramatically improve the food-producing capabilities of the group. If a woman sought a divorce from her husband, the family grouping first attempted to reconcile the couple; if their attempts were unsuccessful, the bride price that had been paid for the woman by her husband would need to be returned, and the economic benefit for the clan would be impacted. This type of familial socioeconomic bond is not unusual among native people, and is also practiced among the Pueblo Indians in the Southwest. The impact of Anglo-American society over time would have a significant effect on this tradition. According to Delfina Cuero, divorce had become easy: the woman who decided to leave her husband need only leave their residence and return to her family.[56]

If a woman engaged in adultery, however, punishment could be extreme. Among the Gabrielinos, a husband had the right to "kill or wound" his bride without fear of retribution if he caught his wife with another man.[57] He could also seek revenge on his wife's paramour and kill him. If anyone attempted to stop him from inflicting punishment on either his wife or her lover, the husband could seek redress through the *net*. Most often, however, the husband abandoned his wife, and may have even sought to claim the woman of his wife's paramour as payment for her loss to the clan. The Gabrielinos were not alone in this tradition: among the Cahuillas, death was also a possible punishment for adultery by women. Anthropologist Lucille Hooper asserted in her study of the Cahuillas, "If a wife misbehaved, she was tied to a tree and beaten by the chief."[58] According to Father Boscana, who recorded his interactions with the Jueneno Indians, "adultery was severely punished."[59] It is not clear whether this same taboo existed for men; none of the literature would support that men were held to the same standard as their wives. Instead, in many of the tribes of southern California, multiple wives would not have been unusual for the elite members of the tribe. Among the Kumeyaays, according to Tom Lucas, if a man wanted to divorce his wife, this issue had to be "taken up with the headman," and if permission to divorce were granted, the man's wife would "keep all the possessions, the house and everything they own."[60] However, this does not mean that women were to be treated as chattel. If a man abused his wife, she was well within her rights to abandon her husband and return to her family. Her actions would still have prompted the need for her clan to return the bride price that had been paid for her hand in marriage.

Despite this rather dismal image of women as little more than economic and social pawns in a larger tribal game, it should be noted that both sexes were integral to the functioning of society. In many cases, the importance of a woman's life exceeded that of a man's in the overall functioning of the society. Following a war between tribes, while male prisoners were often tortured and then killed, women were either kept as slaves or sold to other tribes.[61] Additionally, the fact that native women in southern California so infrequently appear in the records of Anglo society independent of native men indicates a protective society rather than one in which women were little more than chattel. In 1878, the *Riverside Press* reported on an incident between a Mexican man, his wife, and an Indian who returned home following a dance that had "been prolonged into the wee hours." Without apparent provocation, the Mexican man announced his intent to whip his wife, and was first verbally warned not to proceed by the Indian. The Indian's warning was imprudently ignored, and when the Mexican attempted to strike his wife, the Indian struck him in the elbow with the shank bone of a cow. The Mexican quickly called a truce, left the residence, and proceeded into town where he aroused the authorities, who then arrested the Indian for assault. During the trial proceedings, the Mexican was proven to be at fault, but for his chivalrous action, the Indian was still required to pay court costs that totaled fifty cents.[62] It can only be surmised that the Indian man may have been defending his lover from her husband. Whatever his intentions, as a protective lover or a good Samaritan, he found his behavior lauded in the Anglo press, but penalized in the courts.

For many of the tribes of southern California, justice was a private affair—one that was dealt with, if possible, in the extended family or the clan before involving the tribe's *net*. Until the age of puberty, children were under the control of their parents, with men having greater influence over their sons, and women more influence over their daughters. By and large, the punishment of choice was ridicule for minor infractions such as disrespect of elders or minor theft among family members. In the Cahuilla culture, the clan would "publicly announce an individual's real or reputed antisocial actions in songs, thus bringing shame upon him, his family, and his lineage."[63] Forms of public ridicule were common among most tribes, and served as an effective means of social control for the vast majority of the tribe's members. However, despite the effectiveness of shame as a controlling mechanism, more serious crimes were still committed within the tribal groups.

As in all societies, certain forms of antisocial behavior could not be ignored or left solely to the family to contend with, as they impacted the functioning of tribe as a whole. Among the Indians of southern California, these included murder, theft, incest, witchcraft, rape, adultery, and poaching. Punishment for these crimes could often result in death, at the hands of either other clan members or the tribe at large. All of the above crimes impact the reciprocity that was expected from each tribal member and that was necessary to maintain the equilibrium of society. Murder could remove a valued provider and threaten the economic stability of a family, which would place an undue burden on the rest of the clan, or take a mother from her child—forcing another family to assume the responsibility of raising children that were not their own, thereby reducing their ability to provide for their own children. Theft or the poaching of either personal goods or property that served the clan also imperiled the survival of the whole. Incest and adultery were crimes against an individual and against the clan. The progeny of an incestuous relationship had a greater chance of defects and stood as a constant reminder of a violation of stringent laws regarding potential marriage partners.[64] It also prevented the economic interchange among clans. Adultery and rape likewise offended both the individual and the clan as a whole.

Murder, according to Hugo Reid, rarely occurred among the tribes in southern California.[65] However, the punishment for such a crime would be death, with judgment most often being passed by the *net*. In many of the instances where the punishment was carried out among Anglo witnesses, a common thread existed between the crime and the punishment, such as where the execution took place or the method of execution. In 1871, the *Los Angeles Star* reported on the case of two Indians who had fought each other with knives. In the end, one was stabbed to death, and the tribe was allowed to assign the punishment for the murderer. The tribe, or more likely the *net*, determined that the murderer should be hung from a branch of the tree under which the fight had occurred.[66] Within a tribal society, the death of a clan member could adversely affect the survival of the group, and punishment needed to be swift and decisive.

However, at times the tribal society as a whole could be impacted by the actions of an individual, and instead of taking direct action, covert action was resorted to. Tom Lucas, a Kumeyaay, recalled an incident in which

a young man went a little "crazy." He would shoot the water jugs the women were carrying from the spring and shoot at children just to watch them scatter. They found two or three people dead, and this man, who was suspected of killing them, turned up with items that belonged to the deceased. . . . The council decided his fate and the entire village was in on the plot. Everyone kept telling him he looked sick and that he should see the medicine man. After a few days, he believed he was sick and went to the medicine man who gave him something to drink. He simply went to sleep and never woke up. Survival of the whole group had top priority.[67]

The possibility for a private rather than a societal punishment for murder is something that has a tradition in Anglo society, but finds little mention in native accounts of tribal culture. While murder was punished, the *net* and the council appear to have served as the primary judge and jury. This stands in contrast to a report by Bancroft in which he remarks that among the Indians of southern California, "A murder's life was taken by the relatives of his victim, unless he should gain access to the temple, in which case his punishment was left to their god. Vengeance was, however, only deferred; the children of the murdered man invariably avenged his death sooner or later, upon the murderer or his descendents."[68] Bancroft's account, while appealing to the larger Anglo-American society of the time, may not represent traditional Indian culture so much as Old Testament lore.[69] For people who valued harmony and equanimity in their daily relations, the idea of a tribal member permanently hiding out in a temple to escape punishment would have denied the tribe a productive member of society and would have required that other tribe members pick up the slack, providing for him as well as the rest of the clan. The assumption that revenge between the two clans could wait for generations is also unlikely in such a society. However, neither can his account be disregarded out of hand. As tribal society crumbled in the face of Anglo expansion, structures that had previously given the society coherence were eroded. The authority of the *net* was diminished, and Indians were so marginalized by Anglo society that the death of an Indian often warranted only casual mention in the weekly newspapers. Native people who resorted to private justice instead of relying on traditional law or the Anglo-American courts would not have been outside the realm of possibility.

While murder could devastate a clan, so too could witchcraft. Shamans held important positions among the tribes of southern California. Unlike other members of the tribe, a shaman was not under the control of the *net*, because a true shaman was said to converse with the Great Creator. Since tribal leaders had no delusions of godhood, they recognized that they could not effectively judge someone who was in contact with the Creator, and left the responsibility for this to the other shamans. In the event of a shaman who did not appropriately use his powers, other shamans could ceremonially take his power from him. However, if a shaman had devolved into evil and practiced witchcraft, he imperiled the entire tribe. It was assumed that an individual cursed by the shaman would be unable to fulfill his responsibilities to the clan or tribe. In other instances, the witchcraft could impact the tribe as a whole, such as in the case of prolonged drought or disease. In these cases, judgment was as swift and as severe as if the shaman had committed murder: death. In 1858, the Indians in San Diego County— possibly responding to the influx of Anglo-Americans onto their lands, or the decimation of their population from smallpox epidemics that had ravaged the native population several times during the 1840s to 1850s— prepared to punish a chief named Manuelito for witchcraft. However, the sheriff intervened and prevented the punishment from continuing. In all likelihood, the sheriff's actions saved Manuelito's life.[70]

Despite the apparent communal nature of punishment among the tribes in southern California for severe crimes, in most cases assault appears to have been a private matter, unless it impacted the functioning of the tribe as a whole. When this occurred, the *net* was again called in to restore the social equilibrium. In 1851, approximately one hundred Cahuilla Indians were involved in a significant row in the city of San Bernardino. In late October, the Cahuillas appeared in town and requested permission from the city marshal to play a game called *peon*.[71] The marshal refused, citing city ordinances that prohibited the game. Not to be discouraged, the Indians then approached Juan Sepulveda, the justice of the peace, with the same request and were granted permission to proceed with the game. The accommodating Sepulveda even detailed six guards to ensure that the game would be peaceful, and accompanied the players to the field. That evening, as the game was being played, an Indian named Cayote attempted to forcefully take alcohol from the wife of the man on whose property the Indians were playing. The woman's husband intervened, overpowered Cayote, tied him up, and prepared to remove him to the city jail. However, before Cayote could be removed from the premises, several Indians intervened to protect Cayote from the Anglo authorities. The authorities retreated, and the Indians began to threaten to set fire to the house. Justice Sepulveda, recognizing that he had lost control of the situation, went into town for help and returned a short time later with seven men, all armed with guns. In contrast, none of the Indians had firearms. By this time, the number of Indians who were gathering had swollen to one hundred. A five-minute gun battle ensued during which eight Indians were killed; the rest of the Indians then quickly dispersed. The Anglo authorities pursued those involved in the melee, eventually arresting and jailing twenty-one Indians. Each of those Indians received sentences of twenty-five lashes and a one-dollar fine. Juan Antonio, the Cahuilla captain acting as the *net* for the tribe, secured the release of the prisoners.[72] To lose so many men from the tribe would have resulted in economic and social disarray. Antonio's focus, therefore, was to ensure that the disruption to the tribe's functioning was minimized. Another incident, which also occurred in San Bernardino, involved two Indian men who had been fighting. Under the authority of the *net*, each man was forced to lie face-down in the dirt and receive thirty lashes.[73] There is no mention of the men's tribal affiliation, or the name of the captain who ordered their punishment. Still other instances indicate that while all the particulars of the crime were not known, the tribe was determined to proceed with its judgment. In the early years of Anglo-American occupation, it appears the American authorities were content to allow the tribes to police themselves. Often, the Anglo community was only aware that an infraction had occurred when punishment was decreed. In these instances, any interest in determining why an individual was being punished was minimal. An example would be an article in San Bernardino's *Guardian* newspaper in 1873. The reporter acknowledges that an Indian court had judged a case, but the crime was not recorded—only the fine of ten dollars for each offender.[74]

Lastly, theft was a charge that Anglo-Americans widely leveled at the Native Americans in the region. While native people were responsible for the killing of livestock and the occasional theft from a person or store, often they were suspected in the press based on what amounted to flimsy or nonexistent evidence. According to Hugo Reid, "robbery was never known among them."[75] If Reid's assessment is accurate, then the question of Indian theft takes on wider cultural implications. If Indians were reluctant to steal from each other, but willingly took property from non-tribal members, it can be ascertained that the reasons for the theft were myriad, including the simple desire to have property that was denied them, the belief that the property rightly belonged to them, the feeling that they had no other choice in order to survive, or because they were attempting to passively strike back at the Anglo-Americans and Europeans who had invaded their land and condemned them to a life of poverty. All of these issues and more are likely behind the issue of Indian theft from Anglo-Americans, but this provides little insight into crimes that were committed against tribal members.

Despite Reid's assertions, theft was known among the tribes of southern California, but its overall practice was likely limited. In part, this would have been because of the localized societies in which most Native Americans lived. Many Indian villages had between 50 and 150 individuals. With such a small population, if an individual stole anything, the theft would be recognized more quickly, and the repercussions would be more significant on a personal level than if the individual had stolen property in a larger and less intimate society. Another reason for the limited incidence of theft among tribal members would be its impact on the clan of the thief. If an individual stole from the land of another moiety, this opened his entire clan up to ridicule and repercussions. The cascading impact of taking something that did not belong to you could threaten the survival of the clan by exposing them to ridicule and sanction. If carried far enough, the clan could even be forced to remove themselves from the band, which could threaten their survival. It is little wonder that honesty was considered a primary virtue among the native people of the region.

Punishment for crimes were not as clearly defined among the Indians of southern California as they are within an Anglo-American judicial system. This stands in contrast to Reid's assertions that "Laws in general were made as required."[76] More appropriate would be to state that antisocial behavior was clearly defined; however for the Indian, the punishment was tailored to the infraction. Punishment was clearly the purview of the *net* once an individual reached adulthood. According to Reid, whipping, which became so dominant a form of punishment for everything from fighting to theft after the incursion by Anglo-Europeans, had previously been "never resorted to as a punishment; therefore all fines and sentences consisted in delivering money, food and skins."[77] Since so many of the previous traditions of the Indians have been lost because of the concerted efforts of the Spanish and the Mexicans to ensure the assimilation of the tribes, sanctions on the physical punishment of an individual can only be speculated about. However, within a small insular society, if an individual were ordered whipped, those individuals who were called on to impose the sentence might well be subject to revenge from the guilty party if it was felt that they played their role too enthusiastically. In the event of a murder or a threat to the survival of the clan as a whole, exacting revenge did not have the same potential to foster ill feelings toward those inflicting the punishment. They were merely agents in ensuring the dead had their revenge.

The world that the Americans inherited in 1848 was one that was filled with a diverse population of people and customs. Within this mosaic of cultures and societies, different traditions evolved that in many respects mirrored the judicial traditions of the incoming Anglo-American culture. Unfortunately, while the Americans brought with them their legal traditions, they also brought with them their prejudices. Confronted by the possibility of engaging in a multicultural society that was based on mutual respect, or imposing their will on the people that already occupied the state, the Americans chose the latter. At the heart of this imposition was not, as might be expected, the wholesale hatred of Indians; many Americans had great sympathy for the plight of the Indians and recognized the cause of their poverty as being Anglo incursion into tribal lands. Instead, at the core of Anglo-American behavior was greed: an unfettered desire for the land, the resources, and the labor of the people they considered inferior. In order to achieve their ends, Americans often resorted to the law.

Justice and Municipal Courts

OR MOST INDIANS OF SOUTHERN CALIFORNIA, INVOLVEMENT in the Anglo-American judicial system started in the lower courts. In these chambers, justices communicated the prejudices and needs of their communities through their rulings.[1] The first California Convention in 1849 established a multi-tiered judicial system for the state.[2] This included the supreme court, district court, county court, probate court, justice court, and the lower municipal courts, such as the recorder's, police, and mayor's courts. Within this system, the justice and municipal courts served as the primary arbiter in local criminal matters. California statutes in 1850 further defined the role of the local courts in attending to the judicial needs of the local communities. The justice courts would be limited to cases involving less than $200. The following year, California's legislators further defined the role of the lower courts and gave them jurisdiction in criminal cases that included petty larceny, assault and battery, disturbing the peace, and other misdemeanors where the punishment did not exceed $500 or three-months' imprisonment.

For the Indians of southern California, this meant that whoever occupied the bench in these courts expressed his interpretation of the law, and the values and attitudes of the community he served.[3] For the Indians who came under the jurisdiction of these Anglo courts, this could be a significant handicap in their ability to receive justice. As historian Ron Woolsey has noted, during the early years of American control, many Anglos considered the Indian to be the root cause of the lawlessness that plagued their communities.[4] While prejudice against Native Americans was a common trait shared by most Anglo-Americans during the nineteenth century, the expression of this prejudice was most often limited to personal displays of contempt, abuse, or chicanery. Within the local courts, however, the prejudices of the justice of the peace could be expressed through the judicial system. Oftentimes these judicial opinions fluctuated according to the changing demographic, economic, and land-tenure issues that confronted the communities of southern California.

In 1850 the total population of southern California was estimated to be 20,000 people, with Native Americans holding a simple majority.[5] The integration of the Indian into the economic and social fiber of the community under the Mexican regime had resulted in a parasitic relationship in which Indians provided the vast bulk of the labor needed in the region, and the Californios (California-born Mexicans) enjoyed the fruits of the Indian labor. As Horace Bell noted in his memoirs on the early days of America's hegemony in the region, "Indians did the labor and the white man spent the money in those happy days."[6] His sentiments echoed those of Father Guardian Lopez in 1825, who noted that the "colonists . . . are too indolent to work." In fact, without the labor of the Indians, it seems likely that the early European colonists would have starved.[7] As Americans began to filter into the southern California region, the benefits of this nonreciprocal relationship were not lost on them. When Americans seized control of the land in southern California, they widely adopted this parasitic relationship to suit their labor needs.

While there is some controversy over when American influence in the region became pronounced, it appears, as historian Charles Hughes insists, that the influence of Anglos over Hispanics in San Diego occurred far earlier than previously supposed, with Anglos holding key political and financial positions by the early 1850s. Previously it had been supposed that the de facto transition from a primarily Mexican to an American government did not occur until the 1870s.[8] However, prior to the Mexican-American War, Americans were primarily men who came to California to make their fortunes, and who were often accepted into the Mexican families that dominated the rancho period. In southern California, Benjamin D. Wilson, or Don Benito Wilson, was one of the most prominent of these expatriates, and in 1843 he received a land grant of one square league in Los Angeles County, the Rancho San Jose de Buenos Ayres.[9] Wilson was far from alone in securing his grant of land from the Mexican government and in the influence he exerted over the politics and development of the

region. Another prominent expatriate was John Warner, who was granted
a total of ten square leagues in San Diego County between 1840 and 1846.
Out of the 155 land grants that were given by either Mexican or Spanish
authorities, at least thirty-four were given to Anglos.[10] At the time of the
Mexican-American War, many of these individuals, despite spending years
under the Mexican flag, chose to fight with the American forces when the
opportunity came to overthrow their benefactors.

In another example of the growing influence of Americans in the region
after the war, in 1850 the Los Angeles county directory listed seven lawyers
as practicing in the county; ten years later, this number had increased to
twenty-four.[11] With the limited population in the region, the focus of the
work for these men was debt collection and land-title litigation. This work
placed them in a favorable position to acquire land for themselves and
to directly benefit from the happenings in the courts. As their holdings
increased, so too did their influence over local government. For the Indians of southern California, this meant a rapid transition from Spanish to
American legal practices. It also meant exposure to the rabid nativism , or
prejudices against non-Americans by the incoming Americans. Historian
David Langum supports this position in his study of the development of
law in the early American period. Langum maintains that Americans in
California "drew on local law to the extent absolutely necessary," eventually
replacing the prevailing Hispanic system with one of their own choosing.[12]
The influence of Anglo state lawmakers in ensuring the subjugation of the
Indian was clearly expressed through several California statutes, including
the 1850 Act for the Government and Protection of Indians and the 1854
Act to Prevent the Sale of Firearms and Ammunition to Indians. Implemen-
tation of the principles of these statutes would be up to the local communities. However, in southern California, based on the precedent already set
by the state, local ordinances were passed that also ensured the subjugation
of the Indian. In Los Angeles this was manifested in the "slave" market
that operated during the first two decades of American domination. In this
system, Indians were "hired" out to Anglos who had labor needs and were
willing to pay the fines Indians had incurred through the violation of local
statutes.

At the state level, the constitution of 1849 established the judicial blueprint for the state, including the establishment of the supreme, district,
county, and justice courts. The justice courts would receive instruction at a

later date as to what cases they would handle. However, the district courts would have original jurisdiction where the "amount in dispute exceeds two-hundred dollars," and in "all criminal cases not otherwise provided for."[13] The original state legislatures then moved to address the judicial needs of the Indians in the state, through the *Act for the Government and Protection of Indians*. This, on the whole, meant that Indians would be subject to a different judicial system, one that most residents of California bypassed depending on the severity of the crime. Under this statute, "Justices of the Peace shall have jurisdiction in all cases of complaints by, for or against Indians, in their respective townships in this State."[14] The act also made Indians essentially responsible for all costs incurred in the administration of this act. Section 8 of the statute called for the justice of the peace to biannually "make a full and correct statement to the Court of Sessions of their County, of all monies received of fines imposed on Indians." These fees would be paid into the county treasury's "Indian Fund," and the county treasurer would then pay out of the fund for "fees and expenditures incurred in carrying out the provisions of this law."[15] In the years this Indian fund existed, it consistently brought in hundreds of dollars in fines. In 1858, $255.38 had been collected within a five-month period. Since most fines assessed to Indians ranged from one to five dollars, this represented at minimum fifty fines imposed on Indians over the course of less than half a year.[16] By allowing the justice courts original jurisdiction in cases dealing with Indians within the state, the government had essentially left native people at the mercy of local prejudice. In addition to this, the justices had an incentive to bring Indians before their courts in order to assess fines that would be paid into a larger "Indian Fund." While this may have been explained away by the argument that Indians were prohibited from participating in the government of the state and also did not pay taxes, neither explanation is accurate. Under the 1849 state constitution, Indians could—on a two-thirds vote from the legislature—be granted the right to vote within the state, and Indians who owned property did pay taxes on the land, just as Anglo landowners did. What the *Act for the Government and Protection of Indians* amounted to was an additional assessment that was forced on the Indians of the state.

Those criminal cases that were to be heard by the justice and municipal courts were limited to misdemeanor offenses such as petty theft,[17] and assault cases in which no serious injury had been sustained. Fines could not exceed five hundred dollars, and jail time was limited to six months or less; in 1870 penalties were increased to one thousand dollars and one year in jail.[18] The justice courts also held preliminary hearings for more serious crimes such as murder or grand theft,[19] to determine if the case should be referred to a higher state court or to the grand jury. In the absence of a coroner, the state authorized the justices to hold their own coroner's inquests to aid in their preliminary determinations. The authority of the justice court to deal with the vast number of crimes that were committed within a local community was steadily eroded by the state legislature in the first decades of California's statehood in order to dilute some of the autocratic authority that many courts had assumed. This included legislation in 1856 that disallowed corporal punishment for theft, and an 1863 statute that prohibited the justice courts from trying grand larceny cases.[20] However, despite the passage of state legislation, the justice courts frequently overstepped their authority in cases in which Indians were involved.

The men who agreed to sit upon the bench in the justice courts rarely could claim any legal training.[21] Instead, the high positions they held within their local communities as either business or professional leaders supposedly qualified them for the position. The assumption that prominent men would best be able to serve their local communities must also be balanced against the acknowledgment that these were also the individuals who had invested the most in their local communities and therefore had the most to lose if land prices declined.[22] Most, but not all, were literate.[23] Even if the men who assumed the role of justice of the peace had been interested in knowing more about the law they had agreed to uphold, theirs would have been a difficult task. Legal reference books were almost nonexistent in the area due to the limited population and the previous domination of the Spanish judicial system. The American government embraced instead the precepts of English common law, which was not wholly compatible with Spanish legal traditions. While the original 1849 state constitution called for the timely printing and distribution of legal precedents in the state, these decisions often were not distributed to the lower courts. Instead, many new laws were printed in the local papers. This gave the justices no rationales or guidance in the cases they determined.

This dearth of information was compounded by the fact that many communities still had not constructed courthouses or jails by the mid-1850s. In Los Angeles County, the Union Hotel served as the courthouse until 1853, and the jail was "the old adobe house of Dr. Bush . . . there was a big pine log extending from end to end of the long room . . . with staples driven into it at intervals of three or four feet, to which were chained the prisoners."[24] In San Bernardino, the courts were forced to scramble for a place to conduct business until a permanent structure was erected in 1858. Initially, judicial proceedings were heard at the Mormon council house or the Crosby Hotel, and prisoners were boarded in private homes. Up until 1858, attempts to build a city jail had been met with apathy, or had failed due to shoddy construction techniques.[25]

Coupled with these drawbacks came another significant challenge for the judiciary in southern California. Because of the region's limited population and proximity to Mexico, it had earned a deserved reputation for lawlessness by the 1850s. The rich gold fields to the north drew off much of the labor that would have been needed to establish an effective police force. Faced with a limited pool of candidates, those who assumed the role of sheriff often had more in common with the criminals than the judiciary. Even where a police force had been established, the presence of a few officers had limited impact on a desperate criminal element. Judge Benjamin Hayes, who served in the Los Angeles district court, complained of needing to travel with another individual for protection, and of the constant need for firearms when traveling outside the city. In 1857, Los Angeles county sheriff James Barton was killed in an ambush at San Juan Capistrano that had been set up by former inmates who sent word out into the local communities that they were going to seize control of the land from the *gringos*, or newly arrived Americans.[26] Barton was not alone in his sacrifice for the stability of the communities of southern California. It is little wonder that within this volatile setting, "local government's inability to respond to violence created a hostile atmosphere between competing ethnic groups."[27] It should also come as no surprise that the first person hanged in Los Angeles in 1849 was an Indian.[28]

Oftentimes the fear experienced by Anglos translated into prejudicial action within the judiciary. In many instances the victims of this fear were non-Anglos, and while it was considered that the entire region was awash in crime, a different story appears when the records of the state prison are examined. Between 1851 and 1854, the counties of southern California sent nine men to San Quentin, the newly established state penitentiary in northern California. Of these nine, seven came from Los Angeles County and two from San Diego County. Of the seven who were sent to the state prison from Los Angeles, five were Hispanic and one was an Indian. Only one Anglo man was sent to the state prison in a three-year period. In contrast, San Diego County sent two Anglo men to prison during the same period.[29]

In the 1850s and 1860s, the harassment of Native Americans by the judiciary included several cases in which Anglos arrested Indians and held them in jail without charging them with a crime. In Los Angeles, Jose Antonio found himself in jail because he had the bad luck of being near the jail when the sheriff was around.[30] In San Bernardino, an Indian named Manuel remained in the local jail until the grand jury, after determining that no crime had been committed, ordered the sheriff to release him.[31] The harassment of Indians in the local judiciary was pervasive enough that after most Indians had been forced from Los Angeles County in the 1880s because of the coming of the railroad and the increase in land values, the practice of harassment that had been established by the legal authorities continued in the counties where the local Anglo communities still needed to contend with a native population. According to historian Tom Patterson, in his history of Riverside, in 1885 "Recorder Edward Conway made a statement to the board to the effect that a certain Indian had been before him and in the course of examination had stated that he had twice been under arrest within a short time and had been released by C. C. Westerbrook, deputy marshal of the city, by the payment of $5 to said Westerbrook, and without process of law."[32] The power exercised by the police and the judiciary in these instances served no other purpose than to harass those Indians who were unlucky enough to be available. Unfortunately, these are not isolated examples. Hatred of the authority held by the justices and the police may have prompted an Indian named Jose Antonio to try to burn down the Anaheim city jail in 1872.[33] In another instance, in 1851 an Indian named Jose assaulted a policeman in San Diego during an attempt to take him to jail. Jose pleaded guilty to the offense; however, there is no indication why he had been taken to jail in the first place.[34]

Based purely on numbers alone, the Indian presence in the municipal courts of southern California was an exercise in harassment. While many of the records from the era under consideration have been destroyed, those records that do survive indicate that the Indian presence in the courts occurred in numbers out of proportion to their numbers in society. However, while Indians were brought before the courts more frequently than their numbers in society would suggest, the punishments they received were often only a fraction of what an Anglo or Hispanic defendant could expect to receive. The reason for this can only be speculated on, but it lends credence to the contention that the courts were used either to harass Indians into providing cheap labor, or to prompt them to abandon their traditional homes in a search for less contentious surroundings.

In 1860 the total Indian population in Los Angeles County stood at 2,014.[35] Within this group, the Anglo courts charged nine Indians with crimes ranging from petty larceny to assault with a deadly weapon. Of the nine accused, seven were convicted. The ratio of Indians to those accused stood at one in 223. However, the sentences they received were approximately 75 percent of what a non-Indian defendant could expect. A decade later, the native population in Los Angeles County had declined dramatically. A smallpox epidemic from 1863 to 1864 had literally littered the countryside with the bodies of victims, most of whom were Indians. The attrition of Indians in the southern California area was exacerbated by the continual displacement of tribes by the ongoing influx of Anglo-Americans, and the seemingly perpetual violence that plagued native communities; much of this violence occurred at the hands of Anglos. To avoid harassment, many Indians abandoned their traditional cultures and assimilated into the Hispanic community. These factors are reflected in the 1870 Census, which lists only 219 Indians living in Los Angeles County. Of those 219, seven stood accused of crimes ranging from grand larceny to assault. The ratio of Indians accused of crime stood at one in thirty-one, compared to one in 223 only ten years earlier. Despite their presence in the court system, Anglo juries convicted only one of the seven charged.[36] In part this may be attributed to the growing number of Anglos who came to the region during the boom times of the 1870s and did not as readily embrace the prejudices of those who had been in the area since its transition to American hands.

Farther to the south in San Diego County, a different story developed. While San Diego did not have the slave market that so characterized early labor conditions in Los Angeles, Indians often could rely on receiving lighter sentences than non-Indians who were convicted in the courts. However, in San Diego, the likelihood of this was significantly less than in Los Angeles County. From 1870 to 1880 in San Diego County, the total Anglo population stagnated. In 1870 the Anglo population stood at 2,700, while only twenty-eight Indians were recorded in the census.[37] By 1880 the Anglo population had declined to 2,600 and the Indian population had risen to 1,702.[38] These numbers inaccurately reflect the true number of Indians in the region, and instead are only reflective of the Indians who worked and lived among Anglo-Americans. Since the San Diego area developed at a significantly slower pace than Los Angeles, many of the Indians in the area were able to avoid contact with Anglo society and continued to live within traditional communities. However, those who did have contact with the Anglo communities often found it to be a less-than-pleasant experience. From 1870 to 1880, Indians found themselves before the justice courts eleven times for crimes ranging from petty larceny to assault with a deadly weapon.[39] In comparison to Los Angeles County, the chance of an Indian appearing in the justice courts was one in 154.

The reason Indians were before the courts so much more as the decades of the nineteenth century progressed lies primarily in the demographic shifts that occurred during these decades. As the Anglo population increased, the Indian population decreased. The 1870s started, and faltered, with the creation of two executive-order reservations in San Diego County. By 1871 the land had been returned to the public domain because of Anglo protest. By the middle of the 1870s, some of the reservations had been reestablished, and many Native Americans who had been living in Los Angeles were encouraged to move to the new sites. While this explains the reason for the shift in the native population, it does not explain the presence of the Native American in the courts. For that, the economic development of the community must be considered.

By the end of the 1860s, the people of California saw the potential benefits of a railroad that would connect their isolated state to the rest of the union, and to new markets. The importance of rail travel had already occurred to the residents of Los Angeles County, who in 1861, led by Phineas Banning, Abel Stearns, and Murray Morrison, chartered a railroad that would lead from the harbor in San Pedro to the city itself. The initial attempt to build a rail line to the city was fraught with controversy, however; individuals who had invested in the stage and wagon lines successfully blocked the creation of the railroad for several years. In 1868, Phineas Banning, then a freshman state senator for Los Angeles County, helped push through legislation that ensured a railroad would be built in southern California. The twenty-mile rail line was completed on 26 October 1869.[40]

Banning's boosterism for Los Angeles was not the only rail subsidy passed in 1868; the California legislature also passed a "5% subsidy law which would tax counties as an inducement to further rail construction."[41] Railroads, it was felt, would surely benefit the development of the state.

However, the favored position enjoyed by the railroads in the 1860s was not extended into the 1870s. As a nationwide depression spread throughout the nation, beginning in 1873, the vast fortunes made by the railroad giants forced many to reconsider why the state's population should agree to the payment of subsidies when the railroad magnates would reap the financial benefit. Subsidies, after all, led to higher taxes, and higher taxes resulted in a lower profit margin for farmers and other entrepreneurs. Additionally, the railroad brought in cheap goods from the east, which impacted the ability of the local communities to develop their own manufacturing infrastructure. This backlash against the railroads almost swamped the efforts of southern Californians to bring a railroad to the region.[42] However, the genie had been let out of the bottle, and most believed that rail travel would be the wave of the future, annihilating all that stood in its path. In southern California, arguments against the railroad would fall to the greater call for expansion. With the railroad came people, and this influx of people would raise land prices. As a visitor to San Diego remarked in a letter home in 1873, "San Diego is a pleasant place, but real estate is ten years ahead of commerce. When they get a railroad and good water, there will be business openings there."[43]

In 1876, Los Angeles ended its isolation from the northern part of the state with the completion of the Southern Pacific's southern route. The importance of the railroad in this developing region cannot be overstated.[44] As a largely rural enclave, Los Angeles' development depended on the promotion of its primary resources—namely, as the shipping entrepot of the region for the distribution of its cattle and agricultural products. However, prior to the arrival of the railroad, any expansion in regional production was hindered by the farmer's inability to get his produce to market before it spoiled. In the 1870s, the market for cattle from southern California almost collapsed as production from other regions in the country began to provide better-quality beef. This decline in the cattle market in turn focused the attention of area investors on agriculture. Southern California was blessed with a long growing season and abundant fertile soil. With the railroad came ready access to new markets and the incentive to expand agricultural operations. As agriculture in the region expanded, so too did the value of the land. However, the role of the Native Americans in this new economic scheme had changed from the days when their labor had been coveted. Now their presence was no longer needed because of the influx of Anglo men in search of work. However, removing the Indians from the area would not be easy.

In 1873, the collapse of the national economy sent the southern California economy into a tailspin. The limited regional resources were stressed by an increasing number of men who moved through the countryside looking for work. Many cities forced these tramps out of town; however, many remained in the area. Given the choice between American or Indian laborers, employers chose Anglos. Without the ability to work, Indians were reduced to a state of destitution. It was this debased condition that led to calls for the reestablishment of the reservations in 1875. With that call came a concomitant "encouragement" from the judiciary for Indians to leave town. The high percentage of Indian arrests, coupled with the absurdly low trial rates, points to the use of the courts as one means of making life unbearable for the few Indians still living in Los Angeles.

Unlike Los Angeles, San Diego's hope for a railroad faded in the mid-1870s when a proposed line that would have been built by the Texas and Pacific Railway failed to materialize. Originally planned to connect San Diego with San Bernardino, the spur line drew considerable opposition from the Southern Pacific. However, the financial panic of 1873 doomed the project's financing, and the scheme collapsed. Another decade passed before San Diego finally received its railroad connection to the surrounding southern California cities. Following the arrival of the railroad to the city in 1883, it could be anticipated that the presence of the Indian in the courts would have soared, as it had in Los Angeles; but the opposite was true. The reason for the declining presence of the Native American in the California courts was the assertion of the federal courts and the solidification of the Indian agent as the overarching authority among reservation Indians by the 1880s.[45] This removed Indians in San Diego County from state to federal jurisdiction. As has been previously discussed, this transition of authority was a two-edged sword, leaving the Indians of southern California subject to the personal whims of the Indian agent while also protecting them from the prejudice of the local courts.

Throughout the latter half of the nineteenth century, the propensity of the justice courts to hear cases involving Indians without sustaining convictions proved to be a common occurrence in all three counties. The courts frequently arraigned Indians on charges of grand larceny to determine if the case should be referred to the grand jury for further proceedings. In San Bernardino, many of the cases presented did not warrant referral to a higher court, or even the initial charge of grand larceny. In one instance, the court heard a complaint against an Indian woman named Maria, who had been accused of stealing a hat and an undisclosed amount of money from a drunken bar patron. Several witness reported that the patron had been gambling and drinking heavily and did not have any money by the end of the evening. Despite this, the lower court found sufficient evidence to convict Maria, and the case was referred to superior court. The upper court upheld her conviction, but the judge recognized the trivial nature of the charge and released Maria with time served.[46] In another case, the authorities in San Bernardino accused an Indian of grand larceny and then transferred his case to San Diego County for prosecution. San Diego apparently refused to pursue the case.

The rationale for charging Indians with felony versus misdemeanor crimes meant higher bail amounts could be demanded. Since most Indians could not make bail, they remained incarcerated until the conclusion of their trials. In San Bernardino County, where Indians also routinely served as a labor source for the community, the longer an Indian remained in jail because he could not make bail, the more his labor could be exploited.[47] In 1853, Bill Jenkins, one of the Los Angeles Rangers, reportedly begged his fellow rangers not to kill any Indians they found on a raid, as he "proposed to capture about a dozen or so of stout young bucks, as he proposed to commence the planting and cultivation of a vineyard."[48]

In San Diego, between 1857 and 1881, ten cases involving Native Americans accused of theft came before the justice courts, but authorities never pursued six of these cases. Of the four remaining cases, one Indian confessed and the court referred another to the grand jury. The grand jury later refused to recommend this case to the upper courts.[49] The remaining two cases resulted in two guilty convictions. One was heard in the state court,[50] and in the other, the defendant received a $500 fine.[51] All ten cases involved the theft of livestock.[52]

In Los Angeles, the justice and municipal courts heard six grand-larceny cases involving Native Americans from 1861 to 1872; in half of those cases, the Indians confessed to the charge. Despite these confessions and the referral of all three cases to the grand jury, only one individual was convicted.[53] Of the remaining three cases, the court reduced the charges in one case to petty larceny, and the defendant received a $400 fine or six months in jail.[54] The court refused to pursue prosecution in the other two cases.[55] In four of the six cases involving Native Americans, the alleged theft involved livestock. The poor conviction ratio for grand larceny with Native American defendants is surprising when considered against the frequency with which Indians were accused of this crime. The possibility exists that grand juries refused to refer cases for several reasons—the first being the difficulty in determining the true ownership of the livestock, and the second being the declining value of the livestock in the region by the 1870s. A more humanitarian possibility was that since most Indians who were accused of stealing livestock converted the animal to food for their families, the juries were more lenient in their decisions.

In contrast to the grand-larceny charges that permeated the lower courts, the rate of Indians charged with petty larceny for the same time period was abnormally low. From 1851 to 1885, two petty-larceny cases came before the justice courts in San Diego. In both cases, the court found the Indians guilty as charged. In the first case, an Indian woman stood accused of stealing some silk from a local store. She received a sentence of three months in the county jail.[56] The second case involved two Indian men who had broken into a home and taken a violin. The charge against them was changed to burglary, and their case was heard in the district court.[57] The court found both guilty of burglary. From 1860 to 1890, Los Angeles heard one petty-larceny case involving an Indian who was eventually concicted. In Los Angeles, bail rates for petty larceny were not recorded, most likely because the cases were heard and decisions rendered during a single court appearance.

The issue of Indians being charged in the courts, but in many instances not tried for their alleged crimes is puzzling until two factors are considered: what had been stolen and when. The majority of the cases that involved the theft of livestock had all occurred at a time when Indians were being displaced from their lands, from the 1850s to the 1870s. During the early 1870s, jobs were scarce because of a downturn in the economy. When reservations had been arranged for the native people in southern California, their presence in the courts declined significantly. In most of the cases involving the theft of livestock, the identity of the owner was not noted. It is possible that without a complaining prosecution witness, the courts felt they could not sustain a verdict of guilty. It is also equally possible that the livestock had not been properly branded, and therefore it would have been almost impossible to find the rightful owner. During the latter half of the nineteenth century, the lower courts heard numerous cases of Anglo men who petitioned the courts for ownership of livestock they found on their property. The idea that an Indian may have also run across a stray animal did not seem to have been considered when the courts charged Indians with theft.

In several cases in which Indians claimed livestock as a possession, the courts responded with considerable skepticism. An example occurred in Los Angeles during the trial of an Anglo, Santos Silvas. Silvas had come to the attention of the authorities after Tomas, an Indian man visiting from San Bernardino, saw Silvas riding a horse that had been stolen from him. Before the court would consider the horse his property, the court required Tomas to locate the man who had originally sold him the horse and have him appear in court. This done, the court charged Silvas with grand larceny for the theft of Tomas's horse, but later abandoned the grand-larceny case in preference for a burglary charge brought by another Anglo man.[58] Had their roles been reversed, it is doubtful Tomas would have needed to go to such lengths to prove his ownership of the animal.

Anglo insistence that Indians could only occupy the lowest social rungs of the new state was compounded by the theft of Indian lands. This prevented Indians from gathering the foods that had once been the mainstay of their diet. Additionally, the land Anglos converted to agriculture sharply reduced the areas where these traditional foodstuffs grew, and as new plants began to take hold in the region, many native plant species that the Indians had relied on previously for their survival disappeared. In the harsh economic climate of the 1870s, Indians found the availability of wage labor to meet their subsistence needs nearly nonexistent because of the prejudices of potential employers. Those employers who considered hiring Indian laborers faced pressure from Anglos to exclude Indians from their employment rolls. For many Native Americans, the only option available was to take from the livestock that now ranged on their traditional homelands, or starve.

Despite the appearance of Indians in the courts to answer charges involving a crime against property, judicial records indicate that Indians in southern California did not receive sentences that were harsher than those received by members of other ethnic groups who were similarly convicted. In San Bernardino, during a six-month period from October 1864 to February 1865, the court sentenced two Indians charged with burglary to one year in state prison.[59] In contrast, an Anglo man named James Maddison also stood accused of burglary; Maddison admitted to his crime, and the court sentenced him to a two-year term in state prison.[60] The trend toward harsher sentences for Anglos continued with the 1867 sentencing of James Marshall, who received two years for burglary.[61] The justice-court tendency to charge but not pursue cases against Native Americans, and to afford lesser sentences in some crimes, is an enigma. However, clues to solving this puzzle may lie in the nuisance charges brought against Native Americans.

The use of the municipal courts as a barometer to determine Anglo attitudes toward Indians is best illustrated by examining the nuisance cases that clogged the courts. Only San Bernardino County has extensively preserved the records of nuisance complaints made during the latter half of the nineteenth century.[62] By far the most frequent charge brought against Indians was the charge of being drunk in public. Within a two-year period, from 1873 to 1875, the justice court of San Bernardino heard seventy such cases. Fines ranged from $1 to $7.50, with men receiving fines that were twice what women received. However, men considered to be too old or infirm were either discharged without a fine being levied, or ordered to pay a fine consistent with that paid by the women.[63]

The system that found it so easy to focus its attention on Native Americans who had too freely imbibed routinely turned a blind or even a sympathetic eye to Anglo men similarly accused. An illustrative instance occurred in 1871 when an American named John Wolf came to San Bernardino with friends to purchase horses. While in the city, Wolf "indulged freely in drinking." After sleeping briefly in the stable, Wolf wandered into the street to "obtain something to drink." Fearing he may have been suffering from delirium tremens, his friends initiated a search. Two days later, Wolf's body was found with his head smashed in. The same night that John Wolf staggered through the streets of San Bernardino, three Indian women were arrested for being drunk in public.[64] Had the authorities in San Bernardino applied the law against public drunkenness to all ethnic groups instead of focusing their attention on native people, John Wolf could have spent the night in the local jail sleeping off his liquor. Instead, Wolf fell victim to a murderer's rage.

The reason for the dominance of Indians in the justice courts of San Bernardino lay in the collective needs of the Anglo community. By mid-1870, San Bernardino had weathered two decades in which it had tried to establish an identity apart from Los Angeles or San Diego.[65] However, since the county's economy was agriculturally based, this would prove impossible so long as the local cities remained the primary outlet for their produce. Boosterism and land speculation started an early tradition in the area during the 1870s, when San Bernardino began advertising in out-of-state newspapers for settlers who were "intelligent, industrious and enterprising." To increase the county's image as an agricultural haven, residents of the new city of Riverside began clearing a canal in 1870 in order to ensure a year round water supply, and in 1872 county residents began damming the Santa Ana River to irrigate anticipated croplands. The effect of these activities would prove to be disastrous to local native communities. The land being sold off to the newly arriving farmers had once been used to sustain native people. On the remaining lands, Indians tried desperately to eke out a living by planting subsistence crops. However, the diversion of water to the new farms prevented the Indians from being able to grow their own food.

These issues had been circumvented from the 1850s to the 1870s because the county lacked adequate transportation to ship San Bernardino's produce to markets outside the region. As a result, extensive use of the land by Anglos did not occur, and Indians in many areas were still able to subsist on their own crops or by gathering their traditional foods. However, Americans were not content with this arrangement and constantly sought a product that would allow them to increase production while avoiding spoilage. To accomplish this, increasing areas were irrigated and crops planted. Attempts to grow citrus, grapes, and wheat had been made, but spoilage continued to be a persistent problem. In 1873 the United States Department of Agriculture shipped two navel-orange saplings to Mrs. Eliza Tibbets in San Bernardino County to determine their likelihood of survival in the arid region. From this limited inception, the navel orange soon came to dominate the agricultural industry of the county.[67] Picked green, this nearly seedless orange could be transported by wagon to Los

Angeles, and thanks to the developing rail system could then be shipped to northern markets in time for the fruit to ripen.[68]

The only thing lacking in San Bernardino's grand scheme was the development of the irrigation, warehousing, and transportation corridors to grow, house, and ship the oranges. To achieve this, extensive amounts of labor would be needed. In the depressed economy of the 1870s, it would have been next to impossible for farmers to pay a large labor force to achieve these goals. The community needed a collective labor pool that would cost little to nothing and be available when needed. The solution to this dilemma lay in the judicial system.

In a system not unlike the "slave market" that existed in Los Angeles in the 1850s, Indians who were unable to pay their fines were held in the county jail. During this time, prisoners would labor for the city, or be hired out to farmers if no city work was available. In contrast to the system developed in Los Angeles in which prospective employers literally bid on the prisoners, those incarcerated in San Bernardino exchanged their labor at the rate of one dollar per day. There is no evidence to suggest that any other race except the Indian was used extensively in this manner.[69] Several news accounts from San Bernardino discuss the progress of the "Indians [who] have been put to work on the Cajon Pass," or who have been "shoveling dirt."[70]

Most of the Indians who found themselves laboring unwillingly for the Anglo communities had been charged with nonviolent nuisance offenses. These offenses resulted only in small fines or a few days in jail. Despite the prevalence of these cases, their impact on the functioning of native society would have been minimal. Individuals who had been incarcerated would have returned to their homes in a few days. It is perhaps because of this reason that no protests were recorded from the Indian tribes over the treatment that they received. In a tenuous economy, it is possible local Indians felt the "free" labor they provided was one way of getting along in the Anglo communities, and that protesting their treatment would have resulted in reprisals that could have been more devastating to the tribes. In many cases, local tribes in the southern California region actively participated in the legal system that had been established by the Americans by bringing in tribe members who had been accused of crimes, or in actively assisting Anglo-American authorities in meting out punishments. This makes it also possible that many Indians in southern California had assimilated to the dominant Anglo-American culture and had also adopted its norms as their own. Regardless of the reasoning employed by Indians at the time to accept the punishment and treatment of the American authorities, this did not always occur in cases that had a more lasting impact on native communities, such as when an Indian stood accused of a violent crime.

Of the cases charging Indians with the commission of a violent crime, a significant proportion involved other native people. The propensity for Indians to be both the perpetrators and the victims of violent offenses, especially in light of the fact that southern California Indians came from cultures that by most accounts were not violent, indicates that the stresses endured by Indians over the loss of lands, lack of food, and the loss of cultural autonomy had a profound effect on native peoples. The presence of Indians in the court system is even more galling since many of the cases involved the use of alcohol. Because Anglos were the almost exclusive distributors of alcohol, Anglo men provided the means through which native societies were being destroyed from within, and then provided the jails to exploit the havoc they had wrought.[71] According to Horace Bell in his recollections about the development of the region, "The cultivators of vineyards commenced paying their Indian peons with *aguardiente*, a veritable firewater. . . . The consequence was that on being paid off on Saturday evening, they would meet in great gatherings called peons, and pass the night in gambling, drunkenness and debauchery. . . . About sundown the pompous marshal, with his Indian special deputies who had been kept in jail all day to keep them sober, would drive and drag the herd to a big corral in the rear of Downey Block . . . and in the morning they would be exposed for sale."[72] While Bell's tale recounts the image of Indians being coerced into drinking alcohol in a humorous light, the results were far from funny. According to the *Act for the Government and Protection of Indians*, anyone caught furnishing an Indian with liquor would be subject to a fine of not less than twenty dollars for each offense, or would be imprisoned for not less than five days.[73] Clearly, the local judiciary made a conscious decision not to enforce certain provisions of the act in favor of the local community's needs. For the Indians, the justice's decision to ignore provisions of the legal code to suit the needs of the community resulted in disaster. With their inhibitions lowered by the alcohol and faced with being perpetual slaves, or at best second-class citizens in the Anglo-American communities, many Indians resorted to violence to express their frustration. It is not surprising that a significant number of the violent assault cases wherein Indians were the perpetrators involved Anglo men as victims.

In the eighteen assault cases that were heard in the San Diego justice courts from 1851 to 1880, seven involved Indians who assaulted Anglos, while seven more involved Indian-on-Indian attacks. In the four remaining cases, Anglos assaulted Indians. Of those four cases, the rate of conviction was fifty percent.[74] Of the seven cases in which an Anglo man was the victim of an Indian assault, at least three of the cases involved the use of alcohol; four convictions were sustained in the justice courts, and their cases were referred to the county courts. In each case, the guilt of the Indian was sustained in the higher court. In the case of Indians who were involved in assaulting Anglos, the conviction rate was 57 percent versus 50 percent for Anglos who assaulted Indians.[75] Of the seven remaining cases involving Indian-on-Indian crime, five involved the use of alcohol. Four of those five cases listed Indian women as victims of the assault.[76] In the cases in which violence occurred against tribal members, the effect of the assault would have torn the fabric of tribal life. Forced to endure the loss of their lands and a restructuring of their society, the one haven most Indians had was their tribal affiliation. When violence erupted between two tribal members, this impacted the group as a whole. The fact that Indian men were almost as likely to attack an Indian woman as an Indian man would also indicate further stressors on the tribal society.

A review of the surviving cases for violent offenses that involved Indians in Los Angeles confirms the same trend toward alcohol-induced violent offenses and the propensity for the victims to be other Indians. From 1861 to 1889, eleven cases of assault and assault with a deadly weapon were heard in the lower courts. Only two of these cases involved an Anglo assaulting an Indian. Eight of the victims in these cases were other Indians. Sentences for those convicted of assaulting another Indian ranged from five dollars to one year in prison.[77] Of the sole case involving an Indian who assaulted an Anglo man, the punishment was four hundred dollars or six months in the county jail.[78] Of the two Anglo defendants in these assault cases, one pled guilty and received seventy-five hours in the county jail, while the other case was referred to the upper courts.[79] Despite the referral, the case was never heard.[80] Of the eight cases in which Indians were the victims and the perpetrators of the assault, five involved the use of alcohol. The significance of the above cases lies not only in charting the increasing incidence of violence among a previously peaceful people; the incidence of violent crime also serves as a manifestation of the stressors that confronted native people. For many natives, alcohol provided a brief escape from the confusing and rapidly changing world around them. Unfortunately it also lowered inhibitions that eventually led several tribal members to attack their own people.

Despite their presence in the American courts, Indians were not always neophytes when they entered the courtroom. Many lived and worked with the Anglo men who would also serve as their judges and juries. As such, they would have been aware of that individual's prejudices toward them. In facing the courts, the Indian needed to consider whether he would be better off pleading his case before a lone justice or to a jury of Anglo men. Given the prejudices Anglo-Americans harbored against Indians, it is not surprising that the majority of them pleaded not guilty when brought before the justice courts. By doing so, they had a chance of convincing at least one man in the jury of their innocence.[81] In San Bernardino County, the percentage of Native Americans who pleaded guilty in non-nuisance cases, or those where the crimes would have netted the defendant either a significant fine or a prolonged incarceration, was only 25 percent.[82] For nuisance crimes such as being drunk in public, where small fines or minimal jail time was the norm, the number of guilty pleas jumped to 100 percent. In San Diego and Los Angeles counties, the percentage of Indians who pled guilty to non-nuisance charges dropped to 17 percent. As Indians so frequently found themselves before the courts for alcohol-related crimes, it is possible that since Indians knew ahead of time what the penalty for their behavior would be, they were not overly concerned with the punishment they would receive. In cases involving non-alcohol-related crimes, this same level of comfort could not be attained, as sentences and convictions now depended on a variety of factors, including the justice of the peace, the jury, and in many cases the competency of their lawyer.

The percentage of Native Americans who pleaded guilty in justice-court trials is indicative of a degree of savviness with the American judicial system that has not been acknowledged before. In most proceedings, the presence of a lawyer or interpreter to serve as a mediator between the two cultures is not mentioned. However, the willingness to use the system indicates a level of agency that previously has been ignored by many non-Indian historians. Intimately aware of the prejudices within the Anglo population, Indians also frequently waived a jury trial to limit their exposure to the vagaries of an all-Anglo jury made up of individuals whom the Indian likely knew, or at least had secondhand knowledge of. This data can be supported by the work of historians George Harwood Phillips and Richard Carrico, which reveals that Indians in California not only actively participated in the development of the region but also had a significant degree of understanding of the Anglo system. This has often been ignored in preference to the interpretation made popular during the nineteenth century that Indians had a limited capacity to understand or to function within the Anglo-American society. As we have seen with the land disputes in previous chapters, Native Americans in southern California were well aware of the conditions they faced, and attempted to use whatever tactics needed to ensure their survival within the white courts.

Overall, in cases in which an Indian victimized another Indian, or where theft involved something that could be converted to food, Indians fared better in court than Anglos did. The regularity with which Indians found themselves before the justice courts on nuisance charges indicates a desire by the local communities to exploit the labor of native people without properly compensating them for their labor. As the last decades of the nineteenth century wore on, the impact of the justice courts on the lives of native people became more punitive. The justice and municipal courts often held preliminary trials in cases where felony charges were being considered. In these instances, the justices could reduce the charges to a misdemeanor, immediately refer the case to a higher court, or refer the case to the grand jury. In this way, the justice courts were able to impact the dockets of the higher courts and further impact the effect of the judiciary on the aboriginal people of California. While most courts gave the option of bail to defendants in lieu of jail time, for an individual with limited resources, making bail often proved to be impossible. Men made up the vast majority of defendants appearing before all levels of the judiciary. In an economy in which the labor of the male was compensated at a higher rate than that of a female, the removal of a family breadwinner could prove to be damaging both to the accused and his family. In cases where an individual was accused of stealing food, the significance of this is even more compelling.

While removal may not have been a concerted and overt policy among the judiciary, the perpetuation of this idea appears to have guided judicial decisions in the justice courts. As prominent individuals within their communities, those who sat on the benches of the justice courts knew that the further development of the region could create great wealth and personal profits for the business and community leaders—wealth that they, as the founders or at least investors in their communities, could use to enrich themselves. Initially, the presence of Indians served as an obstacle to this development through their land claims. Once the land issue had been squelched, the presence of starving or drunken Indians living on the outskirts of a community that sought to represent itself as successful would have been a blow to the boosters who were trying to entice new settlers into the area. Historian John Stanley has maintained that the arrival of the railroad resulted in a rise in the number of cases before the justice courts. In this, his assessment appears correct, but while Stanley focused his attention on Anglo defendants, the impact on the Indian communities was also significant.[83] In part this was because of the now ready access to the community from the outside, but also because of the internal desire of the community to rid itself of its less desirable elements. In many instances, these undesirable elements were the aboriginal people.

Several news accounts following the arrival of the railroads support this position. In 1871, after successfully petitioning to have the executive-order reservations closed because Indians occupied lands that Anglos considered to be part of the public domain, the number of complaints about the conditions endured by the Indians increased in the press. However, Anglo complaints were not solely the result of altruism; for the most part, Anglos were concerned with property prices. Concerns over the "suffering condition" of the Indians mingled with concern over land prices and the potential for criminal activity among the tribes.[84] As seen in the previous chapter, attitudes of Anglos toward the Indian were based on expediency. When a labor source was needed, the Indian served as a ready source of strength. When land was needed, the traditional homelands of the natives served as a ready source of available land. In all of these scenarios, the Indian was never considered part of the community. Despite the treatment he received in the lower courts and the attitudes of the local communities, the treatment of the Indian in the district and county courts would not get any better.

County and District Courts

THE DISTRICT AND COUNTY COURTS MADE UP THE CENTER tiers of the state's judicial hierarchy. Instead of the nuisance cases that plagued the lower courts, the district and county courts focused primarily on felony and appeal cases. According to the California State Constitution, the "District Courts shall have original jurisdiction, in law and equity, in all civil cases where the amount in dispute exceeds two hundred dollars, exclusive of interest. In all criminal cases not otherwise provided for, and in all issues of fact joined in the probate courts, their jurisdiction shall be unlimited."[1] Initially, the county court was called the court of sessions and heard criminal cases that included assault and battery, breach of peace, riot, petty larceny, and other misdemeanors where the fines exceeded $500. In 1851 the jurisdiction of these courts was extended to address indictments provided by the grand jury, and to clarify that they had appellate jurisdiction over the inferior courts—the justice, mayor's, and police courts. In 1863 the court of sessions was abolished in favor of the county court.

The district court was also known as the superior court of the county and stood as the epitome of the local court system; in these courts, felony criminal cases such as murder and assault were heard. The courts as established by the initial constitution of the state created a blueprint from which all citizens of the state could seek redress for criminal and civil matters. However, their jurisdiction, while affording protection to the citizens of the state, would not extend equally to all residents of the state. Crimes that involved Indians would be dealt with primarily through the lowest courts: the justice, mayor's, and police courts.

This would pose some issues regarding Indians and the law. According to the *Act for the Government and Protection of Indians*, justices of the peace would "have jurisdiction in all cases of complaints by, for or against Indians, in their respective townships in this state."[2] It would appear that local law would trump the state's constitution. The *Act for the Government and Protection of Indians* did not make provisions wherein a justice would refer a case involving an Indian to a higher court; however, it is apparent from a review of the court records that this did occur. Nevertheless, Indians were often forced to appear before the justice of the peace before their case was referred to a higher court. The result was additional costs incurred by the defendant, and more money for the county treasury. The *Act for the Government and Protection of Indians* was amended in 1860 to increase the authority of the county and district courts over issues involving custody of Indian children, but not in criminal cases.[3]

To a defendant in a criminal proceeding, the district and county courts often seemed interchangeable: each court dealt with felony cases. However, only the district court held jurisdiction in cases where the penalty could result in death, while the county courts held jurisdiction in cases that began in the justice courts, and could sentence defendants to time in the state prison. In contrast to the informal proceedings that characterized the justice and municipal courts, business within the higher courts was conducted in a formal atmosphere. Professionally trained lawyers who understood the nuances of the law staffed the bench and bar. Additionally, the court officers in these higher courts, unlike the justice courts, were paid for their services, instead of collecting fees from defendants. District- and county-court judges were also prohibited from holding any other office, and could not "receive to his own use, any fees or perquisites of office, again in contrast to those individuals who served in the justice and municipal courts."[4] In keeping with the professional environment in which these individuals worked, cases were more judiciously recorded, and in some cases evidence was preserved.

Despite this formal atmosphere, the men who oversaw the district and county courts were also members of the communities in which they practiced, and were victims of all the same prejudices that were prevalent in Anglo-American society. However, these cultural traits were often, but not always, offset by their cognizance of the legal principles involved in the cases they oversaw, and of the rights of the accused. Even within the higher courts, a perverse logic prevailed when it came to Indians and the courts. Indians could expect to receive sentences that were less than those received by non-Indians, but could also expect to find themselves in the courts out of proportion to their numbers in society. In additional to this perversity, crimes against Indians—especially violent crimes—often went unreported and unpunished.

Historian Richard Maxwell Brown has written extensively on violence and American values. In his work *No Duty to Retreat*, he argued that a "reinterpretation" of English common law resulted in the acceptance of the legal concept whereby an individual had no duty to retreat from an adversary, even if that confrontation could result in death.[5] This interpretation of the law played out mainly in the frontier states and helped to shape a unique aspect of American culture, one that was almost exclusively male and embraced traits that more developed societies would have recoiled at. Violence, drinking, and whoring were aspects that came to exemplify "manly" behavior. Any man who could not stand toe-to-toe with another and defend his rights, whether presumed or codified, did not measure up to this new standard of behavior. In the early years of California, this pattern of behavior evolved largely because of the massive numbers of men, especially young men, who flooded into the state in search of their fortunes during the gold rush. In some areas, Anglo men outnumbered Anglo women nine to one. With this lopsided gender balance, a youthful population, and the desperate search for wealth, trouble was not long in following these argonauts to the state.

Most of the immigrants came in search of gold, which they felt rightly belonged to Americans by right of conquest following the Mexican-American War. Any attempt to preempt that perceived right was often met with violence. As many of the forty-niners who scoured the state in search of gold laid claim to the land, they saw Indians and Mexicans as interlopers instead of as legitimate residents who also had a right to the gold being extracted from the rivers and streams. Faced with a challenge to their hegemony over the gold fields, miners began to pass what would collectively be known as "miner's laws," essentially vigilante laws that were specific to the region and the individuals who passed them. Through the use of these laws, non-Anglo people, including Indians, were forcibly pushed from the land. Indeed, as historian William G. Robbins has observed, "genocide, intimidation and the removal of native people characterized the migration to

California in the 1850s and 1860s."[6] Aspects of these miner's laws were often reflected in the legal practices of established communities. While many Anglo men enforced their "rights" with a gun, others used the judiciary. However, to ensure that Anglos always had the advantage, the California legislature passed a law in 1854 that forbade the sale of guns or ammunition to Indians. This statute effectively left Indians unable to defend themselves in the face of well-armed Anglos.[7] As one traveler through the region noted in his diary in December 1860,

> This southern California is still unsettled. We all continually wear arms—each wears both bowie knife and pistol [navy revolver], while we have always for game or otherwise, a Sharp's rifle. . . . Fifty to sixty murders per year have been common here in Los Angeles and some think it odd that there has been no violent deaths during the two weeks that we have been here.[8]

The absurdly high murder rate in the first decade of the state's existence offers a practical application of the idea of vigilante justice, with Indians often suffering attacks that they could not defend themselves against. Much of the reason for the animosity that existed between Anglo-Americans and Native Americans was the pervasive belief among Anglos that Indians were little more than subhuman brutes, and therefore worthy of killing. In his diary, William H. Brewer, a professor of agriculture who had been sent to California in 1860 to survey the state, quickly picked up and adopted the prejudices that existed among Anglos in the region, calling the Indians he encountered "a miserable thieving set" and reserving any grudging praise for the aboriginal population to those who were "half-breeds."[9] With such virulent opinions displayed so casually within Anglo society, it is a wonder that any crimes against Indians were reported at all. It might have been more expedient for the local community to take matters into their own hands and avoid the cost of bringing an Indian to trial, costs which the Anglo community would have absorbed. This can only mean that the trials that involved Native Americans were often held, not just to mete out justice, but to also "send a message" to the Indian community at large. While justice was often absent on many of the occasions that Indians found themselves before the American courts, several cases were brought before the Anglo authorities. Of those cases that survive, those that involved murder most often reflected the core values held by the local communities with respect to issues between racial groups. In addition, both then and now, murder often has a salacious tendency to draw our attention to events, from a safe distance, that expose the most barbaric aspects of our natures. Therefore, these cases will be examined in some detail.

Of the 171 murder cases from 1850 to 1890 that survive in the records of the district court of Los Angeles, seventeen involved Native Americans.[10] However, it must be noted that these relatively few cases are not reflective of the conditions that existed at the time. Most murder cases that involved Indians went unsolved, or were never investigated to begin with. According to historian John Boessenecker, from September 1850 to September 1851, thirty-one homicides occurred in Los Angeles County alone. While this number is not further defined as to the particular ethnic groups impacted by murder, it does bring attention to the unparalleled violence that characterized southern California during the early years of statehood. With a population of only 2,500, this meant that an individual in Los Angeles County during this time had a one-in-eighty chance of dying violently.[11] However bad things were for the general population of Los Angeles, things were worse for the Indians of southern California. The following year, 1852, five Indians were reported dead in the streets of Los Angeles.[12] No investigations into their deaths were ever made. The apathy that seemed to pervade the investigation and punishment of individuals for murder is exemplified in the number of criminal defendants sent to San Quentin. From 1851 to 1854, according to the inmate registers for San Quentin, Los Angeles County only sent one man to prison for manslaughter; he was not charged with killing an Indian.[13]

While Anglo-Americans in Los Angeles County were clearly upset with the lawlessness that characterized the early 1850s and 1860s, their focus was not on the Indians in their midst. Indians were clearly not intended to be included in the Anglo community as a whole, and as such they were not entitled to any of the benefits a citizen of the county could expect. This appeared to include the services of the police to protect and avenge them, as well as the services the county could provide upon their deaths. In 1861, the citizens of the city complained about the request from the coroner to spend $25 to bury an Indian. The city council declined to approve such an extravagant cost and referred the burial of the body to the "Indian Alcalde," who would "discharge such duty free, gratis, for nothing."[14] Even when Indians were buried within the city limits by the American authorities, their bodies, like those of other non-Anglos, were buried in a separate, more remote area of the cemetery.

As the years progressed, neither time nor distance improved conditions for the Native American population in southern California. In 1873 the San Bernardino daily newspaper, the *Guardian*, published a "mortuary report" to extol the beneficial effects of the weather in the county. This report maintained that in San Bernardino County, only thirty people had died from 1 January to 6 December. Out of a county population of 9,000, this meant that the chance of dying in the county stood at one in 300. However, it seemed to be a climate that favored Anglos over Indians. Of those who died, three committed suicide, seven died from old age or infirmity, and another seven were under a year old. That left thirteen remaining deaths that are presumed to have been either violent or accidental. Only two of the remaining deaths were reported to have been the result of a pistol shot, and seven of the bodies were of strangers. So accordingly, the chance of a violent or accidental death for a county resident was reduced to one in 1,500.[15] What the report does not mention is that at least two murders involving Indians occurred in the county that same year. Additionally, the same year saw three Indians murdered in Los Angeles County and another killed in San Diego County. This made San Bernardino's boast, "What sanitarium in California can make a better showing than this?" a somewhat hollow endorsement for the region.[16]

The gross underreporting of the number of Indians who had been killed, and whose murders had not been investigated, is exemplified in newspaper reports: from 1850 to 1860, at least twenty-five cases involving Indians were reported in the press. The vast majority, twenty-three, reported Indians as the murder victims, but in only one case was an individual charged with murder. In that case, Heath, an "angelic" looking American, "with no other motive, apparently, than an antipathy to Indian proximity, violently drove from his august presence two unoffending Indian women;" having achieved this goal, Health then ordered an Indian man from his presence. The man refused to leave and the two fought on the public street, with the Indian gaining the upper hand. Not wanting to push his advantage, the Indian left the street and the fight. Heath reportedly returned to his home, borrowed gunpowder from a friend, and then spent the next several hours molding bullets for his gun. Later that night, when the unnamed Indian man lay down to sleep with his wife, Health stole in upon the man, leveled his gun at the man's chest, and fired.[17] Health was arrested and held in the San Bernardino city jail while his trial for murder commenced. However, despite widespread coverage and condemnation of the crime in the newspaper, he was acquitted of the murder and released.[18]

Despite the number of incidents that appear in the local papers that mention the murder of an Indian, even these reports must be assumed to be relatively low. Personal accounts from earlier settlers would indicate that the frequency of Indians being murdered was considerably higher. In his reminiscences of life in early southern California, pioneer Horace Bell reported on the 1853 hanging of an Indian near the San Gabriel Mission, which was nine miles from the city of Los Angeles, by a mixed group of Mexicans and Indians. No reason for the Indian's murder or record of his crime can be found in any newspaper, judicial, or personal account.[19] Historian Sherburne Cook estimated that as many as half of the Indians in California died at the hands of Anglo-Americans in the first years of American occupation. His estimates, while boggling to the mind, may not have been that far off, as many Americans considered the Indian to be inferior, racially and culturally. In 1859 one news account in the *Los Angeles Star* reported on a fictional story that had appeared in the *San Fernando National*: "The settlers in that region of the country seem to think little of knocking down an Indian, and it is said, that a party of three sportsmen, who went out shooting for a week, returned the other day after bagging no less than thirty Indians. For three men that is considered a pretty fair result for one hunting excursion." While the *Star* scolded the *National* for its flippancy, the complaint was less about the racist inclinations of the *National* and more that this type of "criminal conduct . . . has precipitated most of our Indian wars."[20] For the Americans in southern California, the life of an Indian had little value. The prevalence of this attitude can be seen in the few murder cases involving an Indian that did make it to the courts.

Over a forty-year period, from 1850 to 1890, Indians appeared in the courts in Los Angeles County seventeen times in cases that involved murder. In thirteen of those seventeen cases, Indians were the victims. Four of the cases list an Anglo man as the perpetrator of the crime. Of those four Anglo men accused of murdering Indians, Anglo juries convicted only one man.[21] The poor conviction rate of the courts of Los Angeles, however, are not the issue in this instance. Overall, the courts only had a conviction rate of 31 percent for all murder cases, only slightly higher than the 25 percent conviction rate that for cases where an Anglo had killed an Indian. The underlying issue for the Indians of southern California was that the courts did not pursue cases against individuals who did violence against them as they would have for an Anglo. In cases where an Anglo was the murder victim, 59 percent of the cases were pursued by the authorities through the courts. Reasons for the limited prosecution of Indian murder cases in the county included not only the racist beliefs of the local communities, many of whom saw the Indian as a hindrance to civilization and therefore disposable, but also a provision in the *Act for the Government and Protection of Indians* that declared, "In no case shall a white man be charged on any offence upon the testimony of an Indian."[22]

Many Indians undoubtedly felt it was not worth their time to protest the treatment they or other tribe members had received. Had they chosen to pursue charges against a white man for the murder of an Indian, they may have been forced to suffer through a preliminary trial to determine whether an Anglo witness could be secured, and if not, they would have been forced to leave the courthouse without the justice they deserved. Several newspaper reports in the early 1850s relate stories of Indians who approached Anglo-American authorities to complain that Anglos had either squatted on their land, stolen their children, or abused their women. Nothing ever appears to have been done to curb the antisocial behavior of the Anglo community. As such, it is remarkable that any cases involving the murder of an Indian ever went to trial.

In the one instance where an Anglo was convicted of murder, the murderer, Michael G. Lachenias, almost got away without penalty. The events that brought him to trial took place in 1866 in Los Angeles County. Lachenias's victim was Pablo Moreno, one of his employees. According to the testimony given by Lachenias during his trial, on 22 October he returned to his rancho and ordered Moreno to unsaddle his horse. However, Moreno was too drunk to complete the task, and Lachenias surmised that the Indian had stolen wine from him. Lachenias reported that Moreno fell twice in the attempt to tend to the horse, but wound up face down in the dirt instead. In disgust, Lachenias left the Indian where he lay and retired to his house. During Lachenias's absence Moreno expired, still face down in the dirt. Lachenias reported that he was not aware until the next day that the Indian was dead. Had Lachenias's testimony been the only evidence that was heard in his trial, it is likely that Moreno's murder would have gone unnoticed. Instances of Indians being drunk were commonly reported in the press, and the prejudices of the day would have supported the contention that Moreno had been drunk.

Other Indians buried Moreno, and the matter would have been forgotten had a priest not been summoned to bless Moreno's grave. The priest questioned why he had not been called to confess Moreno before he died, and the other Indians reported that they did not think Moreno would die so soon. The priest who oversaw Moreno's funeral testified he thought the Indian had died of natural causes. However, if he had been told Moreno had died as a result of being beaten, he "might not have recollected it."[23] From the remaining court records, it is difficult to determine why Moreno's death then attracted the attention of the Anglo authorities, as it does not appear that the priest or the Indians reported his death. However, when news of Pablo's death reached the authorities, the sheriff called a coroner's inquest and Pablo's body was exhumed.

A physician called to the gravesite to examine Moreno's body testified that the Indian had been beaten so severely on the head with an iron bar or pistol that his head had three permanent indentations where the blows were sustained. One of the blows he received fractured his skull so severely that brain matter oozed from his head. Moreno sustained a wound above his left eye, a second on top of his head which was three inches deep, and a third on the back of his head—hardly the injuries expected to be incurred in a fall.

During the trial, several prosecution witnesses called Lachenias's testimony into question. Witnesses reported that Lachenias had told them he had come home at nine in the morning and instructed Pablo to unsaddle his horse. However, "it seemed the Indian was heavily drunk and was unable to do it."[24] Pablo subsequently fell several times, thus injuring his head. By the next day, Lachenias reported to them that he woke to find Moreno dead in the courtyard. Why Lachenias remained isolated in his home through the entire day, and how all residents of the rancho had missed the presence of a man lying in the courtyard were not discussed in the court records. However, Lachenias must have considered the implausibility of his story, and when it came his turn to testify, he insisted instead that Moreno had died of venereal disease and alcohol abuse, just as Moreno's wife had. To complicate the story further, Lachenias's wife testified that she had been caring for Moreno for several days prior to his death, and that he had told her other Indians had beaten him. The couple later insisted that Moreno had regularly been stealing wine from a cask they conveniently kept in the courtyard, and that they had taken him into the house to care for him after his beating because he lived in a shelter made of branches. No reason why other Indians would want to beat Moreno was given. In light of Moreno's wounds, it is unlikely that he would have been able to provide anyone with many (if any) details of his assault. However, had the testimony of either of the Lacheniases been accurate, the Christian charity they reported having shown the wounded Indian left much to be desired.[25]

A medical examination indicated that Moreno had received no such care, and that he had no venereal disease. This contradictory evidence ensured Michael Lachenias's conviction on manslaughter charges. The death of Pablo Moreno highlights several of the issues prevalent between Anglos and Indians. The first was the tendency of Anglos to look upon the Indian as being inferior. Throughout the examination of witnesses, Moreno is referred to primarily as "the Indian," thus denying Moreno both his identity and humanity at the same time. This tendency to dehumanize Indians is also present in state laws, which occasionally refer to an Indian as "it."[26] While it is obvious that much of the testimony in this case was fabricated, the statements made by the defense played on the preconceptions Anglos had of Native Americans. The defense attorney portrayed Moreno, and by extension all Indians, as a drunken, sexually promiscuous, violent man who lived in a hovel—hardly the image of a civilized person.[27] The image of Moreno as a lascivious, subhuman creature was clearly an attempt to dehumanize him, and thereby minimize the crime that had been perpetrated against him. This tactic was not unusual in southern California trials involving Anglos accused of some violent action against an Indian. The tactic had some effectiveness with juries as well. Lachenias was eventually convicted of manslaughter instead of first-degree murder. He later appealed his conviction to the state supreme court, but his appeal was denied.

The lenient treatment Lachenias and other Anglos received in court when accused of murdering an Indian no doubt confirmed that the life of an Indian held little value in American society, and in many cases Anglos could get away with murder. The ability to dehumanize Indians in court trials and play to the prejudices of the juries also accounts for the rise in the number of Indian murders as the nineteenth century progressed. In the 1860s, the frequency with which an Indian was the victim of murder in

Los Angeles County occurred at a rate of one in every 251 Indian people. By the 1870s, the chance of becoming a victim had risen to one in every 73 for Indian people.

The Lachenias case highlights another glaring problem with the judiciary in southern California during the last half of the nineteenth century—namely, the weight (or lack of it) given to Indian testimony. State law prohibited the conviction of "a white man" based on the testimony of an Indian. This law presumed either the inability of the Indians to understand the significance of the issues they were brought to testify about, or presumed that all Indians would lie and therefore corroboration was always needed. It was only because other Anglo men stepped forward to testify that the Lachenias case was ever brought to trial. In the Lachenias case, even when Indian witnesses confirmed testimony that had been provided by an Anglo, little cross-examination ensued, and in many cases the courts only requested brief written statements about what the Indians knew.

In the few cases in which Indians were listed as witnesses in murder cases that involved Anglos in Los Angeles County from 1850 to 1890, their testimony in court was clearly discounted unless it served the purpose of the court. An example is the case against a Hispanic man named Jose Domingo for the murder of Robert Parker in 1865. During the trial, the testimony of Massalina, Parker's Indian widow, helped to convict the man who had killed her husband. Domingo was found guilty in the case, but the court neglected to record his sentence.[28] In the Domingo case, the Anglo jurors willingly considered the testimony of an Indian in order to avenge the murder of a white man.

In all of the remaining murder cases that came before the district courts in Los Angeles during the last half of the nineteenth century, both the victim and the murderer were Indians. Two of the Indians accused of murder were women, and as such will be discussed in more detail in the final chapter. Of the seven final cases in Los Angeles County from 1850 to 1890, all but one of the male Indian defendants was found guilty. In cases where the victim was another Indian, those convicted received sentences ranging from three to thirteen years in state prison, for an average sentence of nine years.[29] In one case the jury determined the defendant, who had been charged with the death of an Indian women, to be "guilty of manslaughter in the mildest form."[30] In the two cases in which an Indian man stood accused of murdering an Anglo man in Los Angeles County, both sustained convictions. When Anglos fell victim to Indian violence, it appeared that a conviction could be almost guaranteed. A few cases will highlight the prejudices Indian men endured in the courts of southern California.

In 1871, Jesus Venegas, an Indian, stood accused of the murder of Frederick Rupp. Information in the trial case is limited, and no motivation for the crime is preserved in the surviving documents. Most of the witnesses who protested Jesus's innocence were Indians. This fact alone may have condemned him. Two weeks after he had been arraigned on the murder charges, a jury found Jesus guilty. However, five days after Jesus's conviction, an Anglo named Daniel Saptano came into court and stated he had heard from his brother that Rupp had been killed by a Sonoran Indian, not Jesus. Despite the new evidence being hearsay, and the individual presenting it being thrice removed from the actual events, because an Anglo had presented it, Jesus was granted a new trial.[31]

The findings regarding murder cases in the district courts were consistent with the conclusions drawn from the justice courts. Indians during the 1870s increasingly found themselves as the victims of crime, in numbers out of proportion to their numbers in the population. What is not recorded in these statistics are the numbers of Indians who were murdered, but whose murders resulted in no investigation from authorities. Despite the despicable treatment received by Indians in the Los Angeles County courts, other southland courts were worse.

Indians who were accused of murder in San Bernardino County from the 1860s to the 1890s stood a greater chance of being found guilty and sustaining a longer sentence than in any other county in southern California. Of the two cases in which Indians were convicted of murder, juries determined that one would receive a twenty-year sentence and the other would be condemned to die.[32] A third case involved an Indian man who had been brought before the court for trial, but had the charges dismissed when the district attorney admitted he was unable to determine if a murder had even taken place.[33] In San Bernardino County, the lone Anglo-American accused of murdering an Indian was found guilty and sentenced to seven years.[34] This sentence was significantly less than those received by the Indians who had been similarly convicted, and also considerably less than the average sentence meted out in Los Angeles County. In that county, the average sentence for all whites convicted of murder (excluding life terms and death sentences) was 8.7 years. For Indians convicted of murder, the average sentence was 9 years.

Of the two Indians accused of murder in San Bernardino, one had reportedly killed an Anglo man. As in Los Angeles, his conviction seemed predetermined despite some extenuating circumstances. In the trial against Prospero, witness testimony indicated that he was likely insane at the time of the crime. According to trial testimony, Prospero wandered onto the Watkins Ranch in June 1872. During his stay, which seemed to be several hours in length, Prospero babbled incoherently, lit "matches on his leg," and pulled the blankets off a sleeping Indian worker. Despite Prospero's intrusion onto the ranch, little was done to move him along or determine what he needed or wanted. In spite of his bizarre behavior, a ranch hand only sought assistance in dealing with Prospero after he took a potshot at the Watkins family dog. In the interlude between the time assistance was called for and when it arrived at the ranch, Prospero entered the ranch house and shot Watkins, the ranch owner, in the chest. It would take Watkins three weeks to die. Prospero's behavior clearly indicated he did not have all his faculties. Despite this, he received a twenty-year sentence in San Quentin.[35]

It should also be noted that in southern California, facilities existed for the treatment of mentally ill individuals, and on several occasions Indians were committed to these facilities. However, in the records surveyed, no cases survive in which a white man who displayed some level of diminished capacity was charged with murder. During this era, judges frequently held hearings on whether to commit individuals (both Indian and Anglo) who were considered insane. Unfortunately, the case against Prospero is not unique from the perspective of an Indian with mental-health issues being shown no sympathy in the American courts. In 1859, during the waning years of the Tejon Reservation, an Indian named Tomas stood accused of stabbing his wife and child to death. Tomas's case went to trial in September of 1860, when a jury found him guilty and sentenced him to death. Prior to his hanging, a number of prominent citizens—including the presiding judge in the case, Benjamin Hayes—considered sending a petition to the governor requesting that Tomas's death sentence be commuted to life in prison. However, despite his moral revulsion at sending an insane man to the gallows, Hayes neglected to act. Most likely his personal feelings conflicted with the norms that had been established within the Anglo community about the treatment of Indians.

In deference to these community standards, Hayes did not pursue his petition idea. However, Hayes did empanel a second jury to confirm whether Tomas was insane. After a brief deliberation, another jury concluded that Tomas had been sane at the time of the murders, and his execution date was scheduled. Hayes's distaste at having participated in the conviction and execution of Tomas is almost palpable in his diary: in the record of his thoughts on the day of Tomas's hanging, he pens, "A feeling of *awe* appeared to rest upon society—of doubt and fear—lest this poor man after all should have been found guilty originally when insane, or executed in that state, even if his conviction was right." A newspaper account Judge Hayes preserved in his diary indicates his moral revulsion at executing an insane man. However, Hayes's moral quandary appeared to be a minority position.[36] As the previous two cases indicate, when an Indian man was involved, Anglo juries would give no quarter in regard to their treatment in the court.

The idea of using insanity as a defense in criminal trials received considerable attention during the nineteenth century. Trials in which the sanity of the defendant played a role were frequently judged by juries, and in these cases "the jury was free to apply its 'unwritten laws' to which justice was, in theory tailored to the individual case."[37] In other words, the sanity of the defendant was taken into account, and the accused could be acquitted of the crime because of insanity. However, in the cases involving Indians, the "unwritten law" appears to have been to ignore the affliction. For Indian men entering an American court accused of murder, conviction seemed a foregone conclusion. An Anglo pleading diminished capacity in the murders of Indians appeared to have received more sympathy from Anglo juries.

In contrast to the previous cases, the lone Anglo man convicted of murdering an Indian in San Bernardino between 1850 and 1890 was Charles Shettler. During his trial, Shettler claimed he had been asleep in his hotel room when he had awoke to find Maria, a local native washerwoman, standing near his bed with a knife. In an acrobatic maneuver, Shettler reportedly lurched out of bed, grabbed a pistol, and shot Maria dead. The deed done, Shettler found himself still wishing to return to his bed, so he dragged Maria's body to the top of the stairs, cleaned up the blood in his room, and returned to his dreams. In the morning, the grizzly discovery caused a panic in the hotel. At first Shettler denied any knowledge of the murder, but as evidence continued to implicate him in the crime, he relented and confessed to the killing. With his confession in hand, Charles Shettler was sentenced to seven years in state prison, far less than what would have been handed down had the roles of the victim and murderer been reversed, and less than the sentence he might have received had his case been heard in Los Angeles County.

Despite the sentence received by Charles Shettler, his conviction may have had more to do with the fact that he was a stranger in town than the color of his skin. In the 1870s, the worsening economic picture in the state, and nation, had resulted in large numbers of men tramping around the countryside in search of work. In many communities, all strangers were viewed with suspicion. Many transient Anglos in southern California were arrested on vagrancy charges and forced from the city's limits to avoid the local community being forced to pay for services that might need to be rendered. Shettler, despite having enough resources to afford a hotel room, was potentially among these vagrants. Additionally, Shettler had taken something from the community. Maria had been a fixture in the community; most likely she served the Anglo population by taking on small jobs, which would have included cleaning or possibly prostitution, as this would have been the most likely reason why she was in Shettler's room during the middle of the night. In several news accounts in which Indians are featured, many are referred to in a possessory sense, such as "our Indians." Shettler, as an outsider, had taken not only the life of Maria, but also a "possession" of the community.

Of the twelve murder cases that involved Indians who went to trial in San Diego, six involved Anglo men who killed Indians, two involved Indians accused of killing Anglos, and five involved Indian-on-Indian assaults. In the remaining case, an Anglo man was successfully convicted of killing another Anglo man based on the testimony of a ten-year-old Indian boy named Juan Pino.[38] Pino's testimony was accepted by the court only because in 1875, state law had been amended to allow non-whites to testify against Anglos. This simple change in the law allowed justice to prevail. Sadly, it did not result in an increase in the number of cases brought before the court by Indians. Years of mistrust and cultural differences continued to convince many Indians that the Anglo courts were reserved for Anglos. The result of this was that of the six cases involving Anglo defendants, only one ended in conviction.

In this case, the authorities accused Antonio Bertrand of beating two Indians to death, including Maria, a local tribal chief.[39] While the murders occurred near the Mexican/American border, in Mexican territory, the state tried the case in the United States. During the trial, Bertrand admitted finding the bodies, but did not confess to the murders. He suggested other Indians had committed the murders, because he had found barefoot tracks leading away from the bodies. Bertrand's attempt to deflect the blame away from himself and onto an unnamed Indian is reminiscent of the same tactics used by Lachenias in his defense. By playing to the prejudices of the jury, the defendant hoped to escape penalty for his crimes. For Bertrand, the ruse failed to work. A jury convicted him of second-degree murder and sentenced him to ten years in state prison.[40] Bertrand's punishment hardly seems appropriate to the crime. Ten years for beating two people to death represents a light sentence. It is likely Bertrand's ruse would have worked had Maria not been a tribal leader. His loss from the tribe would be an acute loss in leadership. Bertrand's conviction and sentence may have been an attempt to pacify Indian hostility over the loss of their chief. The fact that Bertrand was listed as being Hispanic made the decision to convict him much easier than if he had been an Anglo-American man. At the time of the trial in 1888, a growing movement was taking place in the United States that began to look at the Indian as less of a threat and more of an icon of the west. Concerns abounded that the Indian population as a whole might one day become extinct and, as the Indians posed a limited threat to the Anglo residents, several attempts to preserve them as a distinct group had begun to take shape. Bertrand's trial and conviction may have been an offshoot of this change in Anglo feeling. However, Bertrand's case did not herald in a universal change in the Anglo courts. In other cases involving Anglos who murdered Indians, there was a studied lack of concern on the part of the authorities about the killing of Indians, the message ultimately relayed by the courts to both the Anglo and the Indian communities was that the Anglo judicial system served the needs of the Anglo community, not necessarily the needs of justice.

A case in point occurred in 1857 during the preliminary examination of Maria Antonio Ortega for murder. During the examination, Ortega testified that he shot two Indians he thought had been stealing his livestock. While Ortega did not present any proof that his stock had been stolen, he also did not confirm that the Indians he shot were dead, as he had not bothered to check. It appears Ortega reported the incident more as a warning to other ranchers that potential stock thieves were about, not that he had done something wrong in taking a human life. In his mind, it is possible that Ortega had convinced himself that he had not taken a human life, as he never confirmed the deaths of the Indians. However, his lack of concern speaks volumes about the prejudices that pervaded the Anglo community. The court dismissed Ortega following the preliminary examination, and no further action was taken.

Surprisingly, in the two cases involving Indians who were accused of murdering an Anglo-American in San Diego County, the prosecutors obtained no convictions. In the 1853 case against Manteca, William Williams, an Anglo-American man, accused Manteca of killing "an American." Williams produced no body or other evidence aside from his testimony to back his accusation. Williams likely had assumed that Anglo prejudice against Indians, combined with his testimony, would be sufficient to convict Manteca. Based on this assumption, Williams pursued the charge in court; despite his efforts, authorities were unable to prove a murder had taken place and eventually ordered Manteca released. Instead, the court fined Williams twenty-five dollars in court costs.[41]

The differences between the charging, sentencing, and conviction ratios by each of the three counties indicates overwhelmingly that the Anglo community placed little value on the life of an Indian during the latter half of the nineteenth century. An Indian could be brought into jail and tried for murder, despite the lack of a body or corroborating evidence, based on the testimony of a white man. In contrast, an Anglo who acknowledged his crime would most likely be let go, or would receive a sentence that paled in comparison to those received by Indians. There are no cases in which an Anglo endured incarceration and trial when no body or proof of a murder had taken place. In cases where Anglo men admitted to killing Indians, a preliminary hearing was held, but few indictments based on these hearings were pursued.[42] The number of Indian murder victims in the counties of southern California stands as sad testimony to the violence that characterized the region during the early years of statehood, but it alone does not accurately reflect the degree of violence that permeated the communities. Coupled with the incidence of assault, a more dire picture emerges, especially when it comes to Native Americans.

Within the district and county courts, Indians most often stood before the bench accused of violent crimes against another person. In the majority of these cases, the victims were other Indians. The incidence of these cases in light of the unpopular status of the Indian in Anglo society raises questions about why these cases attracted the attention of the judiciary—especially when considered against the incidence of newspaper reports in the first twenty years of American control of the state that discuss Indian-on-Indian assaults as a common occurrence, and one that the Anglo authorities preferred to not become involved in. As members of a disenfranchised group with waning economic importance, Indians, as we have seen, frequently suffered the brunt of American racism. Their dead bodies were collected at the start of the day and disposed of as quickly and cheaply as possible. Efforts to find their killers were haphazard at best, if not nonexistent. Because of this, it would seem the incidence of Indian-on-Indian assault cases would also be nonexistent in the courts. For the most part, this conclusion would be correct. Several newspaper accounts recount assaults committed by one Indian on another, and in the majority of these cases, no charges were filed. Only when assault charges were brought by an Anglo, or in cases where the assault disturbed the peace of the larger community did these cases make their way into American courts.

In San Diego County, five cases of assault or assault with a deadly weapon involving Indians went to trial in the county and district courts from 1881 to 1886.[43] In three of the five cases, the victims were Indian women, and in two of those instances the perpetrators had been Indian men. In both cases the Indian men were found guilty. One received a sentence of five years for his involvement in an assault with the intent to rape.[44] In the other case, an Indian named Salvador viciously assaulted an Indian woman named Lenore with a bridle and bit because she had refused his advances.[45] Testimony during the trial indicated Salvador had been known to have a pronounced violent streak, and court records indicate a previous arrest for wife beating. However, in the earlier case in which he reportedly had whipped his wife and dragged her around by her hair, the charges were dropped.[46] It is possible that the arrest of an individual like Salvador could have been an efficient way for the community to remove an undesirable element. Salvador obviously had a pronounced violent streak, one that could spill over into the white population, and as such he presented a threat to the Anglo community. The fact that his first arrest resulted in no action being brought against him, despite the severity of the attack, lends credence to the supposition that it was the repetition of the offense that raised the concerns of the Anglo community. In his study of American law, historian Lawrence Friedman discusses several instances in which an individual who raised the ire of a community was subsequently punished through the use of laws that were not commonly enforced.[47] In the case of the Indian man accused of assault with intent to rape, his conviction also could have been partially motivated by concerns within the Anglo community that his behavior might eventually lead him to attack an Anglo woman.

In San Diego, felony cases involving Anglos prosecuted for assaulting Indians were infrequent. The case against Stanislado Setia may illustrate why. On 5 May 1881, Setia approached an Indian named Manuel who had been working at a sidewalk coffee stand in the city of San Diego. Without provocation, Setia pulled out his knife and stabbed Manuel. Manuel was a reluctant witness and initially refused to testify against Setia. Other Indians who were in the area and witnessed the assault were equally reluctant to become involved in the case. Perhaps they, like Manuel, felt it would have been a waste of time.[48] Their reticence was well founded: Setia went to trial but was found not guilty by a jury of his peers. In fully half of the assault cases involving Anglo attacks on Indians that were heard in the lower courts, the court acquitted the Anglo of the offense. In the cases where the court convicted an Anglo, the punishment was most often a fine, which was split between the sheriff and the court. In traditional southern California native cultures, an injured party would have had the right to demand some compensation since he had been the victim of the assault. The fact that the American courts preempted this compensation may have left many Indians to wonder why they bothered to seek redress from the Anglos who assaulted them. Another, more likely possibility is that as Indians came to recognize that the murder of an Indian was only infrequently punished in American society, the chance was that a lesser offense of assault would not generate any response. Since the sole testimony of an Indian was not sufficient to result in the conviction of an Anglo, there was little point in taking the time to report or pursue a case. If the Indian did so and the case was dismissed, the Indian who had sworn out the complaint and then not substantiated it would have been forced to pay court costs.

In Los Angeles County, the same grim story repeated itself. Of the eleven cases from 1869 to 1878 that involved Indians, five were cases in which Indians assaulted Anglos, four were for Indian-on-Indian crime, and three were cases in which Anglos assaulted Indians. The victims in three of the Indian-on-Indian crime cases were women. In all three of these cases, the defendants were found guilty. In the lone case of an Anglo man accused of assaulting an Indian woman, the defendant admitted to the assault and the court fined him $175. The high number of cases in which an Indian assaulted an Anglo man was due to the repeated arrests of an Indian named Jose Maria. Of the five attacks on white men, Jose Maria was accused of three. All three attacks occurred within a six-month period. It is likely the authorities in Los Angeles pursued charges against Maria because he, like Salvador in San Diego County, had become a liability to the community. In his ensuing trials, the court convicted Maria, and he was sent to San Quentin.[49] In the remaining two Indian-on-Anglo assaults, the court found one defendant guilty, and the second admitted to the attack.[50]

In San Bernardino, the records relating to assaults are less clear than those of either Los Angeles or San Diego, but still support the conclusions found in those counties. The prosecution of Indians for assault often stemmed from the needs of the Anglo community to control Indian behavior rather than a desire to protect native people. When the larger community interests were not impacted, the prosecution of Indians occurred infrequently. In San Bernardino from 1864 to 1882, five cases involving Native Americans accused of assault were heard in the district and county courts. Indians were the defendants in four of these five cases. In only one of these four cases was the racial identity of the victim revealed. In this case, Paulino and Pedrito stood accused of assaulting each other. Coyly they each demanded separate trials and then both pleaded guilty to assault.[51] The court sentenced each to one day in the county jail—hardly a punishment for a serious infraction had the community been interested in controlling the violent tendencies of Paulino and Pedrito.[52] Since both men generated little sympathy for their station in life, or concern for their welfare, the most expeditious way of dealing with their case would have been to clear them off the court calendar as quickly as possible. At the time of their mutual assault in 1879, San Bernardino had ceased using prisoners as a wholesale labor source. As a result, any significant punishment of the pair would have adversely impacted the coffers of the community. The case of Paulino and

Pedrito stands in sharp contrast to a case in which the victim of an assault was a valued member of the community. The 1864 case of an Indian named Santiago proves this point. Santiago appeared before the court charged with assault with intent to commit robbery. He pleaded guilty, and the court sentenced him to five years in San Quentin.[53] His sentence, was hardly in accordance with other cases in which an Indian was convicted of assault, the only difference was that his victim was white.

The different values placed on the lives and property of the individuals involved in assault cases are highlighted in the sole case in which an Anglo man stood accused of assaulting an Indian. However in this case, as in the cases that involved Jose Maria and Salvador, the sentence was less likely to be an effort to punish someone who violated the norms of the society, and more likely because he was considered a liability to the larger community. On 21 March 1873, Charles Martin, a man who had already been involved in a shooting scrape with his brother-in-law and who was suspected of stealing cattle and generally wreaking havoc in the community, came into town with a friend, looking for trouble. After a period of time, Martin spied his intended victim, an Indian woman named Maria who had finished her chores in the town and was walking home. Martin watched Maria for a few moments and then spurred his horse until he overtook Maria and knocked her down. Not content with his first attack, Martin wheeled his horse around and attempted to trample Maria again. During the attack, Maria's injuries prevented her from being able to move away from her assailant. Recognizing the situation, another Anglo man, named Henry C. Dodson, interceded and prevented Martin from causing further harm to Maria. Despite Dodson's intercession, Martin continued to pursue his attack on the wounded woman; however, Dodson continued to defend Maria until Martin backed off the attack. While Dodson was clearly Maria's rescuer, he was also the reason that charges were preferred against Martin in court. Maria's testimony alone would have been insufficient to bring Martin to trial. During the trial, Dodson testified that at the time of the attack, when he demanded to know why Martin was attacking the woman, Martin had responded he thought he had done something "damned smart." Martin's case languished in the courts for months, and initially it was thought that murder charges would be brought against him as Maria's injuries were severe. However, as Maria recovered, the outrage that had characterized the community's initial reaction to the attack waned. In the end, Martin received a fine of only twenty-five dollars.[54]

The high incidence of assault and murder cases among Native Americans in southern California is significant for many reasons. They demonstrate the position Native Americans occupied within the larger Anglo community. The predominance of violent crime where Native Americans, especially women, were the victims indicates the stress and deterioration of native culture. While no culture can be held up as being without fault, certain behaviors are less acceptable in some cultures while they are more accepted in others. Prior to contact, the people of southern California ritualized violence in the form of warfare directed against outsiders, while they considered violence against their own members unlawful.[55] Additionally, while reports of women being beaten by their husbands because of infidelity exist, an arbitrary assault on an Indian woman was not considered appropriate.

This was not the only cultural norm that came under attack following the movement of Americans into the region. For the Indians of southern California living within their traditional cultures, crimes against property, like crimes against tribal members, were rare. In 1852, Hugo Reid, a self-proclaimed authority on Indians, commented in a report about the aboriginal people of southern California that theft was "never known among them."[56] Living within a reciprocal society that valued relationships over movable property, the incentive to steal had been quashed. Because of this, it is not surprising that so few cases of burglary or petty theft came before the courts.[57] However, Indians were often associated with rapacious thefts throughout the early decades of American domination in the region. These crimes were most often considered to be grand larceny in Anglo-American courts, and involved the theft of livestock. In many cases, the courts acknowledged that the Indians killed the livestock in order to feed their families. In most of these instances, the court was lenient in its sentencing. Predictably, when environmental or economic factors impacted the availability of jobs or available game, the number of cases of theft involving Native Americans grew.

In San Diego, the majority of grand larceny cases against Native Americans occurred in the late 1880s. All involved the theft of livestock. During this decade, San Diego was anxiously waiting for the railroad to connect it to the rest of the state and to the markets beyond. Land prices increased as the date for the railroad's completion neared, but in order to reassure other Americans who considered investing in the community that their investment was sound, assurances that their property would be protected became paramount. Additionally, the influx of Anglo-Americans into the area challenged the already limited resources of the Indians; many lost what employment they had previously had, while others were prevented from collecting food as they had before the increase in the population. The choice for the Indians in many cases was simply steal or starve. Because of this, the courts and the Anglo juries tended to be somewhat lenient in the sentences they recommended. In San Diego, sentences for an Indian accused of grand larceny ranged from one to three years.[58] In one instance the jury found the defendant guilty, but recommended the "shortest term fixed by law" in a case involving the theft of a heifer.[59]

In San Diego, of the seven grand-larceny cases that survive, only two resulted in convictions.[60] In 1871, an Indian named Juan stood accused of stealing a horse from Hancock Johnson. An Anglo jury found Juan guilty during his trial, but his lawyer filed a demur, or protest, in the case, maintaining the horse did not belong to Johnson, or to anyone else for that matter. Apparently the idea it might belong to Juan had not been considered. Juan was acquitted.[61] The reluctance of the courts to believe an Indian could hold valuable property has been explored in the previous chapter in the 1878 case against Santos Silvas.[62] However, it seems guilt was always presumed and innocence needed to be proven. When Indians stood accused of taking the personal property of Anglos, their rates of conviction and sentences increased significantly. The most glaring examples of this can be found in San Diego County.

In San Diego County, only three cases involving Native Americans accused of burglary appear in the upper courts. All three of these cases occurred from 1880 to 1885. On 3 April 1880, an Indian named Fred entered the home of "John Doe" Brawley and took ten yards of house lining, which was valued at one dollar. The theft brought him before the superior court in San Diego under the charge of burglary. Brawley, oddly enough, was not present during the trial of the man accused of robbing him. Instead Brawley, who apparently was suspected of a crime in the area, had already skipped town. Fred may well have thought Brawley's property had been abandoned. Despite this, an Anglo jury found Fred guilty and he was sentenced to six months in state prison.[63] In the two other cases, the defendants were not so fortunate. In 1884, Chilchil and Asketo stood charged with burglary of a local store. On 13 April 1884, both men apparently broke into the store owned by Charles S. Hamilton; what they may have stolen, and whether or not they were caught in the act are uncertain. Both were arranged on $1,000 bail and scheduled to appear in superior court on 27 June 1884. However, three days before their trial was to begin, each man pled guilty.[64] Their punishment would be three years in the state penitentiary, San Quentin.[65] The final case occurred in 1885 and involved an Indian named Carlos Dgero, who had broken into a saloon in order to steal a pistol, or possibly just to get a drink. Regardless of his motivation, the court found Carlos guilty of burglary and sentenced him to ten years in prison.[66] The value of the items in all of the above cases was nominal, and had breaking into a residence not been part of the crime, likely would have resulted in petty-larceny charges instead of burglary. However, the prosecution of the cases appears to be motivated more as a means of punishing the Indians for intruding into the personal enclaves of Anglo society. The Indian in each case proved to be well acquainted with the stores and saloons of the larger community. This fact alone may have represented a level of familiarity that Anglos felt they could not abide. The harsh punishments the Indians received would have been intended to send a message to the Indian community to keep its distance.

In San Bernardino, seven cases in which Indians are accused of theft appear in the judicial record from 1864 to 1890. In five of those cases, a jury rendered a guilty verdict and the defendants received sentences ranging from time served to nine years. In the case where the punishment was harshest, the defendant, an Indian named Leleh, also stood accused of burglary, petty larceny, arson, and grand larceny. Leleh pled not guilty to all of the charges, but was convicted of burglary and sentenced to nine years in state prison.[67] The second-harshest sentence, that of five years, went to an Indian named Santiago who stood accused of assault to commit robbery. Because of the additional circumstances involved in his crime, his sentence reflected this. In both cases, the victims were Anglos.[68] The most lenient sentence was given to an Indian woman who was charged with the most serious infraction, grand larceny. The defendant in the case, Maria, stood accused of stealing money and a hat from Juan McKinney, who was also identified as an Indian. On 21 April 1873, Maria and McKinney were at a local tavern drinking and gambling. McKinney testified that he "lost his money yesterday, don't know how much, or who took it, the defendant got my hat, suppose she took it. I had about $1." McKinney further testified that he left the bar and fell down drunk. When he awoke he thought Maria had taken the money from his pocket. Maria testified that she had taken McKinney's hat, but "never touched" his money. Several other witnesses testified that McKinney had been exceptionally drunk that evening and had lost all of his money gambling. Why Maria was charged with grand larceny is not known. The value of a worn hat could not have begun to reach the $200 value needed to justify such a crime. After hearing the testimony of the witnesses, Maria was found guilty and released with time served, one day.[69] In the remaining three cases, the value of the property was not disclosed in the court documents. However, each involved the theft of property from an Anglo man. In two of the cases, the Indian defendant was acquitted of the charge after evidence proved to be inconclusive as to whether a crime had occurred. In the final case, the Indian was convicted of burglary and sentenced to one year.[70] Clearly, race made a difference in the charges that were levied and in the sentences received by the Indians.

The propensity of the Anglo community to punish Indians who crossed over an invisible "color line" by entering into stores and saloons to steal the personal property of Anglos resulted in the same heavy-handed response in Los Angeles as in San Bernardino and San Diego counties. In 1868, an Indian named Gabriel was accused of burglarizing the local saloon after being caught inside the building after hours. Gabriel protested his innocence and maintained that he had entered the saloon through a window in order to have sex with one of the prostitutes living there. Despite the fact that no goods were taken, his testimony had little impact on the white jury's decision, and Gabriel was convicted of burglary. Gabriel's attorney requested a new trial as the "defendant clearly intended to have intercourse with a female occupant of the house," and not to steal.[71] However, Gabriel's request was denied.

The spate of burglaries or charges for grand larceny in each community also rose as living conditions for Native Americans in the area declined. In 1863–64, a smallpox outbreak had decimated the tribes in southern California. In some reports, as many as half the members of the local tribes perished. To compound this awful loss, a severe drought from 1863 to 1864 left the agricultural economy upon which so many Native Americans depended in shambles. As the 1860s continued, the economic outlook for the region improved as Anglo-Americans began to focus their attentions on bringing the railroads to the region. However, just as the economy began to rebound, a depression hit the United States in the early 1870s. By this time, the land that had been previously available for Indians to subsist on should their incomes be interrupted had declined due to the migration of more Anglos to the area. This migration subsequently impacted the traditional food that Indians would have resorted to if they had had the chance. As farmers began to plow the soil, they uprooted the Indians' traditional foods. By the time the depression had abated and the railroad had secured its presence in the region, the boom times that followed were not to be shared with the Indians. Instead of sharing in the bounty of the 1880s, Indians instead found themselves pushed onto undesirable lands; additionally, the influx of Anglos decreased their appeal as laborers, and work became scarce. The result was the steady decline in the living conditions of the native people in the area. For those Indians without work or sustenance, their only option was to steal. However, Anglos often viewed the theft of even trivial items as an affront to their society; as a result, punishments could be abnormally harsh. Only in cases where an Indian stole from another Indian did the punishment actually fit the crime.

In the early years of American occupation, southern California earned a reputation for lawlessness and violence. Alcohol was free-flowing despite local and state ordinances that prohibited distribution to Indians, and competition for the land grew increasingly more draconian. Vigilance committees preyed on individuals that stood beyond the reach of the courts. The activities of these individuals compounded the prejudice against Native Americans and resulted in a high number of cases in which Indians were the victims of violent crime. The stressors imposed by the encroachment of Anglo-American society began to tear and then to shred the fabric of tribal life. The result was a high number of cases involving Indians who attacked other Indians. In many cases women, as the weakest members of the tribe, suffered the brunt of these attacks. However, in all cases the testimony of Indians was considered marginally important in deciding the merits of a case involving a violent offense, and Anglos exploited this prejudice to their own advantage by preying on Indians, in many cases with impunity.

The interruption of traditional subsistence patterns forced many native people to steal in order to survive. When the theft involved something that could be converted to food, the courts were generally more lenient with Native Americans than with Anglos. However, when Indians crossed over an invisible barrier and entered the homes and shops of Anglos to steal, the response was swift and harsh. Through the use of the law, Anglos ensured the perpetuation of what they considered to be norms of conduct. Indians who stepped outside the limited roles that had been assigned to them found themselves pursued in the courts as a way of reestablishing these social norms.

In the few cases in which Indians sought redress for crimes committed against them, their efforts were largely unrewarded. Confronted with so many attacks from all angles, the Indian people struggled to maintain their semblance of self. In the end, the American courts could offer them little justice. In the minds of Anglo-Americans, Indians had not developed beyond a caricature of one-dimensional drunks or thieves, void of humanity and not deserving of the sympathy or protection of the larger Anglo community. Despite the abysmal treatment of the Indian in the courts, women often fared worse than men. Because of this, the presence of Indian women in the legal system in southern California deserves more consideration.

Native Women and the Law

A SEPARATE DISCUSSION REGARDING NATIVE WOMEN AND the law is important because native women have so often been absent from the narrative of American history. That said, their presence is one that must be teased out. By the time the Americans seized control of the region in 1848, Indians in southern California had already been subject to European cultural norms for seventy years. Because of these cultural norms, native women were often invisible—relegated to the status of helpmates, and denied any agency in the development of their tribal cultures. Additionally, much of the information that we have about native culture from the pre-conquest and early American periods comes from Anglo men, who tended to focus on issues that they considered important, such as war and politics. Even when native women participated in these activities, their actions were often ignored or mentioned only in passing. However, Indian women clearly played a dramatic and irreplaceable role in native society—a role they will also play in furthering our understanding of the legal system of southern California.

Women were the most vulnerable members of society during the early years of American domination. The violent, turbulent society of the 1850s and 1860s was truly an era of men. Violence, whoring, and drinking were characteristics of daily life. Anglo men were understandably reluctant to bring their families into this milieu. With a disproportionately high number of men in the region, Anglo men knew that their women would need protection, something many would be incapable of providing. In part, this dearth of Anglo women would result in even greater burdens being heaped upon those women who were part of this society. Indian women had always suffered doubly at the hands of the invading Europeans, as the victims not only of crime but also of their sex. During the first seventy-five years of European domination in the region, Spanish and later Mexican soldiers routinely raped native women. Their actions provoked many of the conflicts between Europeans and the tribes of southern California.

In an attempt to protect their women and the longevity of their tribal societies, women were often left in the village while the men addressed the demands of the invaders. When California transitioned to American hands, conditions would not improve for Indian women. Indian women continued to be victimized because of their sex; however, the greater numbers of Anglo-Americans resulted in a proportionally greater incidence of crime.

The growing number of Anglo-Americans who arrived in southern California in search of land resulted in the dispossession of the southern California tribes and rendered moot the previous strategy used by the tribes to limit access to their women. The presence of these interlopers also severely affected the ability of native women to continue their subsistence-food gathering practices. As women were the primary providers of food and the caretakers of families within the traditional tribal structures, the loss of the land, and subsequently the loss of their ability to provide food for their families, devalued their position within tribal society. This manifested itself in the increasing frequency of violent attacks initiated by Indian men against Indian women. While Indian women were often less visible in the American courts, when they did appear they often received more deference than their male counterparts. Despite the loss of traditional status within the tribal structure, the attacks perpetuated by their own men, and the growing presence of Anglos in their homelands, Indian women did not wither and fade away; most simply endured. A few used the American courts to assert their rights and the rights of their people. Most sought the protection of the reservations in an attempt to preserve the remnants of their besieged cultures. While the fruits of their labors could not be readily seen in the waning years of the nineteenth century, the daughters these remarkable women produced would rise in the next generation to be leaders of their people.

Prior to contact, the cultures that the Franciscans had so ardently tried to destroy had been, by modern standards, sexually equalitarian. Despite the patrilineal descent of most tribal leaders, women had considerable input in tribal political affairs. They maintained their own property, and they could divorce an incompatible mate or have a child out of wedlock without condemnation from their social group. Within native societies in southern California, women could rise to positions of great importance as healers and counselors. The importance of women to the survival of the tribe cannot be understated, because they were primarily responsible for the gathering of grains and the processing of food; women alone were responsible for an estimated 80 percent of the food their families consumed. In addition, the importance of women as the keepers of tribal memories and knowledge in songs, customs, and rituals ensured the perpetuation of their culture.[1]

Despite the importance of Indian women in traditional southern California native culture, within the European worldview, native women were little more than inferior appendages of native men. Since the traditional dress of native women consisted primarily of a skirt, Europeans interpreted this lack of clothing as a sign of sexual promiscuity. During the occupation of California by the Spanish, soldiers would literally "hunt" native women with lassos. Indian men who protested the rape of their wives and daughters were often killed, and their dismembered bodies displayed in Spanish settlements as a warning to other Indian men who would do the same. To the European, native men had value because of the labor they could provide to the settlements of California. Additionally, the patrilineal societies of Europe assumed that men should be the primary contact for all things related to the tribe; however, Europeans would forever remain in authority over them. Native women had value only as sexual partners or house servants. This lack of economic and political power, combined with their numerical minority within the frontier settlements, placed native women at a severe disadvantage in their ability to control their own bodies.[2] These patterns would not change significantly when America assumed control of the region in 1848.

For these reasons, native women were often seen in little more than a sexual light. In the early years of American domination in the state, prostitution was not illegal. For many women, it was the only option available to them to make sufficient money to survive, or to support their own vices. Many women turned to prostitution to pay for the alcohol they craved. In the 1850s, due to the disparity between the sexes, Indian women were largely drawn into this web. However, unlike the Hollywood version of the brothel where prostitutes plied their trade from only one location, for the most part Indian women appeared as independent agents in the selling of their own bodies, and only occasionally operated out of a local brothel. In other instances, Indian women who operated even infrequently as prostitutes often did so with the consent of the men with whom they were involved. This in part supports the contention of historian Sherburne Cook, who maintained that "Native prostitution was, in some cases, a form of economic adaptation which was controlled by village leaders or by the heads of households."[3] It does not appear, however, that prostitution was an organized tribal business, as might be inferred. Rather, it was something that was engaged in to ensure the survival of the familial group.[4] Because of the lack of local or state statutes against prostitution, women who were brought before the courts were not charged with solicitation, but with disturbing the peace or disorderly conduct. In the legal record, women who were prostitutes are often overlooked, as their cases are often packed between other cases in which the defendants are charged with being drunk in public. However, what sets these women apart is the fine imposed upon them in relation to the fines imposed for merely being drunk.

Victorian euphemisms aside, when Indian women appeared in the courts charged with soliciting, the fine was most often five dollars. An Indian woman charged with being drunk in public could expect a fine from between one and two dollars. However, harsher fines and punishment would be imposed on Indian women who were indiscrete in their solicitation, as in the case of an "Indian Maiden" who was charged with disorderly conduct and sentenced to twenty-five days in jail, or another, Theodora Bofanta, who was sentenced to serve ten days in a San Bernardino jail for "exposing her person." Theodora was released after five days for good behavior.[5]

The frequency with which alcohol played a part in the business of prostitution cannot be understated. In the early years of American domination, southern California was renowned for its lawlessness. Within this hypermasculine environment, overt displays of manly behavior became the expected norm. Men were expected to be able to drink, to defend themselves against even the slightest rebuke, and to openly display their virility. The taverns that sprang up in the region served as the perfect petri dish for this type of social experiment. However, the alcohol lowered inhibitions and often led to violence and sexual aggression from men who might otherwise have preferred a more sedate environment. As the communities of southern California grew, each attempted to suppress the business of selling both alcohol and sex in order to present a more promising image to the world. In 1877 the city council of Los Angeles, in response to complaints that the "beer cellar at the corner of Los Angeles and Requena streets was a sort of rendezvous for hoodlums and prostitutes and that disorderly conduct was constantly permitted on the premises," made use of a city ordinance that had been passed two years previously. The ordinance prohibited Indians from obtaining liquor within the establishments, but did not prohibit them from being in the establishments for other purposes.[6] However, in the rough-and-tumble days of the 1850s, any attempt at regulation would have likely been either ignored or met with hostility. In 1851 John Blais, a resident of San Diego, became tired of the lack of decency displayed by fellow Americans. On 19 December, he swore out a complaint against John Bleeker, a local barkeeper, in the justice court. Bleeker was charged with selling liquor to Indians. Blais contended that between October 10 and 16, he had gone into Bleeker's "store" and seen an Indian woman drinking liquor; no money was exchanged between the two, and Blais sourly surmised that Bleeker "got the value of it one way or the other." Whether it was the sale of alcohol to the Indian woman or the sexual favors that were presumably being exchanged cannot be determined from the remaining court documents. However, the case against Bleeker was never pursued.[7] It is likely that Blais's complaint was considered frivolous and unworthy of the court's time.

In another case in Los Angeles County, Robert Owens was charged in county court with being a public nuisance. Owens was arrested for running a brothel, selling liquor to Indian men and women, and allowing the improper exposure of a person. Owens did not contest the charges and was fined $150.[8] As can be surmised by the first two examples, Anglo men often played a large role in the promotion of prostitution. Many operated taverns or brothels and catered to the vices of other Anglo-American men. However, the more formal environment of a brothel was not necessary for the sex trade to flourish, only two willing partners. In two cases in San Bernardino in the 1870s, sex and the sex trade clearly proved of interest for local men. In 1875 a local newspaper reported that Dr. Brenan voyeuristically was "much interested in a display of conjugal affection" between an Indian man and woman.[9] A few years earlier, a euphemistically named

"John Barleycorn" was involved in a fight with another Anglo man who objected to his proposition of an Indian woman for sex in the middle of a local store. "Barleycorn" did not take well to the criticism and a shooting scrape resulted, but no charges were filed.[10]

However, while sex was a measure of masculinity and was available within the boundaries of the brothel or tavern, some men readily violated even these slight norms of behavior. For the men who raped women, Indian women appeared to be the easiest target and the one most readily pursued. Because no white man could be convicted of a crime against an Indian based solely on the testimony of an Indian, Anglo men do not appear in the court records accused of raping Indian women, although they clearly sought Indian women out as sexual partners. John Barton, the sheriff of Los Angeles County, lived with an Indian woman as his wife, as did James Pyburn, a local outlaw who was nicknamed "Buckskin."[11] Theirs are not unusual stories. Unfortunately, neither are newspaper reports that mention the victimization of Indian women by Anglo men. In 1852 the *Los Angeles Star* extensively reported on the rape of several Indian women at the San Gabriel mission by Anglo men. Hearing the cries of the women, several Indian men came to the women's aid and repelled their attackers.[12] Additional reports in the *San Diego Herald* in 1852 and 1853 report on several "outrages" that had been committed on native women in the San Luis Rey area.[13] Since most of these reports occurred in the early 1850s and then disappear from the pages of the local newspapers, it cannot be ascertained whether the incidence of rape decreased because Indian women were more actively engaged in prostitution, or whether the newspapers simply stopped reporting on the outrages.

Instead, when Indian women appear in the records as the victims of rape, it is at the hands of male Indians. In many cases the Indian man, like his Anglo brother, was not prosecuted for the crime, but because a woman could swear out a complaint, their cases are preserved both in the court files and in newspaper stories. Sadly, many of the cases that survive report Indian men raping or attempting to rape young girls. This perpetuated the image of the Indian as a sexually deviant and uncivilized individual. The first case that appears in the record occurred in 1865 in Los Angeles County. An Indian man named Ramon assaulted and attempted to rape a seven-year-old girl on 22 July. Her ethnicity is not stated in the court records. The only witnesses in the trial, however, were all Anglo men. Ramon was convicted of rape and sentenced to San Quentin. In 1873 in San Bernardino, a newspaper reported that Johnny Goodman and "an Indian" had attempted to rape a "little girl." A posse of armed men pursued both Johnny and the unnamed Indian; however, both managed to evade arrest.[14] As the age of the victim involved increased, there was a proportionate decrease in the response from the local community. In 1872 Francisco Martinez and Rafael Valenzuela, both Indians from Los Angeles County, were accused of raping Refugia Botiller. Refugia escaped her attackers and sought refuge in the home of her neighbor, Don Thomas Albrite. When called to testify, Albrite said that he thought Botiller was a "girl of the street," and that she lived with a man named Garcia. The case languished in the courts for several months without a determination. Finally, in a notation for another case in which Garcia testified, the recorder noted that the defendants had been acquitted, and accompanied it with a statement from Garcia: "That was five months ago and all is forgotten."[15] One wonders if Refugia had managed to forget that night as easily as Garcia had. Of the cases that involved Indian men accused of raping women, only one resulted in a sentence. That distinction belongs to Francisco, who on 30 March 1884 assaulted and attempted to rape Mary Celishaws. Only other Indians, two of whom were other Indian women, provided testimony in the case. Francisco was convicted and sentenced to five years in San Quentin.[16] It appears that in the courts of early southern California, Indian women were perpetually objectified as sexually available and willing partners, regardless of the reality of the situation.

Despite their presence in the consciousness of early California as sexual beings, Indian women most often appeared in the courts of the region as the victims of assault or murder. Indian men committed the majority of these crimes. On the surface it would appear that Indian men victimized Indian women and deserve condemnation; however, it must be remembered that until 1875 Indians were prevented from testifying against Anglos, and that beginning in the 1870s many Indians were being moved onto the newly created executive-order reservations, which would have limited their contact with the Anglo population. When reviewing the total number of assault cases involving Indians, some surprising patterns appear: the first is that Indian women appear as the assailants of other Indian women almost as often as men. Additionally, in cases where an Indian woman stood accused of assault, it was equally likely that she had assaulted another woman as a man. In most cases where an Indian woman was accused of assault, her weapon of choice, like her male counterpart's, was a knife.

However, in the first case to appear in the court documents, the assailant, Maria Antonia Cornelia, chose an unusual weapon. On 9 January 1866, Cornelia was brought before the county court in Los Angeles on charges of attempting to murder Maria Odon with strychnine. While the use of poison was not unheard of among the tribes of southern California, its use was rare. Maria Odon was the heir of Urbano Odon, who had received a land grant for the "El Escorpion" rancho in Los Angeles in 1845. Odon survived the attempt on her life, and the case against Cornelia was dropped. Cornelia's unusual method of attacking Odon would indicate that each woman had some familiarity with the other. The attack on her also serves as a strange precursor to the next time Odon would appear in court. On her second trip to the courthouse, Odon would again be the victim, but this time a man, Miguel Leonis, was attempting to wrest from her the land that she had inherited from her father. Leonis, like Cornelia, failed in his attempt. However, the dispute over the same land had not ended. In a follow-up case three years later in 1866, two Indians named Odon and Juana appeared in court seeking to force Leonis to transfer the title of the property to them.[17] The court dismissed their suit. It cannot be ascertained whether Leonis and Cornelia had a history together. However, Leonis and Odon were reported to have been married in a Gabrielino ceremony some time in the 1850s, and had a child together (Marcelina) in 1860. By all accounts theirs was not a happy marriage, and the lawsuit may have been Odon's attempt to retain her father's inheritance.[18] Since the dispute between Leonis and Odon was of some duration, it is conceivable that Cornelia's attack was a part of this larger issue.[19] According to historian Leonard Pitt in his study of the Californios, "Miguel Leonis, armed a hundred fellow countrymen and Mexicans at Calabasas and clung to [the] land by brute force, staving off both Yankees and Californians with better claims than his."[20] A man who would arm a hundred men to defend a questionable land claim might also be inclined to encourage murder.

Of the other cases that involved Indian women attacking other Indian women, a knife was the preferred weapon in the attack, and in all but one instance, the case was not pursued. In that case, Maria Carmen was charged and convicted of assaulting Dolores with a knife on 7 February 1862. No cause for the attack is listed in the case file; however, another Indian, Francisco

Bracamonte, is listed as a codefendant. Bracamonte was later charged as an accessory. Carmen was convicted of the assault and served three months in the county jail as punishment.[21] In the cases in which Indian women were accused of assaulting men, their chances for conviction soared. Of the three cases that have been preserved in the court records, all resulted in a conviction. However, the punishment for the assault was likely not extensive, as none of the women were referred to the state prison. In only one case is a sentence revealed, and that was for a $50 fine. In that case, Dolores Arsea was convicted of assaulting Juan Diego, another Indian. During the altercation both were drunk, and in response to some unknown stimulus, Arsea picked up a rock and struck Diego above his eye. It should be noted that Diego had nothing to do with the case against Arsea; the charges were preferred against her by the local constable.[22]

In another case against an Indian woman who was convicted of assault, the woman had previously been accused of assaulting another Indian woman. In this case, Pilar was accused of attacking Manuel Flores with a knife on 23 December 1885. The incident might well have passed under the radar of the judiciary had Pilar's knife not nicked the artery in Flores's right knee.[23] Flores's wound was significant, and Pilar had been accused in the same court three years earlier of attacking an Indian woman named Maria with a knife. In that case the charges were not pursued. However, in the Flores case, it is possible that the courts felt that Pilar presented something of a threat to the Anglo community and decided to punish her for the attack. There is no indication in the record that Flores was another Indian. Additionally, Flores's injury was fairly significant, and the possibility that he could have bled to death existed. While it is unlikely that Pilar had intentionally aimed at Flores's knee, the assault could have easily turned into a murder charge.

In the cases where an Indian woman was assaulted, the majority of the assailants were Indian men. In most cases there was a familial relationship between the two. Newspaper accounts report several attacks by Indian men on their wives during the forty years that have been examined in this study. In these reports, the effects of alcohol are mentioned; however, there is no larger demand for the police to intercede and protect the women.[24] In large part, the silence on the part of the press is reflective of the social standards of the day, which would have allowed a man corporal authority over the members of his family, whether it be an Indian family or an Anglo one.

However, when the assault was severe or involved children, the local courts acted, and their punishment was severe. On 20 April 1869, Jose Rosario, an Indian man, assaulted a woman named Juana and a boy named Juan Bautista. Both Juana and Juan are identified in the record as being Indians; while no direct relationship between the three is specified, it is most likely that Juana and Juan were the wife and son of Jose. The assault resulted in Jose's conviction of assault with a deadly weapon and his incarceration in the state prison.

In another instance in which an Indian man was convicted of assaulting his wife, charges were brought against him not by his wife, but by Anglo men who had witnessed the attack. On 2 July 1878 in Los Angeles County, Juan Espinosa accused Louisa, his wife, of "doing him great damage," and as a result began to assault her. Juan had a history of violence toward his wife and had been previously prevented from continuing his attacks on her. During this incident, Louisa ran from the house and was pursued by Espinosa. Several Anglo men who were in the area demanded that he stop his attack, and Espinosa reportedly did. However, four days after the attack, those same Anglo men swore out a warrant for Espinosa's arrest and he was tried on assault charges. Espinosa was convicted of assault with a deadly weapon and fined $175. Lacking the money, Espinosa was forced to remain in jail at a rate of one dollar per day until his fine was paid.[25] It is possible that Espinosa's complaint against his wife was sexual in nature, and that she had either refused his advances or had engaged in prostitution. The fact that Indian women were often the temporary sex partners of other men, either willingly or unwillingly, attacked the core beliefs of the native people of southern California in which adultery was considered taboo for women. These stressors may have played a role in another incident in San Diego County a few years later. In this case, Salvador was accused of assaulting Leonora with a "bridle and hands" because she would not see him. Salvador savagely attacked Leonora and threw her into a corner of the house by her hair. Unable to vent his rage with the attack, Salvador then reached for a gun, but was prevented from shooting Leonora when her father entered the house and protected her. During the trial, Salvador admitted that he had previously attacked Leonora four or five times, and readily admitted to the most recent attack. He was found guilty in the justice court, and the case was referred to the superior court in San Diego County two months later. However, the superior court refused to hear the case because Salva-

dor and Leonora were married, and the charges were not pursued.[26] Two
things stand out in regard to the case against Salvador. The first is that
Leonora's abandonment of her husband was within the norms of the tribal
culture that she had been raised in. Within the cultural norms of the tribes
of southern California, an Indian woman could divorce her husband and
return home without seeking approval of the tribe or any other entity—a
privilege denied Anglo women at this time. The second issue concerns
the Anglo courts. In refusing to pursue the case further, the court could
have been mindful of two things. The first was that Salvador had already
been incarcerated for two months and additional time would not likely
be assigned, and the second was that this was a domestic complaint, and
within the norms of Anglo society a man had the right to beat his spouse.

Despite the image presented so far that Indian women were considered
to be little more than chattel, and that the Anglo courts refused to protect
them, this was not universally the case. Indian men and Anglo men often
interceded to protect Indian women, as can be seen in the case against Juan
Espinosa. A report in the *San Jacinto Register* in 1888 described an incident
in which an Indian woman was being "burned at the stake" by tribe members and was rescued by Anglo men.[27] Another example occurred during
one of the most racist and inhuman attacks recorded in southern California. On 21 March 1873 in San Bernardino County, Charles Martin intentionally rode his horse over an Indian woman named Maria. Martin's goal
was to kill the woman; however, he gave no rationale for his attack other
than that he thought it would be a "damned smart" thing to do. Martin had
no previous relationship with Maria; his actions were motivated purely by
his hatred. Martin's plan to kill Maria was thwarted when Henry Dodson
interceded and protected her. Dodson later preferred charges against Martin to ensure that he was prosecuted for the crime.[28] Indian men were often
no less valiant in the protection of native women. In 1874, Jose Marque
attacked a woman during a gathering at the home of the tribal captain.
An Indian man intervened and prevented the attack from continuing. For
his trouble, the Indian then had to contend with an enraged Marque, who
turned his attack on his wife's rescuer. The case was referred to the sheriff
to determine if charges should be preferred in a higher court, but the decision was to close the case.[29] In another incident, an Indian man came to the
defense of a woman who was being beaten by her Mexican husband. The
husband had the Indian arrested and the case proceeded to trial. However,

when the court realized what had happened, the Indian was released and the Mexican was forced to pay court costs.

Despite the fact that some men came to the rescue of Indian women who were under attack, the majority of the cases involving assault in southern California deal with Indian men who assaulted Indian women. In these cases, an Indian man had about a 50 percent chance of being convicted of the crime. Also, the conviction rate was not dependent on the testimony of the woman assaulted; instead, the rate of conviction increased when the witnesses in the case were Anglos.[30] As with the previous assaults, a knife was the weapon of choice. This undoubtedly reflected the 1854 law that prohibited Indians from owing guns or being sold ammunition.[31]

In several of the cases where an Indian stood accused of a felony, his lawyer would argue, unsuccessfully, that the courts had no jurisdiction in the case. A typical example of all these elements can be found in the case against Antonio. On 20 April 1871, Antonio assaulted Maria with a knife. Antonio was arrested and remanded to the county jail. Despite the attack, when it came time for testimony against Antonio, Maria was nowhere to be found. Instead, J. J. and Andrew Warren, two Anglo men who had witnessed the attack, preferred the charges against Antonio. During the trial, Antonio's attorney argued that the county court had no jurisdiction in the case since it involved two Indians. The court disagreed, and Antonio was convicted and sentenced to state prison.[32] The argument that the local or state courts did not hold jurisdiction in cases involving Indian-on-Indian crime stopped being a defense argument by the 1870s.

In areas where intense concentrations of Anglo-Americans occurred early on, high numbers of Native Americans appeared in the courts charged with violent crimes against each other. This indicates that the destabilizing factor in the relationship between Indian men and women was the presence of Anglo-American culture. In Los Angeles County, where the Anglo population saw its first major increases, violence toward native women occurred in a seesaw fashion. As the native population declined due to external factors and the Anglo population increased, violence against Indian women jumped. In 1852 the Anglo population of Los Angeles County was approximately 4,093. Eight years later, the Anglo population had only risen slightly to 4,400. During this time, the courts heard no cases in which Indians assaulted each other. However, by 1870 the Anglo population of Los Angeles had increased to 5,700 and the native presence had declined to 219. From 1862 to 1871, seven assaults and two murders of native women occurred in the county.[33] Following this rash of violent crime against native women, it would be another seven years before another Indian woman appeared before the courts in Los Angeles as the victim of a violent offence.[34] The defendant in this case was a Mexican man who had been living with an Indian woman.[35]

The sharp decline in the number of offenses affecting native women occurred at a time when the federal government was establishing the executive-order reservations in San Diego County and Indians in Los Angeles County were being encouraged to leave the county for the reserves. While this demographic shift reduced the contact between Anglos and Indians, it would prove to be only a temporary measure. As the Indian population shifted into the southern portion of the region, the Anglo population soon followed, and the same pattern of abuse reappeared.

In San Diego County, the Anglo population in 1870 was 4,951. Up until this time, Indian women had not appeared in the courts as the victims of violent offenses perpetrated by native men. Unfortunately, this would not last. By 1880 San Diego County's Anglo population had doubled to 8,618, and by 1890 it had increased to 34,987. This tremendous increase in the Anglo population had a significant impact on the presence of Indian women who appeared in the courts. From 1874 to 1884, six assaults involving native women were heard in the courts.[36] The incidence of violent crime perpetrated against native women had been mitigated to some extent by the presence of the federal reservations that had been established starting in the 1870s. These allowed native people to limit their contact with Americans. However, some contact was required in order to ensure the wages that were necessary for their survival. For native women, violent crimes against them appear almost as a wave. As the Anglo population began to spread inland to San Bernardino County, and southward into San Diego County, violence against native women increased. However, the defendants in these crimes most often were not Anglos, but Indian men. The incidence of murder cases clearly exemplifies this point.

In the early years of development in Los Angeles County, a number of cases involving the murders of Indian women occurred, while no such claims could be made in either San Diego or San Bernardino counties.

In 1859 an unnamed Indian man was being held in the county jail in Los Angeles County. Accused of the murder of his wife and child, the man was to be charged and would likely have been hung. However, before the case went to trial, the Indian escaped from jail and was never seen again.[37] Seven months later, another Indian, Tomas, stood accused of murdering his wife and mother. He later was hung near Fort Tejon.[38] In 1864 an Indian named Jose was convicted of beating an Indian woman named Maria to death with a stick, after which he threw her body into a drainage ditch. When the Anglo jury passed sentence on Jose, they advised the court that they had found Jose "guilty of manslaughter in the mildest form."[39] While these cases occurred in Los Angeles County, it should be noted that native men were themselves often the victims off violence during this same time period in San Diego or San Bernardino counties. Since Indian men were most often the individuals who had contact with the Anglo-American community because of work or politics, they suffered for this familiarity disproportionately to Indian women.

There are two cases in which Indian women appeared before the Anglo courts accused of murder. In both cases the women were acquitted. The reason for this probably involved Anglo assumptions regarding gender, and the fact that their victims were other Indians. The first case is illustrative of both points. In 1874, an Indian woman named Celsa stood accused of killing her newborn child. Celsa was brought before the district court in Los Angeles and tried before a jury of white men. The jury later acquitted her of the crime.[40] Infanticide was a crime in which poor women were almost exclusively charged as defendants. Faced with oppressive economic conditions, and often lacking the support of husbands, these women chose to end the lives of their children rather than have them join in the misery of their existence. As has already been noted, rape was an all-too-common occurrence in early California, and the scion of such an event could have pushed many an Indian woman to rid herself of any tangible connection to the act. In both instances, the murder of a child was reflective of the breakdown of the society in which these women lived.[41] Within a tribal setting, only other Indians would have been privy to knowledge about a woman's pregnancy and her termination of it. Consequently, these cases would have been dealt with within the tribe, and would not have attracted the attention of the American authorities. It is for this reason that few cases of infanticide ever reached the courts. According to historian Lowell Bean, the occurrence of infanticide was rare among the people of southern California. The underlying reasons behind Celsa's actions can only be speculated on at this later date, but an examination of the conditions that existed in southern California at the time of the murder can shed some light onto her reasons. Southern California in the 1870s was laboring under an economic depression that had a profound effect on native people. The continued migration of Anglos into the area had pushed Indians off their lands, and the harsh economic climate had resulted in a dearth of jobs available to native people. Additionally, the few executive-order reservations in San Diego County had been abandoned because of Anglo protest; this left Indian people with few viable economic options on where or how to live. The entry of a new child into this desperate mix could easily have been another factor that influenced Celsa's decision.

In the other case that involved an Indian woman who stood accused of murder, her victim was another Indian woman. In this case, Maria Grand was accused of stabbing Leona to death with a "ten cent knife" near the Tejon Reservation in 1864. At the preliminary hearing in the Los Angeles County district court, witnesses included several Anglo men and one other Indian woman. In the end, the district attorney decided not to pursue the case. The court did not record the rationale behind this decision; however, the decision not to pursue the case against Maria was in keeping with a noticeable trend in the upper courts of Los Angeles to avoid prosecution of cases in which native women were defendants. Why Anglo-American courts shied away from the prosecution of a member of a group that had routinely borne the brunt of so much prejudice may have more to do with Anglo concepts of womanhood. According to historian Linda Parker in her study of women involved in violent crimes in San Diego County, the Victorian concept of womanhood saw women as passive, nonviolent individuals. Even when confronted with evidence to the contrary, male juries often refused to convict women of violent crimes.[42] It is likely that since the victim in the crime had been an Indian, and the juries traditionally were sympathetic to women defendants, that the district attorney in Los Angeles decided not to pursue the case. This same level of deference is not found in cases in which Indian men stood accused of a violent offense. In cases in which Indian men stood accused of murder, if their victim was another Indian, their sentences were generally light. If the murder involved an Anglo man, the chance for conviction increased significantly.

The last way in which women appeared before the American courts in cases that involved murder were as witnesses. In these cases, Indian women are well represented. In the majority of these cases, the defendants were Indian men. However, this was not always the case: in the first case involving an Indian woman as a witness to a murder, the defendant was a Mexican man. In late 1861, a man named Santa Anna was charged in the Los Angeles County court of murdering an Indian man named Jose Juan. Santa Anna had reportedly borrowed money from Jose Juan, and when he requested it be repaid, Santa Anna stabbed him to death. During his preliminary trial in the court of sessions, Jose Juan's mother, Dolores, testified against her son's murderer. The case against Santa Anna was then referred to the grand jury and later to the district court, but the charges against Santa Anna were not pursued.[43] In another case a few years later, two Hispanic men were accused of murdering an Anglo man, Robert Parker. The men, Jose Domingo and Juan Napomecente, broke into the house Parker shared with his Indian wife, Massalina, and shot him to death. Parker died the next day, and during the trial Massalina served as the chief witness against the two men. At the conclusion of the trial, only Domingo would be found guilty of Parker's murder.[44] In cases in which Indian women provided testimony regarding a murder, there is no evidence that the courts were prejudiced against their testimony in any way. This endorsement of their value as witnesses has its limitations, however, as their testimony was never used in trials where an Anglo man stood accused of murder.

The acceptance of the testimony of Indian women in trials extended to other venues as well. In San Diego in 1884, Antonio Argnello was accused of stealing a horse from A. G. Hall on 20 December 1883. Argnello was convicted of the crime based on the testimony of Christine, an Indian woman, and the horse's owner. Another case in 1877, which also occurred in San Diego County, involved two Indian men, Luis Mocha and Juan, who were accused of arson. The charge against the two men actually started as a shooting fracas between several Indians who were attempting to navigate a road in front of Chatham Helm's home. Helm was well known in the area among native people as a virulent racist. Over the years, both he and his brother Turner would be involved in several incidents where Indians were killed. Neither man would ever serve time for their crimes. On the day in question, Helm had blocked the road in front of his home with his own wagon. This blocked the access route into town and prevented Mocha and Juan from passing in their own wagon. An argument ensued, and weapons were fired. It was apparently a spark from one of the guns that started the fire. Helm then swore out a complaint against the Indians, accusing them of arson. Several Indians provided testimony during the preliminary trial in the San Diego justice court, including Dolores, an Indian woman. While the case was referred to the grand jury for further consideration, no charges were pursued against the Indians for their part in the fracas.[45] While Helm had charged the Indians with arson, and through the force of his personality had managed to get the case referred to the grand jury, it was also apparent that the Indians were telling the truth.

While murder and violent crime have a tendency to immediately draw attention because they represent extremes in antisocial behavior, women also appeared in the American courts charged with other more mundane crimes, such as theft. The charges brought against these women are no less reflective of the stressors affecting native societies in southern California than the more salacious crimes would be. What they also represent is the tendency of Anglo courts to discount the actions of Indian women, even when their behavior was in contrast to social norms. This paternalistic treatment would benefit Indian women, as its manifestation was a reduction in the time they were required to serve for the crimes they committed. Indian women who had been convicted of a crime received sentences that were significantly less than those received by Indian men who had been similarly charged. In most instances, their sentences were light even in comparison to those given out to Anglo men. In almost half the cases, no additional jail time was requested. It is also possible that the Anglo justices who heard cases against Indian women recognized that most crimes that involved theft had been engaged in as a means of aiding women in their daily survival.

Unlike Indian men, who stole livestock, women focused on small, portable items that could be sold. In 1851, an Indian woman named Ursula stood accused of stealing silk from a local store. During her arraignment in the justice court of San Diego, she pled guilty, and the justice sentenced her to three months in the county jail.[46] In contrast, an Indian man accused of petty larceny could expect to receive a sentence of at least six months in the county jail.[47] A further example occurred in 1873, when Anglo authorities accused an Indian woman named Maria of grand theft for the alleged theft of $60 dollars and a hat from another Indian man named Juan McKinney. During a preliminary hearing in the San Bernardino justice court, several Indians testified that McKinney and Maria had been in the tavern that evening, and that they had been drinking heavily. While they drank, McKinney gambled. After several hours, they both staggered out into the street, but before reaching home, McKinney passed out. Maria, who had accompanied him to this point, took his hat and returned to the bar. When McKinney awoke, he realized his hat and his money were missing, but did not remember much of the evening other than that Maria had been there with him. McKinney then swore out a complaint accusing Maria of theft. While Maria admitted to the theft of the hat, she denied she took the money. Instead she advised the court that McKinney had been drunk and gambled away all his money. Two other Indians supported her story. The justice of the peace who heard the case determined that there was no evidence to suppose Maria was guilty of the crime she stood accused of, and she was released.[48] The value of the hat did not justify the charge of grand larceny, and the fact that McKinney was also an Indian may have prejudiced the justice against him. However, if Maria had been a man and the charges against her had been validated, she could have expected a sentence ranging from one to nine years in prison.

From the middle to the end of the nineteenth century, native women, while often only marginally visible in the images we have of the era, proved to have a far greater impact on the budding legal system than may have been previously supposed. While Indian women most often were the victims of violent and sex-based crimes, their presence in the courts speaks of both their vulnerability and their impact on the development of the region. Sadly, these images are also reflective of the destruction of native culture when confronted with the rapacious appetite for land that characterized the Anglo-American presence in the region. Indian women not only became victims of the growing American population, but were also victimized by other tribe members. Native women in the southern California region demonstrate the extent to which this victimization threatened the stability of the tribe as a whole. Many Indian women preferred Anglo or Hispanic men to their Indian brothers as partners. While this fact indicates assimilation, it also reflects a conscious, at least partial rejection of the previous culture. It is perhaps because of this assimilation that Indian women appeared to have been given more consideration in the courts in regard to their testimony. The reluctance of Anglo male judiciaries to prosecute cases in which Indian women were accused of a violent offense was likely due to Victorian notions about feminine conduct, which often held women incapable of such behavior because to do otherwise would have conflicted with the normative patterns that the male-dominated society had established.

Conclusion

(O)VER A FORTY-YEAR PERIOD, AMERICANS MOLDED EARLY California from a Spanish colony into one of the most productive states in the union. The incentive of gold lured thousands to what was once called Eden; however, once here, many Anglo-Americans discovered that the riches to be found in the gold fields were little more than a figment of a powerful dream, rather than a reality. Instead of returning home, however, many remained to see what other dreams could be realized within the state. The "cow counties" of the south were quickly recognized for their mild climate and fertile soil—attributes that made the region a farmer's paradise and a potential source of wealth. With the coming of the railroads, this paradise could generate its own gold rush. However, as in Eden, there was one imperfection to mar this perfect scene. For the early American settlers in southern California, this turned out to be the presence of the Indians.

While Indians were initially seen as a beneficial source of labor for the underdeveloped region, no long-term plans had ever been considered to adopt them into the new American culture. The parasitic relationship that was established between the Indians and the Anglo communities was an extension of practices that had existed under the Spanish. Under the new American regime this relationship quickly soured, helped along by an almost pathological desire among many Americans to degrade the Indians as much as possible. Despite laws prohibiting the sale of alcohol to Indians, it was routinely given out as part of the wages Indians earned on the ranchos in order to cheat the Indians of their earnings and to ensure a steady labor force. The widespread use of alcohol stressed native communities still further as addiction addled formerly productive members of native societies, lowered inhibitions, and forced many Indian women into prostitution.

Endemic violence became the norm in the chaotic society that evolved soon after the signing of the Treaty of Guadalupe Hidalgo, as outlaws coursed through the region virtually unopposed. To preserve their preferred position in this labile society, newly arrived Anglo-Americans used whatever means were at their disposal to not only seize the land but to control those who resided within its borders. Vigilantism became an effective tool for enforcing Anglo social norms. For many Anglo-Americans, the Indians who resided in the area were a challenge to their hegemony, which forced the new settlers to consciously decide on whether to adapt to the presence of the Indians, or eliminate them from the society they hoped to create. For some, the choice was elimination, but the means to achieve this was as varied as the Anglo-Americans who came to the area. Many routinely used violence to drive Indians from homes they had occupied for centuries. The result was a growing abundance of dead bodies, and a steady degradation of Indian life due to the American presence. Indian deaths were dealt with in "the usual way," or glossed over with poorly conceived jokes about "visitations from God."

While direct violence was the choice of a few, its practice was sanctioned by the bulk of Anglo society. Those who chose to indulge in it were rarely forced to answer for their crimes, even though their names were surely known within the Anglo communities. Most Anglo-Americans were less direct in their actions but still focused on their goal to remove any obstacle that prevented their domination of the land, and used the law to ensure their hegemony. These individuals also found ready assistance in the larger community. State and local laws were passed to impede the ability of the Indian to function within the courts, and then Indians were brought, with increasing frequency, before the bench to answer for crimes they often did not commit. The juries, justices, and prosecutors of southern California reflected the prejudices of the communities they served, and their resentment of the Indians.

An impetus for the presence of Indians within the courts was the increasing prosperity of the region. As the region diversified from cattle to agriculture, land values increased. The introduction of the railroad only served to further this development; however, the influx of more Americans altered not only the landscape but the position of the Indian within Anglo society. The need for Indian labor declined, and accordingly the desire increased to remove them from the area. As their numbers declined, Indians increasingly found themselves before the courts. Conviction rates were poor; however, the message was clear. The land had a new master, and the Indian was no longer welcome.

Despite the harassment of Indian people in the courts, Anglo-Americans were not ignorant of the reasons for the degraded position Indians were forced to endure. Recognition of the impact Anglo migration had on the culture and prosperity of the aboriginal societies of southern California was all the more damning, since it did little to alter the behavior of the Anglo communities. Voices were raised to create reserves for the Indians, but what underlay this seemingly altruistic act was the desire to remove Indians totally from Anglo society in order to encourage yet more growth. When the executive-order reservations were created, they were almost as quickly abandoned or amended because of further complaints from those who had insisted on their creation in the first place.

Indian women were doubly victimized by the influx of Americans into the region, objectified as potential sexual partners more than anything else. Women were often the target of rape and violence. The exploitation of Indian women was made all the worse by the complacency of some Indian men. Despite the image of an Indian woman as little more than a sexual partner or a stumbling drunk, when Indian women came before the courts they received surprisingly more-lenient sentences than their Indian brothers, and their testimony was often instrumental in ensuring that justice prevailed, although this applied only in the cases in which the defendant was either Hispanic or Indian.

Overall, the previous assumptions regarding the incidence of Indians in the court system in southern California must be reconsidered. While it would be popular to contend that Indians were given harsh sentences out of proportion to their crimes and were universally victimized by the Anglo-American courts, this assumption does not hold up under scrutiny. However, what can be seen is a concerted effort by the Anglo-American communities in the region to use the courts to harass the Indians in order to further their own desires. Additionally, the courts chronicle the decline of the once-flourishing native populations with each case of drunkenness, assault, or rape that appeared before the bench. Nineteenth-century

American society had little sympathy for the plight of the Indians or for the destruction of their culture. It was felt that the Indians of southern California were unable to adapt to the changing world of the Americans and would subsequently fade from history. While many aspects of their traditional culture have been irreparably lost, the epitaph for the people of southern California has not been written. They are instead attempting to recreate the cultures that were challenged by the influx of Europeans, and later Americans, into their lands. Perhaps this study will help them to further understand the trials endured by their ancestors in order for their modern culture to prevail.

Notes

Introduction

1. Many of the prominent landholders within the state, including those who had defended Mexico, would later serve in the California legislature. At the local level, most *alcaldes* continued to serve their communities as both civil and judicial authorities. As the white population in the state increased, Americans replaced these officers.

2. For an extended discussion about California Indians under Spanish and Mexican rule, see David J. Langum, *Law and Community on the Mexican California Frontier: Anglo-American Expatriates and the Clash of Legal Traditions, 1821–1846* (Norman: University of Oklahoma Press, 1987); and James J. Rawls, *Indians of California: The Changing Image* (Norman: University of Oklahoma Press, 1984), 81–108.

American Law, 1850–1865

1. Gordon Morris Bakken, "Mexican and American Land Policy: A Conflict of Cultures," *Southern California Quarterly* 75, no. 3–4 (1993): 249.

2. Albert L. Hurtado, "Controlling California's Indian Work Force," *Southern California Quarterly* 61, no. 3 (1979): 217–38.

3. *Alcaldes* served as the premier civil and judicial authority in the pueblos and towns; they were often aided in their duties by the *ayuntamientos* or town councils. During the military governorship of California, several serious legal cases which included murder were handled by the civil authorities who had helped govern the state during the Mexican period.

4. Hurtado, "Controlling California's Indian Labor Force," 224.

5. Colonel Richard B. Mason (acting governor) to Jesse B. Hunter (Mormon Battalion), 2 August 1847.

6. Albert L. Hurtado, *Indian Survival on the California Frontier* (New Haven: Yale University Press, 1988), 227.

7. Eight delegates were Californios.

8. The majority of the delegates came from northern states with limited traditions of slavery, while less than one-third of the delegates were from the American South. The combined interests and worldview of the Southerners and the traditional Mexican insistence on compulsory labor were added to the constitution. This would indicate that some of the transplanted Northerners may have altered their worldview after having lived in the state under Mexican rule.

9. Field arrived in California in 1849 and began practice as an attorney in the rough world of the mining camps. He was soon elected as an *alcalde*, then as a justice of the peace.

10. During most of the 1850s, pro-Southern Democrats controlled the legislature in California. By the outbreak of the war, almost 40 percent of California's inhabitants were from slave states. Their proslavery biases are clearly seen in the Act for the Government and Protection of Indians. Their fall from power during the Civil War, coupled with the Emancipation Proclamation, would do away with the official "slavery" of Indian people in the state. For further discussion on the role of California during the Civil War, see Alvin M. Josephy Jr., *The Civil War in the American West* (New York: Alfred A. Knopf, 1991).

11. This statute was later used to prevent Chinese testimony against whites, as the court ruled that Indians and Chinese were from the same Mongoloid race.

12. For boys this was age 18, while girls were released at age 15. Each was to be given $50 and two sets of clothing when they came of age.

13. *California Statutes*, 22 April 1850, section two.

14. Through the 1850s, there was a considerable market in Indian slaves that operated from Utah through to California. Many of the participants were Indians who had captured other Indians during conflicts; others were Mexican and American slave traders who preyed on the Indians throughout the Southwest, and who sold their captives to whites for labor. For an excellent discussion of this practice, see Sondra Jones, *The Trial of Don Pedro Leon Lujan: The Attack Against Indian Slavery and Mexican Traders in Utah* (Salt Lake City: University of Utah Press, 2000).

15. In *Cherokee Nation v. Georgia* (1831), the State of Georgia attempted to extinguish title to Cherokee lands after it had been given assurances by the federal government that it could assume control of the Cherokee land within its state borders if it first relinquished its claims to land beyond its current western border. In the ruling by the Supreme Court, Chief Justice Marshall ruled that tribes were "domestic dependent nations" and "capable of managing its own affairs and governing itself," albeit the tribe was in a perpetual "state of pupilage" to the United States.

16. Hurtado, *Indian Survival*, 119.

17. "Message to the California State Legislature," *California State Senate Journal*, 7 January 1851, 15.

18. Paul Prucha, *American Indian Treaties: The History of a Political Anomaly* (Los Angeles: University of California Press, 1994), 244.

19. Originally $25,000 had been slated for the commission to accomplish its task. However, by the time the negotiations had concluded, a bill for over one million dollars was presented to the Senate for reimbursement.

20. At the time, San Diego County included present-day Riverside and Imperial counties and much of San Bernardino County.

21. Richard L. Carrico, "San Diego Indians and the Federal Government: Years of Neglect, 1850–1865," *Journal of San Diego History* 26, no. 3 (1980): 167–68.

22. This was the title of what later came to be known as the Treaty of Temecula.

23. While William Carey was investigating the land-rights issues in California, he was also speculating heavily in mission land, including the area surrounding Mission San Luis Rey, which encompassed an Indian pueblo. He later resold this land at profit. His actions undoubtedly have added fuel to the rumor of a concerted conspiracy to deprive Indians of their land rights. For further information, see Florence Shipek, *Pushed into the Rocks: Southern California Indian Land Tenure, 1769–1986* (Lincoln: University of Nebraska Press, 1987), 30.

24. Harry Kelsey, "The California Indian Treaty Myth," *Southern California Quarterly* 15, no. 3 (1973): 226–29.

25. *California Senate Journal*, [1852] 3rd sess., 597.

26. Shipek, *Pushed into the Rocks*, 30.

27. Kelsey, "The California Indian Treaty Myth," 225–35.

28. Three other men would serve in the California superintendency, including Pierson Reading, Samuel Sheldon, and Benjamin D. Wilson.

29. In southern California, the Fort Tejon/Sebastian Reservation reportedly reduced the number of cattle thefts in the area. Despite this, the reserve would be abandoned within a few years. Robert Glass Cleland, *The Cattle on a Thousand Hills: Southern California, 1850–1880* (San Marino: The Huntington Library, 1990), 68. Two temporary reservations on the Fresno and Kings rivers and at Nome Cult Valley were also established; however, only Fresno was maintained. See William H. Ellison, "The Federal Indian Policy in California, 1846–1860," *Mississippi Valley Historical Review* 9, no. 1 (1922): 65; and Hurtado, *Indian Survival*, 141–44.

30. Hurtado, *Indian Survival*, 142.

31. *Los Angeles Star*, 18 December 1852.

32. Beale had selected the Fort Tejon area as a reservation because several hundred former mission Indians under the leadership of Tapatero had already established an agricultural community on the site.

33. *The Act to Ascertain and Settle Private Land Claims in the State of California*, 9 United States Statutes 631, 3 March 1851.

34. Shipek, *Pushed into the Rocks*, 30. The fact that Indians did not present their claims before the commission was later used as an excuse by the courts to deny native peoples the rights to occupy their ancestral lands.

35. In the majority of cases, any possible claim for land use by the Indians was ignored in preference to the land claims of the land grantees.

36. Land Commission claim 435, Pablo Apis, claimant for Temecula, granted 7 May 1845; claim filed 1 November 1852, rejected by the commission on 15 November 1853, and dismissal confirmed by the district court on 21 February 1857.

37. Land Commission claim 471, Maria Juana de los Angeles, granted 7 May 1845; claim filed 9 November 1852, confirmed by commission 10 October 1854, and

confirmed by the district court 24 December 1856. Maria Juana's heirs sold the land and began evicting tribal members from the village site at Cuca beginning in 1879.

38. B. D. Wilson maintained there were as many as fifty Indian land proprietors who were waiting for their cases to be settled by the land commissioners. B. D. Wilson, *The Indians of Southern California in 1852* (Omaha: Bison Books, 1995), 24.

39. Following the secularization of the missions in the 1830s, Mexican settlers in the region clamored for the lands that had been attached to the missions in order to assume the benefits of the land improvements made by the Indian neophytes (buildings, wells, and orchards) as well as the livestock that occupied the land. Despite the Mexican government's original intention that the Indians who had served the missions would retain these improved lands, much of the former mission lands fell into non-Indian hands.

40. Lisbeth Haas, *Conquests and Historical Identities in California, 1769–1936* (Berkeley: University of California Press, 1995), 57.

41. Bakken, "Mexican and American Land Policy," 243–44.

42. Haas, *Conquests and Historical Identities in California*, 57.

43. Ellison, "Federal Indian Policy in California, 1846–1860," *Mississippi Valley Historical Review* 9, no. 1 (1922): 46. In 1850 William Cary Jones was sent by the secretary of the interior and the secretary of state to study the land-title issue in California. After a review of the prevailing law, he determined, "In the wild or wandering tribes, the Spanish law does not recognize any title whatsoever to the soil."

44. The total non-native population in Southern California in 1852 was less than 3,500 scattered over hundreds of miles of land.

45. Ronald C. Woolsey, "Crime and Punishment: Los Angeles County, 1850–1856," *Southern California Quarterly* 61, no. 1 (1979): 85.

46. Vigilante justice was not an American phenomenon; vigilante justice was also common during the Mexican period. In 1836, Los Angeles, a pueblo of some 1,800 individuals, created the "Defense Committee for Public Safety," better known as a vigilance committee, to punish the antics of outlaws. In San Francisco, vigilance committees operated through the 1850s.

47. For a review of written accounts of the atrocities committed against Indians in California, see Clifford Trafzer and Joel R. Hyer, eds., *"Exterminate Them": Written Accounts of the Murder, Rape, and Enslavement of Native Americans during the California Gold Rush, 1848–1868* (East Lansing: Michigan State University Press, 1999).

48. Newspaper accounts for the 1850s frequently recount a theft or murder in the area, and often point to Indians as potential suspects. The numbers of incidents are too numerous to recount, but an example can be found in the *Los Angeles Star*, 6 March 1852, p. 2, col. 2.

49. *Los Angeles Star*, 31 July 1852, p. 2, col. 4.

50. *Los Angeles Star*, 26 June 1852, p. 2, col. 3.

51. Ibid.

52. In August 1850, the Los Angeles Common Council passed an ordinance stating that when "the city has no work in which to employ the chain gang, the Recorder

shall, by means of notices conspicuously posted, notify the public that such a number of prisoners will be auctioned off to the highest bidder for private service." *Common Council Minutes* (16 August 1850).

53. George Harwood Phillips, "Indians in Los Angeles, 1781–1875: Economic Integration, Social Disintegration," *Pacific Historical Review* 49 (August 1980): 444–45. Those auctioned off were paid one-third of the price they had been sold for, a price which was often paid in alcohol.

54. The two governors were Peter Burnett and John McDougal. Burnett served as California's first governor from 1849 to 1851; he resigned his position citing "certain personal prejudices" (California had been admitted to the union as a free state). Burnett also held the position that blacks should be barred from the state. Prior to arriving in the state, he had served as council for Mormon prophet Joseph Smith before his murder. Following his stint in the governor's chair, Burnett was elevated to the California Supreme Court. McDougal had served as Burnett's lieutenant governor from 1851 to 1852; his brief administration was mired in corruption. Prior to leaving office, he was forced to admit that the 6,000 citizens of the six southern counties had paid $42,000 in property taxes, while the 120,000 in the north only paid $21,000. Reapportionment did not occur until 1933.

55. Woolsey, "Crime and Punishment: Los Angeles County, 1850–1856," 90.

56. Edward Leo Lyman, *San Bernardino: The Rise and Fall of a California Community* (Salt Lake City: Signature Books, 1996), 196. Most of the marauding tribes were identified as coming from the Mojave Desert, or from northern counties.

57. *Los Angeles Star*, 10 July 1852, 14 May 1853, and 8 June 1853.

58. *San Diego Herald*, 7 October 1853.

59. *San Diego Herald*, 13 December 1856.

60. The previous fine for removing an Indian was $50.

61. "An Act amendatory of an Act entitled 'An Act for the Government and Protection of Indians,'" *California Statutes*, 18 April 1860, sections 3 and 7.

62. "Senate Debate, 26 May 1869," *Congressional Globe*, 36th Congress, 1st session, pp. 2365–69.

63. Richard B. Rice, William A. Bullough, and Richard J. Orsi, *The Elusive Eden: A New History of California* (New York: Alfred A. Knopf, 1988), 186.

American Law, 1865–1890

1. R. F. Heizer and M. A. Whipple, *The California Indians: A Source Book* (Los Angeles: University of California Press, 1971), 71.

2. According to Hurtado, "eighty years of relations with Hispanic people led to a statewide decline in Indian population from an estimated 300,000 to about 150,000. Due primarily to disease, the decline took sharpest effect in the mission and rancho districts." Albert L. Hurtado, *Indian Survival on the California Frontier* (New Haven: Yale University Press, 1988), 196–98.

3. The city of Los Angeles had 1,600 people in 1850 and 5,700 by 1870. The city of San Diego in 1870 had a population of 2,700. The city of San Bernardino's population was 3,064 by the start of the 1870s. Additional families lived in the townships throughout the respective counties. *United States Census*, 1850 and 1870.

4. This statute limited the testimony of all non-whites in court, not just Indians.

5. What the state sought was financial support for the Indians, so the financial burden would not fall to the state residents. As time progressed and the federal government solidified its presence in the region, open conflict over which entity, state or federal, had jurisdiction over Indian criminal affairs began to appear.

6. *Report of the Secretary of the Interior*, 39th Congress, 1st session, p. 283: "Their present means of subsistence is precarious, and as they will steal before they will starve, trouble and difficulty will arise which cannot be avoided unless provision is made for their removal or subsistence." By 1876 conditions had not improved, as reported in correspondence between D. A. Dryden, Indian agent, and the commissioner of Indian affairs: he reported Indians living at subsistence levels with little hope for improvement. *Mission Indians of California: Report of William Vandever, United States Indian Inspector* (1876), 8.

7. Kroeber estimates the pre-contact population of Cahuillas at 3,000; Cupenos at 500; Dieguenos/Kamias/Kumeyaays at 3,000; Juanenos at 1,000; Luisenos at 4,000; Serranos at 1,500; Gabrielinos at 5,000; and Chemehuevis at 1,000. A. L. Kroeber, *Handbook of the Indians of California* (Berkeley: California Book Company, 1953), 883.

8. The ability to pass judgment on their Indian charges was not codified into law, but the agents did increasingly assume this activity.

9. Lisbeth Haas, *Conquests and Historical Identities in California, 1769–1936* (Berkeley: University of California Press, 1995), 63.

10. George William Beattie and Helen Pruitt Beattie, *Heritage of the Valley: San Bernardino's First Century* (Oakland: Biobooks, 1951), 421.

11. *United States Statutes*, 36th Congress, 1st session, 18 June 1860.

12. *San Francisco Bulletin*, 6 January 1865. The *Bulletin* reported extensively on the Congressional proceedings due to California's interest in them.

13. Supreme Court of California, Docket 27, California 404.

14. For an extensive discussion of the national issues surrounding Grant's Peace Policy, see Paul Prucha, *The Great Father: The United States Government and the American Indians* (Lincoln: University of Nebraska Press, 1984).

15. Under this executive order, the Luisenos and Kumeyaays would also receive a tiny portion of their original domain. However, because of the size of their reservation, the government would protect it from further Anglo settlement.

16. United States Department of the Interior, Office of Indian Affairs, *Annual Report of the Commissioner of Indian Affairs to the Secretary of the Interior for the year 1886*, E. S. Parker to C. Delano, 13 February 1871.

17. Richard L. Carrico, *Strangers in a Stolen Land: American Indians in San Diego, 1850–1880* (Newcastle, Calif.: Sierra Books, 1987), 84.

18. Several reports from Indian agents lament the lack of a land base for the Indians that would allow the Indians to farm and remain independent from government support. However, while the agents could see the need for a land base, they often did little to pursue the rights of native people to their ancestral lands. By the late 1870s, Indian agents began to support some government intervention to ensure Indians had a permanent land base.

19. Carrico, *Strangers*, 89.

20. Ibid., 78.

21. In large part, the decision to rewrite the state constitution had been prompted by increasing disaffection with the growing strength of corporations within the state—in particular, the railroads that arbitrarily set freight rates, which caused considerable distress to the local farmers because this impeded their ability to ship their produce. During the constitutional debates, it was proposed that many of the lands that had been given to the railroads as incentive to build their lines should be returned to the public domain. This issue was quashed.

22. Land grants were made to individuals and to tribal groups. Therefore, the Luiseno Indians of Temecula claimed their lands through a land patent that had been granted to Pablo Apis, a former chief. According to Florence Shipek, four pueblos for the San Luiseno and Kumeyaay peoples can be found in the existing records, and there are indications that several others existed, including lands at Las Flores, Pala, San Pasqual, and San Dieguito. On the Cuca Rancho in San Diego County, the original land grantee was an Indian of the village; however, one of her heirs evicted the other families from the village between 1879 and 1889. See Florence Shipek, *Pushed into the Rocks: Southern California Indian Land Tenure, 1769–1986* (Lincoln: University of Nebraska Press, 1987).

23. *San Diego Ordinance Against Public Intoxication*, Section 1, 1874. Prior to this, most fines were between one and five dollars.

24. This topic will be discussed in greater detail in the next chapter.

25. Gordon Morris Bakken, *Practicing Law in Frontier California* (Lincoln: University of Nebraska Press, 1991), 100–103.

26. *Guardian* (San Bernardino), 14 May 1870. Because of the absence of courts in the mines of the state, miners developed their own form of summary justice for individuals accused of a crime. These "courts" presumed to act as judge, jury, and executioner in instances where an individual stood accused of a crime. These extralegal proceedings were little more than vigilante justice.

27. *San Diego Union*, 1 February 1873; and *Guardian* (San Bernardino), 18 March 1873.

28. *Coroner's Inquest Reports*, 1870–1880, file 287, 14 June 1875.

29. For examples and discussion of white perceptions of Indians, see Clifford E. Trafzer and Joel R. Hyer, eds., *"Exterminate Them": Written Accounts of the Murder, Rape, and Enslavement of Native Americans during the California Gold Rush* (East Lansing: Michigan State University Press, 1999).

30. *Guardian* (San Bernardino), 21 January 1871.

31. Ibid., 15 March 1873.

32. Ibid., 22 March 1879.

33. Ibid., 11 May 1887.

34. Chatham Helms found himself in court on two other occasions, both incidents involving Native Americans. In August 1877, he accused two Indian men of setting fire to a house with people in it; *People v. Luis Mocha & Juan*, Justice Court of San Diego (Ballena), 7 August 1877. The second incident occurred in January 1887, when he was charged with assaulting an Indian who tried to move around his wagon, which had been abandoned in the middle of the road; *People v. Chatham Helms*, Justice Court of San Diego (Ballena), 5 January 1887. Helm was acquitted.

35. Helen Hunt Jackson, *A Century of Dishonor* (New York: Indian Head Books, 1994), 471.

36. Prucha, *The Great Father*, 216–17.

37. Shipek, *Pushed into the Rocks*, 37.

38. To accelerate the process of dispossession begun by the Indian Homestead Act and the Dawes Act, in 1906 Congress passed the Burke Act, which allowed the twenty-five years where title to the land was to be held in trust to be waived for those Indians who were deemed to be capable of being independent. The individual who made such determinations was the Indian Agent, who very often was someone who supported Anglo efforts to obtain additional lands from the Indians. The result of the Burke Act was the rapid transfer of lands from Indian hands into those of Anglo ranchers and farmers.

39. For a complete discussion of the allotment and homesteads, see Florence Shipek, *Pushed into the Rocks*.

40. The confirmation of citizenship was not an intentional feature of this act. In 1906 the Burke Act clarified that the allottee would not be granted citizenship following the completion of the twenty-five-year trust state.

41. Vine Deloria and Clifford Lytle, *American Indians, American Justice* (Austin: University of Texas Press, 1983), 10. To prompt those Indians reluctant to fully participate in the program by proving up their lands, an amendment to the Dawes Allotment Act was made in 1891. This amendment permitted the secretary of the interior to lease the lands of an allottee who could not "personally and with benefit to himself occupy or improve his allotment or any part thereof."

42. The issue of allotment proved to be very divisive among the tribes of southern California. By the turn of the century, the allotment process was pursued with a vengeance under the administration of Cato Sells (Indian commissioner) and Franklin K. Lane (secretary of the interior), with little regard to whether Indians retained title to their allotments or not. Protest over the forced allotments prompted the creation of one of the first and most pervasive Indian political groups, the Mission Indian Federation. While not immediately successful in preventing the allotment of Indian lands, the federation eventually succeeded in meeting its goals over the tenure of the organization.

43. *Report of the Secretary of the Interior*, vol. 2 (Washington, D.C.: GPO, 1888), 12–13.

44. C. H. Yates, in *Report of the Secretary of the Interior*, vol. 2 (Washington, D.C.: GPO, 1888), lxx.

45. Legal challenges continued despite previous judgments in favor of the Indians. In 1901 the United States Supreme Court ruled that the Cupas had lost their claim to their ancestral lands because they had neglected to present their claim before the land commission—this despite the Court's acknowledgment that the land commission had actually been in error, as they had not pursued the duties assigned to them. The end result, however, was the same: Indians lost land and whites took it.

46. State of California, *An Act for the Relief of the Mission Indians in the State of California* (Sacramento: GPO, 12 January 1891).

47. Unfortunately, this transition from local jurisdiction to the agent also meant that the agent could impose his own rules of conduct on the reservation.

48. *Riverside Press* (Riverside), 3 October 1889.

49. *San Jacinto Register* (Riverside), 14 November 1889.

50. Cave Couts was accused in the press several times of misappropriating funds for the Indians, and of having caused the deaths of several Indians. See the *San Diego Herald*, 14 July 1855; and *Report on the Mission Indians*, House Executive Document 76, 34th Congress, 3rd session, 1856. Redick McKee billed the government exorbitant fees for cattle owned by his son; see Hurtado, *Indian Survival*, 140. Unfortunately, these are only two examples of the corruption of Indian agents.

51. *United States Census*, 1880 and 1890.

52. *United States Census*, 1870 and 1880.

53. *United States Census*, 1890.

Native American Law

1. According to Nisenan tradition, it was not Marshall but one of the Indians who accompanied him on his search who found the gold nugget that would spark the gold rush. The Nisenan are one of three northern California tribes that are part of the larger Maidu tribal group.

2. The Cupenos are one of the smallest tribes in southern California, but held the water-rich territory from Lake Henshaw in the west to Hot Springs Mountain in the east. To the south, their territory extended to the San Ysidro Creek, and in the north to the San Luis Rey River.

3. The Luisenos have traditionally been associated with the southern Santa Ana Mountains, and their territory extended southward to beyond the San Luis Rey River and eastward to Lake Elsinore in the north and Palomar Mountain in the south. They are also known as the Quechlas.

4. The Gabrielinos occupied territory spreading southward from the Santa Monica Mountains to the Santa Ana Mountains, and eastward to the San Bernardino

Mountains. They occupied the coastal range along the coast, as well as several islands off the southern California coast.

5. The Cahuilla are one of the largest Native American groups in California. Because of this distinction they are often divided into three divisions: the Desert Cahuilla, the Mountain Cahuilla and the Western Cahuilla. The Cahuillas occupied territory from the San Bernardino Mountains in the north to the Chocolate Mountains in the south. In the east they held territory from the Salton Sea to the San Gorgonio Mountains and in the west held lands from Anza Borrego to the San Jacinto Plain.

6. The Serranos are associated with territory that stretches eastward from the Cajon Pass into the Mojave Desert. In the southeast they reached as far as modern-day Palm Springs, and in the north as far as the Yucaipa Valley.

7. The Chemehuevi people primarily occupied land stretching from San Bernardino into the Mojave Desert.

8. The Kumeyaays are also known in earlier literature as the Dieguenos, and are divided into two bands, the Tipai and Ipai. The Ipai primarily occupied the region to the north of the Mexican/American border. The Kumeyaays occupied territory south of the San Luis Rey River along the coast to Ensenada in Mexico. In the east, their territory stretched as far as the Sand Hills.

9. As with the black population in the American South, Indians were not taught to read by the mission fathers out of fear that an educated peon class would result in problems.

10. *Los Angeles Star*, 21 February 1852, p. 2, col. 2. In Hugo Reid's letters to the *Los Angeles Star*, he reports several times that tribe members could recall a few words, but that "the oldest now alive confess themselves ignorant of their meaning."

11. *Los Angeles Star*, 28 February 1852, p. 2, col. 3.

12. *Los Angeles Star*, 26 June 1852, p. 2, col. 3.

13. Joel R. Hyer, *We Are Not Savages: Native Americans in Southern California and the Pala Reservation, 1840–1920* (East Lansing: University of Michigan Press, 2001), 29.

14. *Los Angeles Star*, 2 October 1858, p. 2, col. 1.

15. Hubert Howe Bancroft, *History of California, 1860–1890* (Santa Barbara, Calif.: Wallace Hebberd, 1870), 407.

16. Florence Connelly Shipek, *Pushed into the Rocks: Southern California Indian Land Tenure, 1769–1986* (Lincoln: University of Nebraska Press, 1987), 26.

17. Ibid., 21.

18. Ibid., 28.

19. Hyer, *We Are Not Savages*, 33.

20. *Los Angeles Star*, 6 March 1858, p. 3, col. 1.

21. The Kumeyaays/Dieguenos also refer to this individual as *kwaaypaay*.

22. A. L. Kroeber, "Preliminary Sketch of the Mohave Indians," *American Anthropologist* 14, no. 2 (1902): 276–85.

23. Bruce W. Miller, *The Gabrielino* (Los Osos, Calif.: Sand River Press, 1991), 22.

24. Harry C. James, *The Cahuilla Indians* (Banning, Calif.: Malki Museum Press, 1960), 51.

25. *Los Angeles Star*, 16 August 1851, p. 2, col. 1.

26. *Act for the Government and Protection of Indians*, 22 April 1850, section 9.

27. *Los Angeles Star*, 3 July 1858, p. 2, col. 4.

28. Juan Antonio served as a colorful and powerful leader of the Cahuilla people in the 1850s. When a Cupeno captain, Antonio Garra, led a revolt against Anglo incursion in 1851, Juan Antonio was responsible for his capture and eventual release to the authorities.

29. Benjamin Hayes, letter to Senator David R. Atchison, 14 January 1853, Hayes Scrapbooks, Bancroft Library, California.

30. Geronimo Boscana, *Chinigchinich*, trans. Alfred Robinson (Banning, Calif.: Malki Museum, 1978), 23.

31. *Los Angeles Star*, 20 March 1852, p. 2, col. 2.

32. *Guardian* (San Bernardino), 14 October 1871, p. 2, col. 2.

33. *Guardian* (San Bernardino), 18 February 1873, p. 2, col. 1.

34. John Walton Caughey, *The Indians of Southern California in 1852: The B. D. Wilson Report and a Selection of Contemporary Comment* (Lincoln: University of Nebraska Press, 1995), 29.

35. Bancroft's works were not limited to California, but were very expansive and included the history of Mexico, the United States, and the Indians of the nation.

36. Hubert Howe Bancroft, *Native Races*, vol. 1, *Wild Tribes* (San Francisco: A. L. Bancroft and Co., 1883), 409. .

37. Lora L. Cline, *Just Before Sunset* (Jacumba, Calif.: J and L Enterprises, 1984), 58.

38. Caughey, *Indians of Southern California*, 10.

39. Florence Shipek, ed., *The Autobiography of Delfina Cuero: A Diegueno Indian* (Los Angeles: Dawson's Book Shop, 1968), 41.

40. Bancroft, *Native Races*, 1:414.

41. Caughey, *Indians of Southern California*, 31.

42. *Los Angeles Star*, 21 February 1852, p. 2, col. 1.

43. *Los Angeles Star*, 8 November 1851, p. 2, col. 1; *Los Angeles Star*, 17 February 1852, p. 2, col. 1.

44. *Los Angeles Star*, 17 February 1852, p. 2, col. 1.

45. *Los Angeles Star*, 30 October 1852, p. 2, col. 1.

46. *Los Angeles Star*, 26 June 1852, p. 2, col. 3.

47. *Los Angeles Star*, 6 March 1852, p. 2, col. 3.

48. Lowell John Bean, *Mukat's People: The Cahuilla Indians of Southern California* (Berkeley: University of California Press, 1972), 121.

49. Ibid., 85–86.

50. Ibid., 120–21.

51. *Los Angeles Star*, 28 February 1852, p. 2, col. 3.

52. Bancroft, *Native Races*, 1:417.

53. Bean, *Mukat's People*, 121.

54. Several works discuss aspects of the legal traditions of the Indians of southern California. For further information, see Joel R. Hyer, *We Are Not Savages*; Florence

Shipek, *Pushed into the Rocks*; Florence Shipek, *The Autobiography of Delfina Cuero*; Hugo Reid's letters to the *Los Angeles Star*; or the Smithsonian Institution's *Handbook of North American Indians*.

55. Herbert Eugene Bolton, *Spanish Exploration of the Southwest* (New York: Scribner's, 1908), 85.

56. Shipek, *The Autobiography of Delfina Cuero*, 14.

57. *Los Angeles Star*, 6 March 1852, p. 2, col. 3.

58. Lucille Hooper, "The Cahuilla Indians," *University of California Publications* 16, no. 6 (1920): 354.

59. Bancroft, *Native Races*, 1:412.

60. Cline, *Just Before Sunset*, 70.

61. Bancroft, *Native Races*, 1:407.

62. *Riverside Press*, 26 October 1878, p. 4, col. 1.

63. Bean, *Mukat's People*, 121.

64. Marriage taboos were stringently enforced among the tribes in southern California. Generally, individuals wishing to marry needed to be at least five generations removed before they could consider the possibility. For many tribes, this rule is reinforced in their language, with first, second, third, and fourth cousins often calling each other brother or sister.

65. *Los Angeles Star*, 6 March 1852, p. 2, col. 3.

66. *Los Angeles Star*, 14 October 1871, p. 2, col. 2.

67. Cline, *Just Before Sunset*, 57–58.

68. Bancroft, *Native Races*, 1:409.

69. In Numbers 35–36, the Bible discusses cities of refuge. These towns were places where an individual who accidentally murdered another could flee and be granted sanctuary. The intent of the cities of refuge was to allay the customary blood feud that is common within nomadic or tribal societies. It is most likely that Bancroft, who was often only repeating information provided by others, actually got this information from a text that had been written by Father Geronimo Boscana entitled *Chinigchinich*, which is the name of the Gabrielino deity. Boscana could have been engaging in speculation, or had extended his knowledge of ancient societies to accommodate his sympathy with traditional Indian society.

70. *Los Angeles Star*, 13 November 1858, p. 2, col. 2.

71. The game of *peon*, according to Joel Hyer, involved two teams of four. On one team, each player was given a white and a dark game piece, which were attached to their wrists by a cord. These players then held a blanket in their teeth to conceal their hands. With their hands and arms concealed behind the blanket, these players then moved the stones from one wrist to the other behind the blanket, all the while swaying and moving in such a way that they distracted the other team, hoping to confuse them regarding which color game piece was held on which wrist. To add to the confusion, spectators shouted encouragement or heckled the opposition. When the first team was certain it had succeeded in confusing the opposing team, they would conceal the game pieces in their hands, fold their arms over their chests, and drop the blanket. It was now

up to the other team to accurately guess which hand held the white game piece. Points were granted according to accuracy. The game frequently went on for hours.

72. *Scrapbook of Benjamin Hayes*, vol. 38, Bancroft Library, University of California, Berkeley.

73. *Guardian* (San Bernardino), 18 February 1873, p. 2, col. 1.

74. *Guardian* (San Bernardino), 8 March 1873, p. 3, col. 1.

75. *Los Angeles Star*, 6 March 1852, p. 2, col. 3.

76. Ibid.

77. Ibid.

Justice and Municipal Courts

1. The *justices* that occupied the bench in the lower courts were locally appointed officials who had no legal training. They are not to be confused with the *judges* who occupied the bench in the upper courts. The upper courts will be discussed in the next chapter.

2. John Stanley, "Bearers of the Burden: Justices of the Peace, Their Courts and the Law in Orange County, California, 1870–1907," *Western Legal History* 5, no. 1 (1992): 35.

3. Ibid., 37.

4. Ronald C. Woolsey, "Crime and Punishment: Los Angeles County, 1850–1856," *Southern California Quarterly* 61, no. 1 (1979): 79.

5. *United States Census*, 1850.

6. Horace Bell, *Reminiscences of a Ranger: Early Times in Southern California* (Norman: University of Oklahoma Press, 1999), 2.

7. C. Alan Hutchinson, "The Mexican Government and the Mission Indians of Upper California, 1821–1835," *The Americas* 21 (April 1965): 338.

8. Charles Hughes, "The Decline of the Californios: The Case of San Diego, 1846–1856," *Journal of San Diego History* 21, no. 4 (1975). For a counter-opinion on the status of the Californios in the state, see Leonard Pitt, *The Decline of the Californios: A Social History of the Spanish-Speaking Californians, 1846–1890* (Berkeley: University of California Press, 1966).

9. California Land Claims, nos. 368, 253, and 254.

10. The number of non-Hispanic recipients may be higher, as many individuals such as Benjamin Wilson adopted Hispanic names during their tenure in the region prior to the transition of the state to American control.

11. Bakken, *Practicing Law in Frontier California* (Lincoln: University of Nebraska Press, 1991), 3.

12. David J. Langum, *Law and Community on the Mexican California Frontier: Anglo-American Expatriates and the Clash of Legal Traditions, 1821–1846* (Norman: University of Oklahoma Press, 1987), 267.

13. California State Constitution, 1849, Article 5, section 19.

14. *An Act for the Government and Protection of Indians*, 22 April 1850, section 1.

15. *An Act for the Government and Protection of Indians*, 22 April 1850, section 8.

16. "Report of the Treasurer of Los Angeles County, from October 1st 1857 to February 1st 1858," *Los Angeles Star*, 13 February 1858, p 2, cols. 4 and 5).

17. Petty larceny as defined by the state constitution included all crimes of theft where the value of the property was less than $100.

18. *California Statutes*, 1 April 1870.

19. Theft where the value of the property exceeded $100.

20. Donald R. Beatty, "History of the Legal Status of the American Indian" (master's thesis, University of California, 1957), 21.

21. For a detailed description of the justices in Orange County (which remained part of Los Angeles County until 1889), see John J. Stanley, "Bearers of the Burden: Justices of the Peace, Their Courts and the Law in Orange County, California, 1870–1907," *Western Legal History* 5, no. 1 (1992).

22. The relationship between the founding fathers of many local communities and their financial interests in the expansion of the communities is best exemplified by the founding of the city of Riverside in 1870. Several of the city's most prominent members, including Dr. James P. Greves, John W. North, and Dr. K. D. Shugart, who reportedly planted the first orange tree in the region, were involved in the scheme to draw people to the new city, sell subscriptions to the land, and make a profit as the colony expanded.

23. This fact may account for why so few records from the middle of the nineteenth century exist. The informality of the proceedings would also have encouraged laxity in keeping records.

24. Bell, *Reminiscences of a Ranger*, 38.

25. Edward Leo Lyman, *San Bernardino: The Rise and Fall of a California Community* (Salt Lake City: Signature Books, 1996), 196–97.

26. Barton's murderer was reported to have been Andres Fontes, who a few years earlier had intervened on behalf of Barton's common-law Indian spouse when he tried to beat her in an attempt to force her to return to him. Fontes found himself in court a few days later, convicted of a felony and sent to San Quentin. See Horace Bell, *Reminiscences of a Ranger*, 401–6.

27. Ron Woolsey, "Pioneer Views and Frontier Themes," *Southern California Quarterly* 702, no. 3 (1990): 256.

28. George Harwood Phillips, "Indians in Los Angeles, 1781–1875: Economic Integration, Social Disintegration," *Pacific Historical Review* 49 (August 1980): n. 59.

29. *San Quentin Prison Registers, 1851–1867*. San Diego sent two men, James Lorby and William Harris, to San Quentin on 1 September 1852; both had been charged with grand larceny. In contrast, Los Angeles County sent four men to San Quentin for murder between 1853 and 1854: Jose Rodriguez, Juan Moran, Juan Chapo (Indian), and Lenner Baldez. Two other men, Anastacio Moreno and Henry King, were sent to the prison for grand larceny during the same time period, and lastly Jose Cerbio Bucieus was sentenced to San Quentin for one year in 1854 for perjury.

30. Woolsey, "Crime and Punishment," 83.

31. *In re Manuel*, San Bernardino Court of Sessions, 8 October 1862.

32. Tom Patterson, *A Colony for California*, 2nd ed. (Riverside, Calif.: Riverside Museum Press, 1996), 191.

33. *People v. Jose Antonio*, County Court of Los Angeles, Case 11, 3 June 1872. It is not certain if this is the same Juan Antonio who had been harassed by the police and jailed for being near the Los Angeles jail. The distance between Los Angeles and Anaheim is approximately thirty-five miles.

34. *People v. Jose*, San Diego Court of Sessions, 1 August 1851.

35. *United States Census*, 1860.

36. *United States Census*, 1870 and 1880.

37. This number was undoubtedly much higher. However, since most Indians did not live in the same towns as whites, their populations can only be estimated. Additionally, census takers had little incentive to accurately record the number of Indians in a given area since Indians neither paid taxes nor were eligible to vote.

38. Again, the census numbers were most likely to be an inaccurate count of the total native population in the area; however, the numbers provided show evidence of a demographic shift among the native population.

39. The number of available cases in the justice courts is limited, and it is highly probable that the actual occurrence of Indian cases before the courts was considerably higher. News accounts of the era would support this contention; however, only surviving judicial records were surveyed for this paper.

40. James J. Yoch, *On the Golden Shore: Phineas Banning in Southern California, 1851–1885* (Wilmington Calif.: Banning Residence Museum, 2002), 61.

41. William Deverell, *Railroad Crossing: Californians and the Railroad, 1850–1910* (Berkeley: University of California Press, 1994), 18.

42. Deverell, *Railroad Crossing*, 27–46. The subsidies that had been granted by the state legislature would eventually be revoked in 1879 when California rewrote its state constitution.

43. D. M. Berry to Thomas B. Elliott, 18 September 1873, Thomas Balch Elliott Papers, Huntington Library.

44. For a further discussion of the impact of the railroad on the development of communities and its impact on Native Americans in the Southwest, see Clifford E. Trafzer, *Frontier Crossing of the Far Southwest* (Wichita: Western Heritage Books, 1980).

45. Prior to the establishment of the executive-order reservations in the mid-1870s, Indians continued to live on *rancherias* and in pueblos. However, their claim to the land was not recognized, and Americans who claimed the land as part of the public domain moved several bands off their lands during the 1870s. Whereas the federal presence in the region had been limited prior to the establishment of these reservations, it increased steadily during the last quarter of the nineteenth century. This included the establishment of a southern federal district court in 1880.

46. *People v. Maria*, San Bernardino Justice Court, Case 361, 21 April 1873. The victim in the case had been drinking and gambling in a local saloon. He apparently passed out sometime during the night, and when he awoke, realized his money and hat

had disappeared. Maria admitted to taking the hat while he was out, but maintained that he had gambled away his money. Other witnesses corroborated her story.

47. Bail amounts for all three counties ranged from five hundred to one thousand dollars.

48. Bell, *Reminiscences of a Ranger*, 115.

49. *People v. Jose*, San Diego Justice Court, 27 January 1873.

50. *People v. Ignacious*, San Diego Justice Court, 14 April 1880.

51. *People v. Marcelino*, San Diego Justice Court, Case 180, 23 June 1881.

52. Most Indians accused of livestock theft stole because they were starving and had no other options available. This idea will be discussed in more detail later in the chapter.

53. *People v. Manuel Isidro & Pelon Arguera*, Los Angeles Justice Court, Case 91, 5 June 1871; *People v. Santiago*, Los Angeles Justice Court, Case 51, 28 October 1867; *People v. Jose Maria*, Los Angeles Court of Sessions, Case 242, 6 March 1861.

54. *People v. Jose*, Los Angeles Justice Court, Case 616, 16 March 1864.

55. *People v. Marquis*, Los Angeles Justice Court, Case 122, 10 October 1872; and *People v. Santos Capistian & Ignacio Flores*, Los Angeles Justice Court, Case 82, 8 January 1872.

56. *People v. Ursula*, San Diego Justice Court, Case 230, 2 March 1851.

57. *People v. Carlos & Tomas*, San Diego Justice Court, Case 721, July 1885. They stood accused of stealing a violin from the home of a white woman.

58. *People v. Santos Silvas*, Los Angeles County Court, Case 433, 22 March 1878.

59. *People v. Jose*, San Bernardino Justice Court, 21 October 1864; and *People v. Juan*, San Bernardino Justice Court, 11 February 1865.

60. *People v. James Maddison*, San Bernardino Justice Court, Cases 332 and 346 (1865).

61. *People v. James Marshall*, San Bernardino Court of Sessions, Case 468, 24 July 1867.

62. Sporadic records do exist for Los Angeles and San Diego counties. Most cases for nuisance behavior in these counties were heard in the police courts, and the records have not been preserved. Only cases involving Anglo men who were associated with Indians during the time they were drunk in public have survived. An example would be *People v. James Connors and Two Indian Women*, San Diego Justice Court, 25 February 1874.

63. *People v. Juan & Jesus*, San Bernardino Justice Court, 16 June 1873. Both were fined five dollars for their actions, but Juan was discharged from jail early because of his inability to work. *People v. Old Pablo*, San Bernardino Recorder's Court, 18 February 1877. Pablo was only fined one dollar for being drunk in public. Earlier, he had been charged and released on his own recognizance. *People v. Old Martin*, San Bernardino Justice Court, 24 May 1875. Old Martin was fined one dollar for being drunk in public while the two other men arrested with him were fined three dollars. Anglo men identified as being old received no discounted fines.

64. *Guardian* (San Bernardino), 25 July 1871, p. 3, col. 1.

65. San Bernardino became a separate county in 1853.

66. W. W. Robinson, *The Story of San Bernardino County* (San Bernardino: Pioneer Title Insurance Co., 1958), 335–45.

67. The missions had an extensive history of planting citrus and fruit crops, although the varieties attempted by the mission fathers proved to be of poor quality. The question over who planted the first navel orange in the region has proven to be fraught with controversy. It appears that Dr. Shugart of Riverside planted an orange tree in 1871, while Mrs. Tibbets can be credited with the planting of the navel orange. For the city of Riverside, the issue is not taken lightly in light of the importance of the citrus industry in ensuring the growth of the city.

68. For a discussion on the growing importance of the citrus industry in southern California after 1870, see Hubert Howe Bancroft, *History of California, 1860–1890* (Santa Barbara, Calif.: Wallace Hebberd, 1870), chap. 3.

69. There are rare references to Anglo men being sentenced to "hard labor" in the county jails. However, this appears to be the exception, not the rule.

70. *Guardian* (San Bernardino), 1 March 1873, p. 3, col. 1; and 16 October 1869, p. 3, col. 1.

71. There are rare cases in the court documents where Indians were arrested and charged with selling liquor to Indians. Since most of these individuals were women, it is possible they were reselling the alcohol in order to supplement their meager incomes or that alcohol was consumed while they were engaged in prostitution.

72. Bell, *Reminiscences of a Ranger*, 35.

73. *An Act for the Government and Protection of Indians*, 22 April 1850, Section 15.

74. *People v. Francis Stone*, San Diego Court of Sessions, 10 October 1855; Stone was fined $100. *People v. Louis K. Thompson*, San Diego Justice Court, 14 February 1876; Thompson's guilt but not his sentence was recorded.

75. *People v. Jose*, San Diego Court of Sessions, 1 August 1851; Jose received a $500 fine. *People v. Tomas*, San Diego Court of Sessions, 29 September 1857; Tomas was sentenced to an undisclosed term in prison. *People v. Francisco & Mariano*, San Diego Court of Sessions, 17 October 1857; Francisco received a one-year sentence while Mariano was sentenced to two years in prison.

76. *People v. Salvador*, San Diego Justice Court, 25 June 1881; *People v. Salvador*, San Diego Justice Court, 29 June 1881; *People v. Juan Pine*, San Diego Justice Court, 21 June 1882; and *People v. Pilar*, San Diego Justice Court, 25 September 1882.

77. *People v. Fernando*, Los Angeles Justice Court, Case 40, 6 February 1866; Fernando was fined five dollars. *People v. Jose Maria*, Los Angeles Justice Court, Case 283, 13 October 1862; Jose Maria was sentenced to one year in prison.

78. *People v. Desidero*, Los Angeles Justice Court, Case 612, 22 March 1864.

79. *People v. Ygnacio Albas*, Los Angeles Justice Court, Case 245, 17 May 1861.

80. *People v. Bonifacio Lugo*, Los Angeles Justice Court, Case 318, 14 May 1889.

81. Despite the traditional twelve-man jury that dominates our current judicial system, juries in the nineteenth century often comprised between six and twelve men.

82. These would include charges against property such as larceny or theft, or crimes against another person such as assault. Nuisance crimes would be limited to drunk-in-public charges or disturbing the peace.

83. Stanley, "Bearers of the Burden."

84. *Los Angeles Star*, 18 January 1855, and 2 October 1858; *Guardian* (San Bernardino), 14 October 1871, and 3 February 1872.

County and District Courts

1. *California State Constitution*, 1849, Article VI, section 6.

2. *An Act for the Government and Protection of Indians*, 22 April 1850, section 1.

3. *An Act amendatory of an Act entitled "An Act for the Government and Protection of Indians,"* 18 April 1860, section 3.

4. *California State Constitution*, Article VI, sections 11 and 16.

5. Richard Maxwell Brown, *No Duty to Retreat: Violence and Values in American History and Society* (Norman: University of Oklahoma Press, 1991).

6. William G. Robbins, *Colony and Empire: The Capitalistic Transformation of the American West* (Lawrence: University of Kansas Press, 1994), 31.

7. *Act to Prevent Sale of Firearms and Ammunition to Indians*, California Statutes, 24 March 1854. The sale of weapons or ammunition was considered a misdemeanor offense and could result in a fine of between $25 and $500, and/or one to six months in jail. Clearly these parameters exceeded the authority of the justice courts and would have been heard in the county and district courts. However, no cases involving individuals so charged have been located.

8. William H. Brewer, *Up and Down California in 1860–1864: The Journal of William H. Brewer* (Berkeley: University of California Press, 1974), 14.

9. Ibid., 39.

10. The following discussion is based primarily on the surviving records for the district and county courts. According to newspaper and personal accounts from the early years of the southern California communities, the murder rate was considerably higher. When possible these reports are addressed; however, the authorities did not investigate most murders involving Indians, and therefore any issues with the Indians and the courts were rendered moot.

11. Bell, *Reminiscences of a Ranger*, viii.

12. *Los Angeles Star*, 10 July 1852, p. 2, col. 3; *Los Angeles Star*, 23 October 1852, p. 2, col. 2; and *Los Angeles Star*, 21 February 1852, p. 2, col. 1. *San Quentin Prison Registers*, 1851–1867.

13. The vigilance committee of Los Angeles, the extrajudiciary arm of the law in southern California, was reported to have hung several individuals for various crimes. However, their records and the incidence of private justice at times defies confirmation, as the group had a variable population and did not keep records.

14. *Los Angeles Star*, 25 May 1861, p. 2, col. 2.

15. Assuming the seven individuals were not residents of the county, that would leave only six residents of San Bernardino County as dying from either violence or accident. Indians, of course, had been residents of the county for centuries.

16. *Guardian* (San Bernardino), 6 December 1873, p. 3, col. 3.

17. *Los Angeles Star*, 20 March 1858, p. 2, col. 2.

18. *Los Angeles Star*, 23 October 1858, p. 2, col. 2.

19. Bell, *Reminiscences of a Ranger*, 83.

20. *Los Angeles Star*, 26 March 1859, p. 2, col. 2.

21. *People v. Michael G. Lachenias*, Los Angeles District Court, 14 November 1866. Lachenias's case is discussed further in the text.

22. *Act for the Government and Protection of Indians*, 22 April 1850, section 6.

23. *People v. Michael G. Lachenias*, Los Angeles District Court, 14 November 1866, testimony of Father Duran.

24. Ibid., testimony of Alex Remdan.

25. Lachenias was suspected in another murder in Los Angeles County. In February 1866, he turned himself in to the sheriff of the county after learning that he was a suspect in the death of Henry Delaval, who had died in Los Angeles County in 1862. Lachenias was tried in district court but found not guilty of Delaval's murder. *People v. Michael G. Lachenias*, Los Angeles District Court, Case 61, 2 February 1866; and *Los Angeles Star*, 23 February 1866, p. 2, col. 1. Lachenias continued to appear in the local courts until 1870, when he was brought before the county court in Los Angeles and convicted of malicious mischief. Apparently Lachenias had stolen water from a neighbor. He was found guilty and fined $43. *People v. Lachenias,* Los Angeles County Court, Case 756, 5 July 1870.

26. *Act for the Government and Protection of Indians*, 22 April 1850, section 3.

27. *People v. Michael G. Lachenias*, Los Angeles District Court, Case 59, 14 November 1866.

28. *People v. Jose Domingo & Juan Napomecente*, Los Angeles District Court, Case 50, 5 May 1865. Juan Napomecente was acquitted of the murder during the trial proceedings. Because Domingo could not be convicted solely on the testimony of an Indian, several of the prosecution witnesses were Anglos.

29. *People v. Manuel (an Indian)*, Los Angeles District Court, Case 116, 26 March 1876. Manuel received a sentence of ten years for the murder of Nicolassa. *People v. Fernando & Juan (Indians)*, Los Angeles District Court, Case 40, 19 June 1863. Juan received a sentence of three years in state prison for the murder of Miguel. Fernando's sentence was not recorded. *People v. Jose*, Los Angeles District Court, Case 7, 6 May 1869. Jose received ten years for the murder of an Indian named Pedro. *People v. Manuel Gonzales (Indian)*, Los Angeles District Court, Case 88, 20 November 1871. Gonzales received thirteen years for the murder of Antonio.

30. *People v. Jose*, Los Angeles District Court, Case 48, 17 November 1864.

31. *People v. Jesus Venegas*, Los Angeles District Court, Case 89, 24 November 1871.

32. *People v. Prospero*, San Bernardino District Court, Case 154, 14 September 1872. Prospero received a twenty-year sentence. *People v. Andreas*, San Bernardino District Court, 20 June 1862. Andreas was condemned to death.

33. *People v. Francisco*, San Bernardino Superior Court, Case 303, 12 December 1881. The district attorney requested the case be dismissed "for the reason that it is impossible to obtain witnesses to prove the actual killing or death of the person alleged to have been murdered." The case against Francisco was not an isolated incident in San Bernardino: on 14 March 1871, the *Guardian* reported two Indians had been examined in Justice Wagner's court on suspicion of murder. Each was discharged when the court admitted there "was no evidence" against them.

34. *People v. Shettler*, San Bernardino District Court, Case 183, 18 November 1872.

35. *People v. Prospero*, San Bernardino Superior Court, Case 154, 14 September 1872. Prospero appealed his case to the state supreme court (Case 3392), but failed to have his conviction overturned. The witness in the case against Prospero was an Indian woman named Julia.

36. Marjorie Tisdale Wolcott, *Pioneer Notes From the Diaries of Judge Benjamin Hayes, 1849–1875* (Los Angeles: McBride Publishing Co., 1929), 184–85.

37. Lawrence Friedman, *A History of American Law*, 2nd ed. (New York: Touchstone Books, 1985), 590–91.

38. *People v. Andronico Lopez*, San Diego Superior Court, Cases 375 and 399, 1 November 1882. Juan Pino was a ten-year-old Indian boy who lived "in the hills" and whose testimony was crucial to Lopez's conviction for the killing of Mr. Aguler. Lopez was sentenced to ten years in state prison.

39. Despite the feminine name, the court documents indicate Maria was a man.

40. *People v. Antonio Bertrand*, San Diego Superior Court, Case 2279, 12 October 1888.

41. *People v. Manteca*, San Diego Justice Court, 14 January 1853.

42. Several other cases of Anglo men presenting themselves before the courts having admitted to shooting or killing Native Americans are preserved in the records.

43. This is not to suggest that more assault cases were not presented before the courts, only that those cases have not been preserved.

44. *People v. Francisco*, San Diego Superior Court, Case 556, 5 April 1884.

45. *People v. Salvador*, Los Angeles County Court, Case 181, 9 September 1881.

46. *People v. Salvador*, San Diego Justice Court, 29 June 1881.

47. Friedman, *History of American Law*, 588.

48. *People v. Stanislado Setia*, San Diego Superior Court, Case 166, 21 May 1881.

49. *People v. Jose Maria*, Los Angeles County Court, 1 March 1872. Also see 21 May 1872 and 26 September 1871. Jose Maria appeared to be a violent career criminal. Four separate cases for assault show him as the accused, as do two for grand larceny. His criminal career spans from 1861 to 1872, when he was incarcerated for assault and sent to San Quentin. Maria did return to Los Angeles after he served his time, but afterward lived a much quieter life. He appears in court documents as a witness in the 1880s.

50. In the case of *People v. Polinares*, Los Angeles County Court, Case 711, 1 February 1869, Polinares assaulted Peter Boffer and Peter Maumuo after they had accused him of stealing.

51. *People v. Paulino & Pedrito*, San Bernardino County Court, Case 638, 10 September 1879.

52. *People v. Paulino & Pedrito*, San Bernardino County Court, Case 638, 10 September 1879.

53. *People v. Santiago*, San Bernardino County Court, 7 March 1864.

54. *People v. Charles Martin*, San Bernardino County Court, Case 358, 28 May 1873. The tale of Charles Martin is unique and at no point loses the flavor of the bizarre. Martin was frequently associated with robberies, cattle rustling, assault, and murder throughout his life. Despite this, he only served one five-year stretch in San Quentin in 1877 for assault with intent to commit robbery. In 1917 Martin was appointed police chief of the city of San Bernardino in spite of the fact that he continued to be associated with crime in the area. After two months, an outraged citizenry forced him to resign his post. Charles Martin died in 1927.

55. Alfred L. Kroeber, *Handbook of the Indians of California* (New York: Dover Publications, 1976).

56. Hugo Reid, *The Indians of Los Angeles: Hugo Reid's Letter of 1852*, edited and annotated by Robert Heizer (Los Angeles: Southwest Museum, 1968), 15–16.

57. Burglary involves entering a dwelling or building to steal, while theft involves stealing valuables from a person.

58. Grand larceny was considered when the value of the property exceeded $200.

59. *People v. Antonio Argnello*, San Diego Superior Court, Case 587, July 1884.

60. *People v. Antonio*, San Diego Superior Court, Case 570, 25 May 1884. *People v. Joaquin Eslava*, San Diego Superior Court, 20 September 1889. *People v. Charley, Jose Cabrillo & Bruno Subrino*, San Diego Superior Court, 12 November 1883; Charley received one year, Cabrillo received two years, and Subrino received ten years.

61. *People v. Juan*, San Diego District Court, 1871.

62. *People v. Santos Silvas*, Los Angeles County Court, Case 433, 22 March 1878.

63. *People v. Fred*, San Diego Superior Court, Case 32, 13 April 1880.

64. The tendency for Indians to use traditional names versus anglicized names, while infrequent, began to appear in the court records in the mid-1880s. In the federal cases that were heard from the 1890s on in southern California, this tendency was more pronounced. Federal cases are not discussed in this study.

65. *People v. Chilchil & Asketo*, San Diego Superior Court, 27 June 1884.

66. *People v. Carlos Dgero*, San Diego County Court, 19 August 1885.

67. *People v. Leleh*, San Bernardino Superior Court, Cases 23, 24, 34, 35, and 36, 18 February 1880.

68. *People v. Santiago*, San Bernardino County Court, 10 March 1864.

69. *People v. Maria*, San Bernardino Superior Court, Case 10, 21 April 1873.

70. *People v. John Doe Indian*, San Bernardino Superior Court, Case 66, 29 May 1880; John Doe was acquitted of grand larceny. *People v. Jose Domingo*, San Bernardino Superior Court, Case 27, 13 February 1880; Domingo was charged with burglary, but discharged by the court after the jury could not agree on whether to convict him.

People v. Jose, San Bernardino County Court, 28 November 1864; Jose was convicted of burglary and received one year in prison.

71. *People v. Gabriel*, Los Angeles County Court, Case 689, 21 January 1868.

Native Women and the Law

1. For a greater discussion of the role of women in traditional native societies, see John Lowell Bean, *Mukat's People: The Cahuilla Indians of Southern California* (Los Angeles: University of California Press, 1974); Delfina Cuero, *The Autobiography of Delfina Cuero: A Diegueno Indian* (Los Angeles: Dawson's Book Shop, 1968); and Rudy Modesto and Guy Mount, *Not For Innocent Ears: Spiritual Traditions of a Desert Cahuilla Medicine Woman* (Angeles Oaks: Sweetlight Books, 1980).

2. For an excellent discussion on the impact of gender in the development of California, see Albert L. Hurtado, *Intimate Frontiers: Sex, Gender, and Culture in Old California* (Albuquerque: University of New Mexico Press, 1999).

3. Sherburne F. Cook, *The Conflict Between the California Indian and White Civilization* (Berkeley: University of California Press, 1943), 21: 86–87.

4. U.S. Department of the Interior, Office of Indian Affairs, *Annual Report of the Commissioner of Indian Affairs for 1870*.

5. *Los Angles Daily Times*, 15 December 1881; and *People v. Theodora Bofanta*, Justice Court of Colton, 29 July 1889.

6. *Los Angeles Daily Star*, 21 September 1871, p. 2, col. 4.

7. *People v. John Bleeker*, Justice Court of San Diego, 19 December 1851.

8. *People v. Robert Owens*, Los Angeles County Court, Case 748, 27 July 1870.

9. *Guardian* (San Bernardino), 16 January 1875.

10. *Guardian* (San Bernardino), 10 December 1870. It appears "John Barleycorn" was a euphemism for a young man. Barleycorn was once used as a unit of measure to indicate approximately one-third of an inch. A measurement that reflected the approximate length of a grain of barley.

11. Barton was killed in an ambush in 1858, while Pyburn was killed in 1871.

12. *Los Angeles Star*, 26 June 1852.

13. *San Diego Herald*, 17 April 1852 and 6 August 1853.

14. *Guardian* (San Bernardino), 5 April 1873, p. 3, col. 1.

15. *People v. Rafael Valenzuela & Francisco Martinez*, District Court of Los Angeles, Case 23, 30 August 1872.

16. *People v. Francisco (An Indian)*, San Diego Superior Court, Case 556, 5 April 1884.

17. *Odon (Indian) v. Miguel Leonis*, Los Angeles District Court, 23 February 1871.

18. Leonis was a harsh and particularly unpopular man among the local population. In the last fifteen years of his life, he was reported to have been engaged in over thirty legal cases, all of which were designed to increase his land holdings. Leonis died in 1889 after he fell from his wagon and was crushed beneath the wheels.

19. *People v. Maria Antonia Cornelia*, Los Angeles County Court, Case 646, 20 January 1866.

20. Leonard Pitt, *The Decline of the Californios: A Social History of the Spanish-Speaking Californians, 1846–1890* (Berkeley: University of California Press, 1999), 250.

21. *People v. Maria Carmen*, Los Angeles Court of Sessions, Case 262, 8 March 1862; and *People v. Francisco Bracamonte*, Los Angeles Court of Sessions, Case 263, 8 March 1862.

22. *People v. Dolores Arsea*, Justice Court of San Diego, Case 65, 10 August 1880.

23. *People v. Pilar*, Superior Court of San Diego, Case 805, 2 February 1885; and *People v. Pilar*, Superior Court of San Diego, Case 383, 7 December 1882.

24. *Guardian* (San Bernardino), 7 December 1867.

25. *People v. Juan Espinosa*, Los Angeles District Court, Case 496, 28 August 1878.

26. *People v. Salvador*, Justice Court of San Diego, Case 181, 25 June 1881.

27. *San Jacinto Register* (Riverside), 6 December 1888.

28. *People v. Charles Martin*, District Court of San Bernardino, Case 358, 28 May 1873.

29. *People v. Jose Marque*, Justice Court of San Diego, 7 September 1874; and *Riverside Press*, 26 October 1878.

30. *People v. Antonio*, Los Angeles County Court, Case 787, 6 May 1871; *People v. Jose Maria*, Los Angeles County Court, Case 792, 26 September 1871.

31. *Act to Prevent Sale of Firearms and Ammunition to Indians*, California Statutes, 24 March 1854. The law made it a misdemeanor, punishable by fines from $25 to $500 and/or one to six months in jail for those convicted.

32. *People v. Antonio*, Los Angeles County Court, Case 787, 6 May 1871.

33. *People v. Carmel*, Los Angeles Justice Court, 6 February 1862; Carmel assaulted an Indian woman named Maria Antonia. *People v. Maria Grand*, Los Angeles District Court, Case 46, 26 April 1864; Grand murdered an Indian woman named Leona. *People v. Ramon*, Los Angeles Justice Court, 20 September 1865; Ramon assaulted, with the intent to rape, Merced Coronel. *People v. Gabriella Osuna*, Los Angeles County Court, Case 662, 23 July 1866; Osuna assaulted Maria Concepcion Albanez. *People v. Jose Ropario*, Los Angeles County Court, Case 716, 6 May 1869; Ropario assaulted Juana and Juan Batista. *People v. Jose*, Los Angeles County Court, Case 729, 5 November 1869; Jose assaulted an Indian woman named Juliana. *People v. Antonio*, Los Angeles County Court, Case 787, 6 May 1871; Antonio assaulted Maria. *People v. Manuel*, Los Angeles District Court, Case 116, 26 March 1876; Manuel murdered Nicolassa on 30 January 1870.

34. By 1880 the number of Native Americans living in Los Angeles had dropped to ninety-seven.

35. *People v. Juan Espinosa*, Los Angeles County Court, Case 496, 26 August 1878.

36. *People v. Jose Marquez*, San Diego Justice Court, 7 September 1874; *People v. Salvador*, San Diego Justice Court, Case 181, 25 June 1881; *People v. Salvador*, Case 1, 29 June 1881; *People v. Juan Pine*, San Diego Justice Court, 21 June 1882; *People v. Pilar*, San

Diego Justice Court, 25 September 1882; *People v. Francisco*, San Diego Superior Court, Case 556, 5 April 1884.

37. *Los Angeles Star*, 3 Sept 1859.

38. *Los Angeles Star*, 4 February 1860.

39. *People v. Jose*, Los Angeles District Court, Case 48, 17 November 1864.

40. *People v. Celsa (Aleolsa)*, Los Angeles District Court, Case 115, 10 April 1874. The court documents in this case are limited; as a result, there is no indication as to why Celsa murdered her child. Since many native societies sanction infanticide as a means of population control during hard times, or when the child is deformed, this may have also have influenced Celsa's reasoning.

41. Women with the financial means during the nineteenth century could seek the assistance of a physician or abortionist, or in some areas had access to "baby farms"—a euphemism for a facility that would dispose of unwanted children for a fee. For further information, see Lawrence Friedman, *Crime and Punishment in American History* (New York: Basic Books, 1993), 229–33.

42. Linda Parker, "Murderous Women and Mild Justice: A Look at Female Violence in Pre-1910 San Diego, San Luis Obispo, and Tuolumne Counties," *Journal of San Diego History* 38, no. 1 (1992): 37.

43. *People v. Santa Anna*, Los Angeles Court of Sessions, Case 71, 19 December 1861.

44. *People v. Jose Domingo and Juan Napomecente*, Los Angeles District Court, Case 50, 5 May 1865.

45. *People v. Luis Mocha and Juan, an Indian*, San Diego Justice Court, 7 August 1877.

46. *People v. Ursula*, San Diego Justice Court, Case 230, 2 March 1851. During the 1850s to 1870s, Southern California experimented with the cultivation of silk worms. While several groves of mulberry trees were planted, the droughts of the early 1860s essentially served as the death knell for this budding industry.

47. *People v. Jose*, Los Angeles Justice Court, Case 616, 16 March 1864. Jose received a six-month or $400 penalty.

48. *People v. Maria*, San Bernardino Justice Court, Case 361, 21 April 1873.

Bibliography

Special Collections

Bancroft Library, Stanford, California
Charles F. Lummis Collection, Warner's Ranch Series, Indian Advisory Commission Series, Manuscript Collection, Southwest Museum, Pasadena, California.
The Huntington Library, San Marino, California.
National Archives, Laguna Niguel, California.
Riverside County Library, Historical Archives. Riverside, California.
San Bernardino County Archives, San Bernardino, California.
San Diego Historical Society Archives, San Diego, California.
San Diego Municipal and District Courts, San Diego, California.

Primary Sources

Act to Ascertain and Settle Private Land Claims in the State of California, 9 United States Statutes 631, 3 March 1851.
Annual Report of the Commissioner of Indian Affairs to the Secretary of the Interior, 1870, 1886.
California Land Commission.
California State Constitution, 1849, 1878.
California Statutes. *An Act for the Government and Protection of Indians*, 22 April 1850.
California Statutes. *An Act to Prevent the Sale of Firearms and Ammunition to Indians*, 24 March 1854.
California Statutes. *An Act amendatory of an Act entitled "An Act for the Government and Protection of Indians,"* 18 April 1860.
California Statutes. *An Act for the Relief of the Mission Indians in the State of California.* Sacramento: GPO, 12 January 1891.
Common Council Minutes, Los Angeles.
Congressional Globe, 36th Congress, 1st session, 26 May 1869.

Coroner's Inquest Reports. San Diego: San Diego Historical Society Archives, 1870–1880.

Report on the Mission Indians, 34th Congress, 3rd session, 1856.

Report of the Secretary of the Interior, 39th Congress, 1st session, 1865.

Report of the Secretary of the Interior, 43rd Congress, 2nd session, 1874. Vol. 1.

Report of the Secretary of the Interior, 50th Congress, 2nd session, 1888. Vol. 2. Washington, D.C.: GPO, 1888.

San Diego Ordinance Against Public Intoxication, Section 1, 1874.

San Quentin Prison Registers, State of California Archives.

Thomas Balch Elliott Papers, Huntington Library.

United States Department of the Interior, Office of Indian Affairs. *Annual Report of the Commissioner of Indian Affairs to the Secretary of the Interior for the Year 1886.*

United States Census, 1850, 1860, 1870, 1880, and 1890.

United States Statutes, 1 Stat 138, 1790.

United States Statutes, 36th Congress, 18 June 1860.

Vandever, William. *Mission Indians of California: Report of William Vandever, United States Indian Inspector.* Washington, D.C.: GPO, 1876.

Legal Cases

In re Manuel, San Bernardino Court of Sessions, 8 October 1862.

Miguel Leonis v. Maria (Indian), Los Angeles Justice Court, Case 62, 10 August 1868.

Odon (Indian) v. Miguel Leonis, Los Angeles District Court, 23 February 1871.

People v. Ygnacio Albas, Los Angeles Justice Court, Case 245, 17 May 1861.

People v. Andreas, San Bernardino District Court, 20 June 1862.

People v. Antonio, Los Angeles County Court, Case 787, 6 May 1871.

People v. Antonio, San Diego Superior Court, Case 570, 25 May 1884.

People v. Antonio Bertrand, San Diego Superior Court, Case 2279, 12 October 1888.

People v. Antonio Argnello, San Diego Superior Court, Case 587, July 1884.

People v. Santos Capistian & Ignacio Flores, Los Angeles Justice Court, Case 82, 8 January 1872.

People v. Carlos & Tomas, San Diego Justice Court, Case 721, July 1885.

People v. Carmel, Los Angeles Justice Court, 6 February 1862.

People v. Celsa (Aleolsa), Los Angeles District Court, Case 115, 10 April 1874.

People v. Charley, Jose Cabrillo & Bruno Subrino, San Diego Superior Court, 12 November 1883.

People v. Chilchil & Asketo, San Diego Superior Court, 27 June 1884.

People v. James Connors and Two Indian Women, San Diego Justice Court, 25 February 1874.

People v. Desidero, Los Angeles Justice Court, Case 612, 22 March 1864.

People v. Carlos Dgero, San Diego County Court, 19 August 1885.

People v. John Doe Indian, San Bernardino Superior Court, Case 66, 29 May 1880.

People v. Jose Domingo & Juan Napomecente, Los Angeles District Court, Case 50, 5 May 1865.

People v. Jose Domingo, San Bernardino Superior Court, Case 27, 13 February 1880.

People v. Joaquin Eslava, San Diego Superior Court, 20 September 1889.

People v. Juan Espinosa, Los Angeles County Court, Case 496, 26 August 1878.

People v. Fernando, Los Angeles Justice Court, Case 40, 6 February 1866.

People v. Fernando & Juan (Indians), Los Angeles District Court, Case 40, 19 June 1863.

People v. Francisco, San Bernardino Superior Court, Case 303, 12 December 1881.

People v. Francisco, San Diego Superior Court, Case 556, 5 April 1884.

People v. Francisco & Mariano, San Diego Court of Sessions, 17 October 1857.

People v. Fred, San Diego Superior Court, Case 32, 13 April 1880.

People v. Gabriel, Los Angeles County Court, Case 689, 21 January 1868.

People v. Manuel Gonzales (Indian), Los Angeles District Court, Case 88, 20 November 1871.

People v. Maria Grand, Los Angeles District Court, Case 46, 26 April 1864.

People v. Ramon Guenos, Jose Loco, Chupo Chivas, and Theresa, San Diego Justice Court, Case 67, 11 March 1884.

People v. Chatham Helms, Justice Court of San Diego (Ballena), 5 January 1887.

People v. Ignacious, San Diego Justice Court, 14 April 1880.

People v. Manuel Isidro & Pelon Arguera, Los Angeles Justice Court, Case 91, 5 June 1871.

People v. Jose Antonio, County Court of Los Angeles, Case 11, 3 June 1872.

People v. Jose, San Diego Court of Sessions, 1 August 1851.

People v. Jose, Los Angeles Justice Court, Case 616, 16 March 1864.

People v. Jose, San Bernardino Justice Court, 21 October 1864.

People v. Jose, San Bernardino County Court, 28 November 1864.

People v. Jose, Los Angeles District Court, Case 48, 17 November 1864.

People v. Jose, Los Angeles District Court, Case 7, 6 May 1869.

People v. Jose, Los Angeles County Court, Case 729, 5 November 1869.

People v. Jose, San Diego Justice Court, 27 January 1873.

People v. Juan, Justice Court of San Bernardino, 11 February 1865.

People v. Juan, San Bernardino County Court, 21 February 1865.

People v. Juan, San Diego District Court, 1871.

People v. Juan & Jesus, San Bernardino Justice Court, 16 June 1873.

People v. Michael G. Lachenias, Los Angeles District Court, 14 November 1866.

People v. Leleh, San Bernardino Superior Court, Cases 23, 24, 34, 35, and 36, 18 February 1880.

People v. Andronico Lopez, San Diego Superior Court, Cases 375 and 399, 1 November 1882.

People v. Bonifacio Lugo, Los Angeles Justice Court, Case 318, 14 May 1889.

People v. James Maddison, San Bernardino Justice Court, Cases 332 and 346 (1865).

People v. Manteca, San Diego Justice Court, 14 January 1853.

People v. Manuel, Los Angeles District Court, Case 116, 26 March 1876.

People v. Marcelino, San Diego Justice Court, Case 180, 23 June 1881.

People v. Maria, San Bernardino Justice Court, Case 361, 21 April 1873.
People v. Maria, San Bernardino Superior Court, Case 10, 21 April 1873.
People v. Jose Maria, Los Angeles Court of Sessions, Case 242, 6 March 1861.
People v. Jose Maria, Los Angeles County Court, 26 September 1871.
People v. Jose Maria, Los Angeles County Court, 1 March 1872.
People v. Jose Maria, Los Angeles County Court, 21 May 1872.
People v. Jose Maria, Los Angeles Justice Court, Case 283, 13 October 1862.
People v. Charles Martin, San Bernardino County Court, Case 358, 28 May 1873.
People v. Old Martin, San Bernardino Justice Court, 24 May 1875.
People v. Marquis, Los Angeles Justice Court, Case 122, 10 October 1872.
People v. Jose Marquez, San Diego Justice Court, 7 September 1874.
People v. James Marshall, San Bernardino Court of Sessions, Case 468, 24 July 1867.
People v. Luis Mocha & Juan, Justice Court of San Diego (Ballena), 7 August 1877.
People v. Gabriella Osuna, Los Angeles County Court, Case 662, 23 July 1866.
People v. Old Pablo, San Bernardino Recorder's Court, 18 February 1877.
People v. Paulino & Pedrito, San Bernardino County Court, Case 638, 10 September 1879.
People v. Pilar, San Diego Justice Court, 25 September 1882.
People v. Juan Pine, San Diego Justice Court, 21 June 1882.
People v. Polinares, Los Angeles County Court, Case 711, 1 February 1869.
People v. Prospero, San Bernardino District Court, Case 154, 14 September 1872.
People v. Ramon, Los Angeles Justice Court, 20 September 1865.
People v. Jose Ropario, Los Angeles County Court, Case 716, 6 May 1869.
People v. Salvador, San Diego Justice Court, 25 June 1881.
People v. Salvador, Case 1, 29 June 1881.
People v. Salvador, Los Angeles County Court, Case 181, 9 September 1881.
People v. Santiago, San Bernardino County Court, 7 March 1864.
People v. Santiago, Los Angeles Justice Court, Case 51, 28 October 1867.
People v. Stanislado Setia, San Diego Superior Court, Case 166, 21 May 1881.
People v. Santos Silvas, Los Angeles County Court, Case 433, 22 March 1878.
People v. Charles Shettler, San Bernardino District Court, Case 183, 18 November 1872.
People v. Francis Stone, San Diego Court of Sessions, 10 October 1855.
People v. Louis K. Thompson, San Diego Justice Court, 14 February 1876.
People v. Tomas, San Diego Court of Sessions, 29 September 1857.
People v. Ursula, San Diego Justice Court, Case 230, 2 March 1851.
People v. Jesus Venegas, Los Angeles District Court, Case 89, 24 November 1871.
Supreme Court of California, Docket 27, California 404.

Newspapers

The *Daily Times* (Los Angeles County).
The *Guardian* (San Bernardino County).
The *Hemet News* (Riverside County).
The *Los Angeles Star* (Los Angeles County).

The *Riverside Press & Horticulturist* (Riverside County).
The *San Diego Herald* (San Diego County).
The *San Diego Union* (San Diego County).
The *San Jacinto Register* (Riverside County).
The *San Francisco Bulletin* (San Francisco County).
The *San Francisco Chronicle* (San Francisco County).

Articles

Bakken, Gordon M. "Mexican and American Land Policy: A Conflict of Cultures." *Southern California Quarterly* 75, no. 3–4 (1993): 237–62.

Bynum, Timothy S., and Raymond Paternoster. "Discrimination Revisited: An Exploration of Frontstage and Backstage Criminal Justice Decision Making. *Sociology and Social Research* 69, no. 1 (1984): 90–108.

Carrico, Richard. "San Diego Indians and the Federal Government's Years of Neglect, 1850–1865." *Journal of San Diego History* 26, no. 3 (1980): 164–83.

Carter, Nancy Carol. "Race and Power Politics as Aspects of Federal Guardianship over American Indians: Land Related Cases, 1887–1924." *American Indian Law Review* 4, no. 2 (1987): 197–248.

Coy, P. E. B. "Justice for the Indian in Eighteenth-Century Mexico." *American Journal of Legal History* 12, no. 1 (1968): 41–49.

Dale, Lyle A. "Rough Justice: Felony Crime and the Superior Court in San Luis Obispo, 1880–1910." *Southern California Quarterly* 76, no. 2 (1994): 195–216.

Dolnick, Robert Lee. "Coyote Cowboy: The Story of Charles Frederick Martin." *Quarterly of the National Association for Outlaw and Lawman History* 19, no. 2 (1974): 12–17.

Ellison, William H. "The Federal Indian Policy in California, 1846–1860." *Mississippi Valley Historical Review* 9, no. 1 (1922): 37–67.

Flannagan, Thomas. "The Agricultural Argument and Original Appropriation: Indian Lands and Political Philosophy." *Canadian Journal of Political Science* 22, no. 3 (1989): 589–606.

Goldberg-Ambrose, Carole. "Of Native Americans and Tribal Members: The Impact of Law on Indian Group Life." *Law and Society* 28, no. 5 (1984): 1123–48.

Greenhouse, Carol J. "Constructive Approaches to Law, Culture, and Identity." *Law and Society Review* 28, no. 5 (1994): 1231–41.

Guest, Francis F., O.F.M. "The California Missions Were Far from Faultless." *Southern California Quarterly* 76, no. 3 (1994): 255–307.

Henderson, I. Youngblood. "Unraveling the Riddle of Aboriginal Title." *American Indian Law Review* 5, no. 1 (1988): 75–137.

Hooper, Lucille. "The Cahuilla Indians." University of California Publications 16, no. 6 (1920).

Hughes, Charles. "The Decline of the Californios: The Case of San Diego, 1846–1856." *Journal of San Diego History* 21, no. 4 (1975): 2–18.

Hurtado, Albert L. "Controlling California's Indian Work Force." *Southern California Quarterly* 61, no 3 (1979).

Hutchinson, C. Alan. "The Mexican Government and the Mission Indians of Upper California, 1821–1835." *The Americas* 21 (April 1965): 335–62.

James, M. Annette. "Federal Indian Identification Policy: A Usurpation of Indigenous Sovereignty in North America." *Policy Studies Journal* 16, no. 4 (1988): 778–98.

Kelsey, Harry. "The California Indian Treaty Myth." *Southern California Quarterly* 15, no. 3 (1973): 225–35.

Kroeber, A. L. "Preliminary Sketch of the Mohave Indians." *American Anthropologist* 14, no. 2 (1902): 276–85.

Merriam, C. Hart. "The Indian Population of California." *American Anthropologist* 7 (1905): 594–606.

Miller, Bruce C. "Contemporary Tribal Codes and Gender Issues." *American Indian Culture and Research Journal* 18, no 2 (1994): 43–74.

Parker, Linda. "Statutory Changes and Ethnicity in Sex Crimes in Four California Counties, 1880–1920." *Western Legal History* 6, no. 1 (1993): 69–91.

———. "Superior Court Treatment of Ethnics Charged with Violent Crimes in Three California Counties, 1880–1910." *Southern California Quarterly* 74, no. 3 (1992): 225–40.

Peak, Ken. "Crime in Indian Country: Another 'Trail of Tears.'" *Journal of Criminal Justice* 15, no. 6 (1987): 485–94.

Phillips, George Harwood. "Indians in Los Angeles, 1781–1875: Economic Integration, Social Disintegration." *Pacific Historical Review* 49 (August 1980).

Ruffing, Lorraine Turner. "Navajo Economic Development Subject to Cultural Constraints." *Economic Development and Cultural Change* 24, no. 3 (1976): 611–21.

Shepardson, Mary. "The Status of Navajo Women." *American Indian Quarterly* 6, nos. 1–2 (1982): 149–69.

Sidham, Ronald, and Roberta A. Carp. "Indian Rights and Law before the Federal District Courts." *Social Science Journal* 32, no. 1 (1995): 87–100.

Stanley, John J. "Bearers of the Burden: Justices of the Peace, Their Courts, and the Law in Orange County, California, 1870–1907." *Western Legal History* 5, no. 1 (1992): 37–67.

———. "Criminal Justice, Law, and Policy in Indian Country: A Historical Perspective." *Journal of Criminal Justice* 17, no. 5 (1989): 393–407.

Sutton, Imre. "Indian Land, White Man's Law: Southern California Revisited." *American Indian Culture and Research Journal* 18, no. 3 (1994): 265–70.

Wilkins, David E. "Transformations in Supreme Court Thought: The Irresistible Force (Federal Indian Law & Policy) Meets the Movable Object (American Indian Tribal Status)." *Social Science Journal* 30, no. 2 (1993): 181–207.

Williamson, M. Burton. "Saboba Indians of Southern California." *Out West: A Magazine of the Old Pacific and the New* 30 (January–June 1909): 148–58.

Woolsey, Ronald C. "Crime and Punishment: Los Angeles County, 1850–1856." *Southern California Quarterly,* 61, no. 1 (1979): 79–98.

Books

Anderson, George, et al. *Treaty Making and Treaty Rejection by the Federal Government in California, 1850–1852.* Socorro, N.M.: Ballena Press, 1974.

Bakken, Gordon M. *Practicing Law in Frontier California.* Lincoln: University of Nebraska Press, 1991.

———, ed. *California History: A Topical Approach.* Wheeling, Ill.: Harlan Davidson, Inc., 2003.

Bancroft, Hubert Howe. *History of California.* Vols. 1–7. San Francisco: The History Company, Publishers, 1888.

———. *Native Races.* San Francisco: A. L. Bancroft and Co., 1883.

Bean, Lowell John. *Mukat's People: The Cahuilla Indians of Southern California.* Los Angeles: University of California Press, 1974.

Beattie, George William, and Helen Pruitt Beattie. *Heritage of the Valley: San Bernardino's First Century.* Oakland, Calif.: Biobooks, 1951.

Beatty, Donald R. "History of the Legal Status of the American Indian." Masters thesis, University of California, 1957.

Beck, Warren A., and Ynez D. Hasse. *Historical Atlas of California.* Norman: University of Oklahoma Press, 1974.

Bell, Horace. *Reminiscences of a Ranger: Early Times in Southern California.* Norman: University of Oklahoma Press, 1999.

Bolton, Herbert Eugene. *Spanish Exploration of the Southwest.* New York: Scribner's, 1908.

Borah, Woodrow. *Justice by Insurance: The General Court of Colonial Mexico and the Legal Aides of the Half-Real.* Berkeley: University of California Press, 1983.

Boscana, Geronimo. *Chinigchinich.* Translated by Alfred Robinson. Banning, Calif.: Malki Museum Inc., 1978.

Brewer, William H. *Up and Down California in 1860–1864.* 3rd ed. Berkeley: University of California Press, 1974.

Brown, James T. *Harvest of the Sun: An Illustrated History of Riverside County.* Riverside, Calif.: Windsor Publications Inc., 1985.

Brown, Richard Maxwell. *No Duty to Retreat: Violence and Values in American History and Society.* Norman: University of Oklahoma Press, 1994.

Cadwalader, Sandra L., and Vine Deloria Jr., eds. *The Aggressions of Civilization: Federal Indian Policy since the 1880s.* Philadelphia: Temple University Press, 1974.

Carrico, Richard. *Strangers in a Stolen Land: American Indians in San Diego, 1850–1880.* Newcastle, Calif.: Sierra Oaks Publishing, 1987.

Chapman, Charles E. *A History of California: The Spanish Period.* New York: Macmillan, 1921.

Cleland, Robert Glass. *The Cattle on a Thousand Hills: Southern California, 1850–1880.* San Marino, Calif.: Huntington Library, 1990.

Cline, Lora L. *Just Before Sunset.* Jacumba, Calif.: J and L Enterprises, 1984.

Cuero, Delfina. *The Autobiography of Delfina Cuero: A Diegueno Indian.* Edited by Florence Shipek. Los Angeles: Dawson's Book Shop, 1968.

Deloria, Vine, Jr., and Clifford M. Lytle. *American Indians, American Justice*. Austin: University of Texas Press, 1983.

Deverell, William. *Railroad Crossing: Californians and the Railroad, 1850–1910*. Berkeley: University of California Press, 1994.

Dippie, Brian. *The Vanishing American: White Attitudes and U.S. Indian Policy.* Lawrence: University Press of Kansas, 1982.

Dumke, Glenn S. *The Boom of the Eighties in Southern California.* 6th ed. San Marino, Calif.: Huntington Library, 1991.

Dyer, Ruth Caroline. "The Indians' Land Title in California: A Case in Federal Equity, 1851–1942." Masters thesis, University of California, 1944.

Fogelson, Robert M. *The Fragmented Metropolis: Los Angeles, 1850–1930*. Berkeley: University of California Press, 1993.

Friedman, Lawrence M. *A History of American Law*. 2nd ed. New York: Touchstone Books, 1985.

———. *Crime and Punishment in American History*. New York: HarperCollins, 1993.

Friedman, Lawrence M., and Robert V. Percival. *The Roots of Justice: Crime and Punishment in Alameda County, California, 1870–1910*. Chapel Hill: University of North Carolina Press, 1981.

Garner, Van H. *The Broken Ring: The Destruction of the California Indians*. Tucson, Ariz.: Westerlore Press, 1982.

Gutierrez, Ramon A. *When Jesus Came, The Corn Mothers Went Away: Marriage, Sexuality, and Power in New Mexico, 1500–1846*. Stanford, Calif.: Stanford University Press, 1991.

Haas, Lisbeth. *Conquests and Historical Identities in California, 1769–1936*. Berkeley: University of California Press, 1995.

Harring, Sidney L. *Crow Dog's Case: American Indian Sovereignty, Tribal Law, and United States Law in the Nineteenth Century*. New York: Cambridge University Press, 1994.

Harris, Newmark. *Sixty Years in Southern California, 1853–1913*. New York: Knickerbocker Press, 1916.

Heizer, Robert F. *They Were Only Diggers*. Ramona, Calif.: Ballena Press, 1974.

———, ed. *Federal Concern About Conditions of California Indians, 1853 to 1913: Eight Documents*. Ramona, Calif.: Ballena Press, 1972.

———, ed. *Some Last Century Accounts of the Indians of Southern California*. Ramona, Calif.: Ballena Press, 1976.

Heizer, Robert F., and M. A. Whipple, eds. *The California Indians: A Source Book*. 2nd ed. Berkeley: University of California Press, 1971.

Hurtado, Albert L. *Indian Survival on the California Frontier*. New Haven: Yale University Press, 1988.

———. *Intimate Frontiers: Sex, Gender, and Culture in Old California*. Albuquerque: University of New Mexico Press, 1999.

Hyer, Joel R. *We Are Not Savages: Native Americans in Southern California and the Pala Reservation, 1840–1920*. East Lansing: Michigan State University Press, 2001.

Jackson, Helen Hunt. *A Century of Dishonor.* New York: Indian Head Books, 1994.

Jackson, Robert H., and Edward Castillo. *Indians, Franciscans, and Spanish Colonization: The Impact of the Mission System on California Indians.* 2nd ed. Albuquerque: University of New Mexico Press, 1997.

James, Harry C. *The Cahuilla Indians.* Banning, Calif.: Malki Museum Press, 1960.

Jones, Sondra. *The Trial of Don Pedro Leon Lujan: The Attack Against Indian Slavery and Mexican Traders in Utah.* Salt Lake City: University of Utah Press, 2000.

Josephy, Alvin M., Jr. *The Civil War in the American West.* New York: Alfred A. Knopf, 1991.

Kawashima, Yasuhide. *Puritan Justice and the Indian: White Man's Law in Massachusetts, 1630–1763.* Middletown, Mass.: Wesleyan University Press, 1986.

Kelsey, C. E. *Report of the Special Agent for California to the Commissioner of Indian Affairs.* San Jose, Calif.: Cleveland Printing Co., 1906.

Kroeber, A. L. *Handbook of the Indians of California.* Berkeley: California Book Co., Ltd., 1967.

Langum, David J. *Law and Community on the Mexican California Frontier: Anglo-American Expatriates and the Clash of Legal Traditions, 1821–1846.* Norman: University of Oklahoma Press, 1987.

Limerick, Patricia Nelson. *The Legacy of Conquest: The Unbroken Past of the American West.* New York: W. W. Norton, 1987.

Lyman, Edward Leo. *San Bernardino: The Rise and Fall of a California Community.* Salt Lake City, Utah: Signature Books, 1996.

McDonnell, Janet A. *The Dispossession of the American Indian: 1887–1934.* Indianapolis: Indiana University Press, 1991.

Miller, Bruce W. *The Gabrielino.* Los Osos, Calif.: Sand River Press, 1991.

Modesto, Ruby, and Guy Mount. *Not For Innocent Ears: Spiritual Traditions of a Desert Cahuilla Medicine Woman.* Angeles Oaks, Calif.: Sweetlight Books, 1980.

Monkkonen, Eric H., ed. *The Frontier.* Westport, Conn.: Meckler Press, 1991.

Newmark, Maurice H., and Marco R. Newmark, eds. *Sixty Years in Southern California, 1853–1913.* Los Angeles: Zeitlin and Ver Brugge, 1970.

Paddison, Joshua. *A World Transformed: First Hand Accounts of California before the Gold Rush.* Berkeley: Heyday Books, 1999.

Parker, Horace. *The Historic Valley of Temecula.* Balboa Island, Calif.: Paisano Press, 1967.

Patterson, Tom. *A Colony for California.* 2nd ed. Riverside, Calif.: Museum Press, 1996.

Phillips, George Harwood. *Indians and Indian Agents: The Origins of the Reservations System in California, 1849–1852.* Norman: University of Oklahoma Press, 1997.

———. *Indians and Intruders in Central California, 1769–1849.* Norman: University of Oklahoma Press, 1993.

Pitt, Leonard. *The Decline of the Californios: A Social History of the Spanish-Speaking Californians, 1846–1890.* Berkeley: University of California Press, 1966.

Pourade, Richard F. *The People Cabrillo Met.* San Diego, Calif.: Cabrillo Historical Society, 1976.

Prucha, Paul. *American Indian Treaties: The History of a Political Anomaly.* Los Angeles: University of California Press, 1994.

———. *The Great Father: The United States Government and the American Indians.* Lincoln: University of Nebraska Press, 1984.

Quimby, Garfield M. *History of the Potrero Ranch and its Neighbors.* Fresno: California History Books, 1975.

Rawls, James J. *Indians of California: The Changing Image.* Norman: University of Oklahoma Press, 1984.

Reid, Hugo. *The Indians of Los Angeles County: Hugo Reid's Letters of 1852.* Edited and annotated by Robert F. Heizer. Los Angeles: Southwest Museum, 1968.

Reid, John Phillip. *Law for the Elephant: Property and Social Behavior on the Overland Trail.* San Marino, Calif.: Huntington Library, 1980.

———. *Policing the Elephant: Crime, Punishment, and Social Behavior on the Overland Trail.* San Marino, Calif.: Huntington Library, 1997.

Rice, Richard B., William A. Bullough, and Richard J. Orsi. *The Elusive Eden: A New History of California.* New York: Alfred A. Knopf, 1988.

Robbins, William C. *Colony and Empire: The Capitalist Transformation of the American West.* Lawrence: University of Kansas, 1994.

Robinson, W. W. *Land in California: The Story of Mission Lands, Ranchos, Squatters, Mining Claims, Railroad Grants, Land Scrip, Homesteads.* Berkeley: University of California Press, 1979.

Robinson, W. W. *The Story of San Bernardino County,* San Bernardino, Calif.: Pioneer Title Insurance Co., 1958.

Shipek, Florence Connelly. *Pushed into the Rocks: Southern California Indian Land Tenure, 1769–1986.* Lincoln: University of Nebraska Press, 1987.

Trafzer, Clifford E. *As Long as the Grass Shall Grow and Rivers Flow: A History of Native Americans.* New York: Harcourt Brace Publishers, 2000.

———. *Frontier Crossing of the Far Southwest.* Yuma, Ariz.: Western Heritage Books, 1981.

Trafzer, Clifford E., and Joel R. Hyer, eds. *"Exterminate Them": Written Accounts of the Murder, Rape, and Enslavement of Native Americans During the California Gold Rush, 1848–1868.* East Lansing: Michigan State University Press, 1999.

Vickery, Joyce Carter. *Defending Eden: New Mexican Pioneers in Southern California, 1830–1890.* Riverside: Department of History, University of California, Riverside, 1977.

Washburn, Wilcomb E. *Red Man's Land, White Man's Law: The Past and Present Status of the American Indian.* 2nd ed. Norman: University of Oklahoma Press, 1995.

Wharton, George James. *Through Ramona's Country.* Boston: Little, Brown and Co., 1909.

Williams, Robert A. *The American Indian in Western Legal Thought: The Discourses of Conquest.* New York: Oxford University Press, 1990.

Wilson, B. D. *The Indians of Southern California in 1852.* Edited by John Walton Caughey. Lincoln: University of Nebraska Press, 1995.

Wolcott, Marjorie Tisdale. *Pioneer Notes From the Diaries of Judge Benjamin Hayes, 1849–1875.* Los Angeles: McBride Publishing Co., 1929.

Wunder, John. *Inferior Courts, Superior Justice: A History of the Justices of the Peace on the Northwest Frontier, 1853–1889.* Westport, Conn.: Greenwood Press, 1979.

Yoch, James J. *On the Golden Shore: Phineas Banning in Southern California, 1851–1885.* Wilmington, Calif.: Banning Residence Museum, 2002.

Index